THE SPIRIT OF ENTERPRISE

George Gilder is Programme Director of the International Center for Economic Policy Studies in Manhattan and Chairman of the Economic Round Table at the Lehman Institute.

He is the author, amongst other books, of *Sexual Suicide* and *Visible Man* and has contributed to the *Wall Street Journal* and *Harper's Magazine*.

D0785605

GEORGE GILDER

THE SPIRIT OF ENTERPRISE

PENGUIN BOOKS

Penguin Books Ltd, Harmondsworth, Middlesex, England
Viking Penguin Inc., 40 West 23rd Street, New York, New York 10010, U.S.A.
Penguin Books Australia Ltd, Ringwood, Victoria, Australia
Penguin Books Canada Limited, 2801 John Street, Markham, Ontario, Canada L3R 1B4
Penguin Books (N.Z.) Ltd, 182–190 Wairau Road, Auckland 10, New Zealand

First published in the U.S.A. by Simon and Schuster 1984
Published in Great Britain by Viking 1985
Published in Penguin Books 1986
Copyright © George Gilder, 1984

Portions of *The Spirit of Enterprise* originally appeared in different form in
the following magazines: Chapter 3, "The Explorer," in *The Yale Literary Magazine*;
Chapter 8, "The Curve of Growth," in *Public Opinion*; and Chapter 10,
"America as Number One," in *Policy Review*

Reproduced, printed and bound in Great Britain by
Hazell Watson & Viney Limited,
Member of the BPCC Group,
Aylesbury, Bucks

For Walter and Reese

CONTENTS

CONTENTS

Prologue: The Entrepreneur

ACKNOWLEDGMENTS

One day in the depths of the recession of 1982 I returned to my home in the Berkshires in Massachusetts from a conference of economists who were almost unanimously predicting stagnation or collapse as the fate of the U.S. economy. On the main street of Stockbridge I met my friend Nick Kelley, who had taken his small paper company, kicking and screaming, into the computer age—from rudimentary paper cutting and preparation into the development of wipers and other gear for semiconductor-industry clean rooms. He was beaming. I asked him what was the matter, didn't he know about the great depression ahead? "If this is a depression, give me more," he said. All he knew was that he had so many orders at Berkshire Paper he couldn't begin to fill them.

It occurred to me at the time that Nick Kelley's smile was a better leading indicator of economic prospects than all the aggregate numbers I had heard recited at the conference. I had told the conference that the country was in the midst of a great entrepreneurial boom that would assure rapid growth and progress for the next decade. Yet the economists were totally uninterested in the statistics I presented on venture capital and new business starts. It was obvious to me that the United States was leading the world move into the computer technologies of the new age—indeed, that was the reason for the booming demand for clean-room wipers. But the eminent economists quoted statistics of lagging capital formation and sluggish productivity and depicted the United States economy as a slough of declining innovation. It seemed to me that the experts in economics not only were ignorant of the entrepreneurial dimension of the economy but were uninterested in it. Yet, as I had contended in *Wealth and Poverty*—and Irving Kristol had long maintained—what entrepreneurs make and manage, not what economists measure, is the real economy. Compared to an entre-

9

preneurial smile, most of those depressing numbers cited by the experts were mere symbols of shadows in the groves of academe.

For my discovery of the entrepreneurial economy—and its celebration in this book—I owe initial thanks to Peter Sprague, a neighbor of mine, who as chairman of National Semiconductor Corporation first intrigued me with the silicon chips that animate the computer age. Nick Kelley then took me to a Dataquest Conference on the industry, where my interest was further whetted. Much of the proceedings was over my head, but I learned enough to decide that this industry—with its entrepreneurial flair and technological ferocity—was central to the future of the U.S. economy.

In addition, I managed to place fourth in the Sevin-Riley 10 K running race, without learning who Sevin or Riley was. Nonetheless, L. J. Sevin became a key figure in Chapter 11 of this book ("The Rise of Micron"), and I researched part of Chapter 10 ("America as Number One") in Riley's Decathlon Club in Sunnyvale, California. And I knew that Peter Sprague and Nick Kelley, neither of them a scientist or engineer, were playing a significant role in this crucial arena from the hills of western Massachusetts. It seemed to me that this industry, like all other major industries before it, was driven less by abstruse science than by the spirit of enterprise and entrepreneurship.

That germ of an idea grew into this book and into a subsequent book on the semiconductor industry itself. In writing this work, I had the help of many friends. Steve Forbes and James Michaels of *Forbes* magazine sent me out to Boise to write the amazing story of Micron Technology, and there I discovered the equally amazing story of J. R. Simplot. These two stories form the narrative core of the book. At a New Year's Eve party at Peter and Tjasa Sprague's, I found myself seated next to Tjasa's father, Milos Krofta. His entrepreneurial story became the theme of Chapter 4, "The Man Who Wanted to Clean the Water." A friend of my wife Nini's invited us to Clearwater Beach, Florida, where I would be able to write free of distractions. The friend's name was Genie de Alejo Garcia. Distractingly charming herself, she distracted me further with the incredible story of Cuban immigrants in Florida. Her story and the saga of her friends became the inspiration for Chapter 5, "The Cuban Miracle." (Its Spanish, English, and statistics were improved by my brother-in-law, Jim Brooke of the *New York Times*, a polyglot reporter who also can write and was then with the *Miami Herald*.) John McClaughry, one of my oldest and altogether wittiest friends, called me from the White House, where he was working as a presidential adviser, and told me I should meet Wayne Copeland, who had a terrific entrepreneurial tale to tell. He gave me a ride in his Sabre Liner and the gist of Chapter 6: "A Sad Heart in a Personal Jet." His story got better as time passed.

John Masters of Canadian Hunter sent me a copy of his book *The Hunters* (Vancouver, B.C.: Evergreen Press, 1980); it provided the essence of Chapter 3, "The Explorer." I learned from an interview that Masters kept a copy of Nick Lyons's *The Sony Vision* (New York: Crown, 1976) for inspiration. I saw it on the shelf of an entrepreneurial English friend, Dennis Stevenson, and borrowed it, and it—along with the equally impressive Sol Sanders's *Honda: The Man and His Machines* (Rutland, Vt.: Charles E. Tuttle Company, 1977)—provided valuable material for Chapter 9, "Japan's Entrepreneurs." Then I met the editor T. George Harris and he introduced me to the works of A. David Silver and Thomas J. Fatjo, which enriched my sense of the self-sacrifice in entrepreneurship. And so it went, a book serendipitously emerging from a life, in much the way a company emerges from the experience and inspiration of entrepreneurs.

Perhaps most important to the ultimate shape of this book, however, was not anybody whom I found or met but an entire company that found me. That firm was Bain and Company. It hired me to speak in Boston the day after I had spoken in Denver and the day before I left on a trip to Great Britain. The company was full of brilliant experts on business and the economy, and I was a jet-lagged speaker, but the company didn't seem to mind for some reason and invited me back to learn about its experience in the consulting trade. Bill Bain, Coleman Andrews, and others in the company became good friends and introduced me to the experience curve, which they correctly identified as the real microeconomic foundation of supply-side economics. The result was Chapter 8, "The Curve of Growth," and a central theme of the book: the key to joining the economics of entrepreneurship to the economics of national economic growth and progress.

Finally I learned, in Chalmers Johnson's *MITI and the Japanese Miracle* (Stanford: Stanford University Press, 1982), that Tanzan Ishibashi, the engineer of the Japanese economic upsurge, had explicitly espoused the connection between tax strategy and price cuts in the early 1950s and it became the crux of the Japanese economic miracle. Further aid in developing these points came from Chuck Kadlec at Laffer Associates, Alan Reynolds at Polyconomics, and Dick Rahn at the Chamber of Commerce.

A book, however, is not written in simple fits of inspiration. This one represents approximately one-third of a giant pile of manuscript deposited on the desk of my initial editor, Erwin Glikes, who had brought the book to Simon and Schuster and provided valuable conceptual aid in its beginnings. He looked at the pile and shortly thereafter suffered a heart attack. He recovered completely and went on to head the Free Press at Macmillan. The pile of manuscript passed on to an independent editor, Midge Decter, the marvelous writer and friend who had edited two of my previous books. Among other valuable counsel, she provided the idea that the pile of manuscript comprised not one but two books: this one and a history and analysis of semiconductor technology (to be published by Simon and Schuster in 1985).

Then the book passed on to its final editor, Bob Asahina, who entirely reconstructed it, chapter by chapter, and is so heavily responsible for its present shape that I think in this case I will happily suspend the usual author's assumption of responsibility for any flaws that survive.

Most of the typing, as usual, was performed on her Osborne by Sally Bergmans, who also provided needed advice and corrections. A fine editor, Joan Taylor of the Manhattan Institute, was generously given time by her boss, Bill Hammett, to edit the manuscript in first draft; she offered a host of discerning observations. Tom Bethell, a master stylist for the supply side and spearhead against the hive, for National Review, the American Spectator, and other discerning publications, read much of the manuscript in its most ramshackle form and made many useful suggestions. Adam Meyerson and Sally Atwater of Policy Review gave valuable help on Chapter 10.

Esther Dyson of RELease 1.0 showed the entrepreneurial confidence to hire me to write the semiconductor sections of her splendid computer industry letter; the experience greatly strengthened the computer and semiconductor chapters of this book. Deric Washburn gave indispensable counsel and diversion for getting through the Berkshire winter without taking an axe to my Apple III disk drives.

David and Peggy Rockefeller provided inspiring places to work in difficult times and offered their own continual inspiration and hospitality. Joshua Gilder, Louisa Gilder, Mellie Gilder, and Richard Gilder gave encouragement in bad times—Richard, for example, by being born two days before the deadline for final submission of the manuscript.

Kay Palmer kept the fort financially, fending off the IRS and other distractions while also maintaining the computer while I wrote. Bruce Chapman defended the Washington front and provided continual advice and encouragement and a possible title. Bill Leigh also provided a title and with Danny Stern smoothly kept the speeches coming; Georges Borchardt enriched his legend and my account; Gilly, Reese and my mother kept the farm. And Nini built the octagon wing and kept me together in it, which was best of all.

George Gilder
Tyringham, Mass.
21 May, 1984

PROLOGUE:
THE ENTREPRENEUR

The prevailing theory of capitalism suffers from one central and disabling flaw: a profound distrust and incomprehension of capitalists. With its circular flows of purchasing power, its invisible-handed markets, its intricate interplays of goods and moneys, all modern economics, in fact, resembles a vast mathematical drama, on an elaborate stage of theory, without a protagonist to animate the play.

The prevailing assumption is that at any particular time the economy is a problem with a small number of solutions—limited by tastes, technologies, and natural resources—which can be expressed as a set of simultaneous equations. Within this scheme, the acknowledged role of the capitalist or entrepreneur is to mediate marginally among all the limiting conditions. Even his leading academic advocates see him as a mere "scout of opportunities," a puppet of price signals, a servant of sovereign consumers. A dependent variable, the entrepreneur rapidly vanishes into the shadows of such imperious factors of production as land, labor, and capital, such massive numbers as money and aggregate demand.

The Marxists, surprisingly, have provided a grander and in some ways more accurate view. Karl Marx himself acknowledged the supreme productive genius of the bourgeoisie and assigned to the capitalist phase a central, if transitory, role in economic progress. But the left fantasizes a tiny elite of tycoons wielding the powers of enterprise rather than an immense class of entrepreneurs and aspiring businessmen—perhaps 30 million in the United States alone—who comprise a near majority of working citizens.

Nonetheless, Marx's theory of the dynamic and creative force of the bourgeoisie was more accurate than Adam Smith's concept of the economy as a great invisibly guided "machine" in which capitalists are tools of the "market." Even the vulgar Marxism of today retains the important virtue of recognizing the crucial creative role of business. The problem is that the left sees the power of business as evil and selfish in spirit and purpose.

Even on the right, however, the entrepreneur is of low moral stature. The prevailing conservative view exonerates him from the leftist charge of being a vicious exploiter of workers only to present him as a plodding pursuer of his own self-interest. Adam Smith sometimes avers that self-love leads to social good, that greed brings prosperity. Nonetheless his theory of the invisible hand leaves the entrepreneur as a blind tool of appetite, who looks beyond himself only to scour the scene for signals of the appetites of others.

In Smith's view, it is only from the capitalist's "luxury and caprice," his desire for "all the different baubles and trinkets in the economy of greatness," that the poor "derive that share of the necessaries of life, which they would in vain have expected from his humanity or his justice." In perhaps Smith's most famous lines, he wrote of capitalists: "In spite of their natural selfishness and rapacity, though they mean only their own conveniency, though the sole end which they proposed from the labours of all the thousands they employ, be the gratification of their own vain and insatiable desires . . . they are led by an invisible hand . . . and without intending it, without knowing it, advance the interest of society."

It is a tribute to the centrality of *The Wealth of Nations* in our intellectual life that Smith's view underlies both the claims and the criticisms of the system. For a critique of capitalism, the left merely espouses Smith's dim view of entrepreneurs but leaves out the miracle of markets. For a celebration of capitalism, the right embraces his theory of markets but sometimes edits out his attacks on entrepreneurs. Both partake of the same British intellectual tradition of disdain for "men in trade." Surveying all the literature of economics, the best we can say for the businessman is that while Smith denied we could expect anything much from his humanity, John Maynard Keynes did see benefits in his "animal spirits."

The problem with all these theories of capitalism is their scientific ineptitude. Even if we do not ask economists to perform as moral philosophers, we should demand that they accurately observe the world. Observing the world, one can see scarce factual foundation for the prevailing view of entrepreneurial activity. The capitalist is not merely a dependent of capital, labor, and land; he defines and creates capital, lends value to land, and offers his own labor while giving effect to the otherwise amorphous labor of others. He is not chiefly a tool of markets but a maker of markets; not a scout of opportunities but a developer of opportunity; not an optimizer of resources but an inventor of them; not a respondent to existing demands but an innovator who evokes demand; not chiefly a user of technology but a producer of it. He does not operate within a limited sphere of market disequilibria, marginal options, and incremental advances. For small changes, entrepreneurs are unnecessary; even a lawyer or bureaucrat would do.

In their most inventive and beneficial role, capitalists seek monopoly: the unique product, the startling new fashion, the marketing breakthrough, the novel design. These ventures disrupt existing equilibria rather than restore a natural balance that outside forces have thrown awry. Because they can change the technical frontiers and reshape public desires, entrepreneurs may be even less limited by tastes and technologies than artists and writers, who are widely seen as supremely free. And because entrepreneurs must necessarily work and share credit with others and produce for them, they tend to be less selfish than other creative people, who often exalt happiness and self-expression as their highest goals.

The virtual absence of these vital and creative, tenacious and sacrificial men from the economic and moral ledgers of society depletes and demoralizes the culture of capitalism. It leads to a failure to pass on to many youths a notion of the sources of their affluence and the possibilities of their lives. It leads to a persistent illusion on the part of intellectuals that we live in an age without heroes. It leads to a widespread sense of entitlement to the bounties of "society," to a "social surplus," which in fact is the product of the labor and ingenuity of particular men and women. Society is always in deep debt to the entrepreneurs who sustain it and rarely consume by themselves more than the smallest share of what they give society. But like the barbarians of Ortega's vision in *Revolt of the Masses*, many children of the West assume that they are entitled: that the comforts of life are natural and inevitable while its hardships are an effect of the malignity of leaders, that goods are summoned by invisible hands or disembodied social dialectics or exogenous sciences rather than contrived by the specific exertions and sacrifices of men and women on the frontiers of enterprise.

There is nothing abstract or predictable about them or what they do. Some are scientists, some are artists, some are craftsmen; most are in business. Although they act as individual men and women, they are nearly always driven by familial roles and obligations.

They are not always kind or temperate, rarely elegant or tall, only occasionally glib or manifestly leaders of men. By fleeing their homes and families to go to far-off lands, many inflict and suffer a trauma of loss—and fight to justify and overcome it. As immigrants, many deliberately seek an orphan's fate, and toil to launch a dynasty. Many lose their fathers, early fill their role, and transcend it gloriously in the world. Ugly, they wreak beauty; rude and ruthless, they redeem the good and true. Mostly outcasts, exiles, mother's boys, rejects, warriors, they learn early the lessons of life, the knowledge of pain, the ecstasy of struggle.

In their own afflicted lives, they discover the hard predicament of all human life, threatened always by the creeping encroachments of jungle and sand. From their knowledge of failure, they forge success. In accepting risk, they achieve security for all. In embracing change, they ensure social and economic stability.

These men and women—who see that civilization is not routine or natural, that it swiftly declines and decays on forty-hour weeks, who know that to maintain a net profit in the world's accounts is a titanic cause—these men and women are entrepreneurs.

While the entitled children speak of an absence of worthwhile work, the entrepreneurs hold three jobs at one time. While the entitled children ache at the burden of laboring nine to five, the entrepreneurs rise before dawn and work happily from five to nine. While the entitled children complain that success comes from "contacts" with the high and mighty—and talk of the frustrations of "politics"—the entrepreneurs ignore politics and make their contacts with workers and customers. While the entitled children see failure as catastrophe—a reason to resign—the entrepreneur takes it in stride as a spur to new struggle.

While the entitled children think riches come to the gambler or the Scrooge, to the ones blessed with genius or good connections, who exploit labor or political links, who are gifted with talent or land, natural resources or unnatural luck, entrepreneurs know that genius is sweat and toil and sacrifice and that natural resources gain value only by the ingenuity and labor of man.

The perennial preening of generals and politicians, bureaucrats and revolutionaries—and their reflected glow in the media and the academy—fosters the prevailing impression that history progresses through elections and wars, mass meetings and militant movements. But these events, dramatic as they are, gain long-run significance for the future of the world largely to the extent that they advance or retard the creative work of entrepreneurs.

It is they who chiefly create the wealth over which the politicians posture and struggle. When the capitalists are thwarted, deflected, or dispossessed, the generals and politicians, the guerrilla chieftains and socialist intellectuals, are always amazed at how quickly the great physical means of production—the contested tokens of wealth and resources of nature—dissolve into so much scrap, ruined concrete, snarled wire, and wilderness. The so-called means of production are impotent to generate wealth and progress without the creative men of production, the entrepreneurs.

It is the entrepreneurs who know the rules of the world and the laws of God. Thus they sustain the world. In their careers, there is little of optimizing calculation, nothing of delicate balance of markets. They overthrow establishments rather than establish equilibria. They are the heroes of economic life. To them this book is devoted, in the hope that the entitled children around the world may come to see and follow their example and earn their redemption and their happiness, reconciled with the world of work and risk on the perpetual frontier of human life.

I

THE
ECONOMY
OF
HEROES

1

A PATCH OF SAND

Lease a man a garden
And in time he will leave you
A patch of sand.
Make a man a full owner
Of a patch of sand
And in time he will grow there
A garden on the land.

Such ancient wisdom cleaves some of the clearest lines among the lands of the world: between wasted barrens held only on lease from an all-powerful state and fruited plains worked with full rights to property and profit. But this ancient law of the garden met a harsh test in early 1909 on the fully titled homestead of Charles Richard Simplot. A hard-bitten farmer of Scotch and Huguenot forebears, with a wiry frame, keen eyes, and a long bulging nose, he fought for food from dry scrubby sands amid the tough sagebrush of the Idaho frontier.

Some weeks before, he had left behind in Iowa a fertile spread and a young wife, heavy with child. Seeking more space and freedom, he had traveled northwest in two "immigrant" boxcars filled with his horses and cattle and machinery for his new farm, and a stove, beds, and a piano for his house. He had unloaded in Burley, in the midst of the Idaho "desert," and moved eight miles up the Snake River toward his holding in Declo.

He had chosen a hard land to farm, with a climate of extremes, for long months near zero to summer stretches above a hundred degrees. It was laced with fierce winds that in winter blinded the traveler with snow and in other seasons whipped up even more devastating blizzards of dirt and sand. Sagebrush ruled everywhere, a shivering gray sea, reaching toward the mists and mountains on the horizon, clinging with tenacious roots, bristling with sharp and scratchy claws, balking passage with gnarled woody stalks. Between the bushes, Russian tumbleweed scuttled dryly over patches of sandy loam. The only signs of life were an occasional cottontail bouncing in the brush, a meadowlark chirping in the midday breeze, and numerous rattlesnakes lurking among the rocks and lava. Even near the river itself, there were very few trees—a rare spindly clutch of cottonwoods or willows. Often they bore in a cleft the bulky nest of a bald or golden eagle.

Arriving at a black lava bluff and peering down at the rocks and sand and sagebrush below—what he had been given to believe was potential farmland—Simplot could see no glint of green except the Snake itself. Warmed by the sixty-mile passage of its "Lost River" tributary underground from a source in Yellowstone, the river was rich with algae: a khaki soup weaving its way incongruously through the bleak barrens of brown and black and gray like a tantalizing symbol of a long-lost fertility.

Clambering and creaking down the steep slope, with his horses and wagons, Simplot finally reached the flatland below. After erecting a tent by the river, he set to work with a friend on the initial challenge of securing water and lodging. They had to dig a well by hand, some eighty feet deep. They had to build a cabin with logs and a thick sod roof. A few weeks later, after they had finished these tasks and were beginning to open a clearing in the sagebrush, Mrs. Simplot arrived by train from Iowa. In her arms she held an infant son, named John Richard Simplot.

It was in this one-room cabin in the wilderness that Jack, as he came to be known—before his name resounded widely through the region as J.R.—first exercized his echoing voice and sturdy limbs. By the end of his first summer, his father had added a barn for the animals. By the time Jack was two, they had cleared the sagebrush off their 120 acres and were harvesting significant crops of vegetables, barley, and hay.

Their way of clearing the land was arduous but effective. After burning a stretch of sage, they would flatten the bush and drag off the tops with a heavy iron rail pulled by a team of horses. Then they would "grub out" the roots with hoes and pull out the rocks by hand. Finally they would begin plowing the soil, harrowing it and planting it, riding the various farm implements through the dry dirt behind a team of horses.

On their arrival, they had expected water from a federal irrigation project. But help did not come for two years, until 1910. Up to then Simplot had to dry-farm the unyielding land.

Nonetheless, their adversary, the sagebrush, had preserved from the Idaho winds and snows a rare bequest: the sand itself. The color of malt when they arrived, it richened with irrigation into a milky chocolate topsoil of loam that J. R. Simplot—some seventy years later—still delights in running through his calloused fingers. Stripped of brush and rocks, the dry soils of the Snake River Valley turned out to be a perfect host for the famous elongated russet Burbank potato. Soon the Simplots were harvesting fields of spuds for themselves and forage for cattle, sheep, and pigs. By the age of six Jack was working hard on the farm and had begun service in the dairy helping with the morning chores.

In photographs, he appears as a happy, freckled youth with a cloth cap, bulky overalls, and work shoes several sizes too large—a Norman Rockwell image of Huckleberry Finn. Although the elder Simplot was known for his fierce discipline of his sons, there is no hint of a boy battered or beaten down by his father, no sign of a dull drudge. But already Jack had learned that life consisted of stern duties: waking in the dark at four to help with the milking, walking two miles to the one-room schoolhouse, returning in the afternoon in time for the chores. If he dallied to play with friends after school, his father would grimly reproach him. The child was needed at home. Except for an occasional dip in an irrigation ditch in summer, or singing and prayers at Sunday School, and songs at night at the piano with his mother, he spent his early life as he would the rest of it—at work.

The one break in the routine was hunting. From the time of their arrival, the Simplots had gained a large share of their food from shooting and fishing. With elaborate seriousness and ceremony, his father taught Jack the rules of firearms from early childhood. The keenest joy of the boy's early years was shooting ducks and cottontails around the farm and along the Snake River. Later he would become a legendary pursuer of elk and other large game in the hills beyond.

In time, however, the elder Simplot, then in his fifties, tired of the remorseless farm life and decided to leave the Idaho plains. The Simplots had become a family of four children: Jack, Myrtle, Peggy, and a younger brother, Bob. In 1917, when Jack was eight, his father subdivided the land into three forty-acre ranches, sold them, taking the mortgages, and left for an easier life on a chicken ranch in Venice, California. Perhaps Jack at last would experience the diversions of conventional youth.

Without the duties of the farm, though, he simply invented new work. Somewhere in his thick Scotch Presbyterian bones, the eight-year-old Jack Simplot was an irrepressible entrepreneur. He took a nickel he had cadged for candy and bought two newspapers, sold them, and with the profit bought two more. He knew at eight the process of investment—forgoing present candy for future bags of lollipops and then forgoing the lollipops as well. Eventually he built up an extensive paper route, and when he was driven from it by older boys who claimed it for their own, Jack began selling the papers in offices in the town. He also collected scrap—bones, rags, and metal—in a wheelbarrow and sold it to dealers. Every weekend he walked four miles to caddy at a local golf course. When a movie company commandeered the lot across the way to film the first version of *The Greatest Show on Earth*, he and his brother snagged jobs as extras.

Jack usually managed to have a pocketful of cash. Still, his father remained skeptical. "Jack, you're moving too fast," he would say. Jack, though, already knew where he was going. On his paper route, at four in the morning, he would keep awake by counting sheep. His dream, remembered from Idaho, was one day to own a flock: "A field spotted with puffy balls of nice white yarn. . . . I always loved the sheep. I thought if I could get a band of sheep and a place to run them, I'd be sitting on top of the world."

For two years the Simplots enjoyed California. But Mr. Simplot's retirement plans failed when the new owners of the Idaho property stopped meeting their mortgage payments. The family had to return to Idaho to foreclose. In 1920, Jack Simplot was back in Idaho, for good, for life.

Once again his father drove him mercilessly, getting him up before dawn to milk the cows, working him in the fields all summer and making him run home immediately after school to do the afternoon chores. With "no sports, no dancing," no other adolescent diversions, Simplot's life revolved around the barns and fields of the expanding farm and around finding a way to escape it. It took him but a year.

In the dynamic of the entrepreneurial life there is nearly always a crisis of breaking away. Whether it is physically leaving family and country, as for many immigrants, or betraying the expectations of parents and the bonds of existing work, as for most native American entrepreneurs, the breaking away entails guilt and anxiety and produces a drive to vindicate the departure. Jack Simplot managed to break away for the first time in 1922, at age fourteen. Leaving a mother he loved and a father he feared and a farm that needed his labor, he suffered all the guilts and anxieties that entrepreneurs everywhere report when telling of their crucial moves. And he showed the same ability to transform his troubles into an implacable drive to succeed.

His method of getting the wherewithal to leave was to collect "bum" sheep from neighboring farms. These were extra lambs, from broods of twins and triplets too numerous for the mothers to suckle successfully, lambs that would otherwise be killed. Over several months, the boy collected some forty of them and raised them to the point where they could be sold back to the farmers. He earned some $140 by these means, a sizable stash for a teenager in 1922. He bought a broken-down Model T pickup, "with a Rexel axle," brought it back to working condition, and drove off into town to live in a room at the Inyard Hotel in Declo (room and board for a dollar a day). Then he began noticing the slaughter of pigs.

It was one of those episodes, frequent in the history of American agriculture, when the price of a product—in this case pork—dropped below the cost of producing it. In desperation, farmers killed their young pigs and pushed them into mass graves. The young Simplot recoiled at this waste and sprang at the opportunity. He told the farmers that he would raise the pigs. He collected hundreds, some for free, some for a few dollars of his sheep winnings. By December that year he had some 700 hogs. His father thought he was crazy and at first refused to help with the project. These were not sheep, which could be sustained with hay and a little grain. These were pigs, hundreds of hungry beasts, who needed protein and starch and carbohydrates to make it through the winter. If it wasn't worthwhile for established pig farmers—with long experience, ample feedlots, and economies of scale—to raise the animals, how could it be possible for a teenager? Even if he got them through the winter, fat enough to sell, he would go broke; everyone knew pork was a glut on the market. The outcome most widely predicted by farmers in the area was a quiet massacre of famished and skeletal pigs one cold February afternoon, followed by Jack's skulking return to his father's spread.

Nonetheless, the boy set eagerly to work, building pigpens and troughs on his father's back forty. He had a plan to feed the pigs for nothing, with a giant savory stew of local refuse. It was not altogether a good plan, but it was enough to launch him into the pig business.

Using sheets of heavy metal flattened from old iron barrels, he contrived a cooker, sixteen feet long by four feet wide, with a firebox underneath and a ten-foot chimney. For fuel, he assembled huge piles of sagebrush, and old tires. Then he went out in his pickup to find food for the ravening pigs. He began with cull potatoes, rejects from neighboring farms, mixed with water from the river and cooked into a murky soup with hay and other available vegetable matter. Piling up sagebrush, bringing water from the river, collecting potatoes and edible garbage, he scarcely had time to sleep. But this concoction, running him into the ground, would do no more than keep the hogs alive; and there was a limited number of reject potatoes. He began adding barley to the soup. But he could not afford enough, and the pigs continued to languish. If there was no market for fat hogs, skinny pigs would be worthless. He had to figure out some better source of protein. Instinctively, as during all previous food crises on the farm, he reached for his gun, a 42-30 Remington rifle. This time, however, he would not shoot ducks and rabbits.

In the hills and along the river, there ran large packs of wild horses, totaling thousands. They were fast and elusive, but they could be reached and run down in a pickup truck. Simplot decided to feed his pigs on horsemeat. It would entail a lot of driving and expensive gasoline, but it would provide the necessary protein to fatten the hogs. During the course of the winter he killed some fifty horses, stripped their hides and sold them for $2 apiece to pay for the gas, and cooked the quartered meat with the culled potato brew for a rounded and rounding diet for the animals. It all cost him nothing, beyond a harrowing investment of labor. It would be richly repaid.

The teenaged Simplot had sensed a key principle of contrarian entrepreneurship: The crowd is always wrong. In the farm panic of the mid-twenties, they were killing pigs; Simplot fed them. He had learned well the poor man's investment strategy; he capitalized his labor. By the spring, when the glut of pork had become a severe shortage, he was ready to reap his return. Jack Simplot's 700 pigs sold for 7 cents a pound, bringing him a check for $7,800 from a local trader named Grow Husky. He had become at age fourteen, for that time and place, a rich man.

He went into farming, buying land, harnesses, plows, harrows, planters, cultivators, and eight horses. For three years, he grew potatoes, beans, grain, and hay and carted them by wagon to market in Burley; he raised and traded pigs, sheep, horses, and cattle. Still, to make it through the winter, he had to work sorting potatoes at a local warehouse, shaking out the small ones through a screen, picking out the deformed ones on top. It was a tedious, inefficient, and low-paying process that seriously retarded the pace of potato production. But it permitted him to set aside some small savings during a hard time.

Then one winter day, in 1927, he was invited to come along as a cook and handyman with some local businessmen on an elk hunt near Yellowstone Park. There, sitting by a tent in the snow in a circle of hunters swigging their way through seven gallons of moonshine, he heard a marvelous thing. A man near Shelley, south of Idaho Falls, so it was said, was building an *electric* potato sorter. Simplot resolved on the spot to buy one. He persuaded one of the hunters, a successful farmer named Lindsay Maggart, to join him in the purchase, each paying $345. They planned to use it for their own crops: Simplot's twenty acres and Maggart's forty. But that was not the way it turned out.

Single-handedly installing and running the first sorter in Cassia County, the burly young farmer soon discovered that it portended not a minor improvement but a revolution in the Idaho potato business. He hired a crew, created his first storage cellar, and then began processing potatoes for other farmers as well. Soon the protests, indignant and contradictory, came pouring in as fast as the potatoes. The device was "destroying jobs," it was said. Simplot's facility was too small to accept everyone's potatoes. Some influential friends of Lindsay Maggart's were left out. One afternoon in the winter of 1928, the older farmer stormed into Simplot's warehouse—"pretty well lit up"—and told him he was out of business. It was half Maggart's sorter, and he ordered Simplot to limit its use to their own crops and thus avoid all the protests and tribulations of economic change. The young man would simply have to leave his warehouse and processing trade and go back to full-time farming. Simplot refused. He had his building investment and crew to consider. It was an impasse: the crusty gray-haired farmer confronting the tough and bumptious young entrepreneur.

Finally, almost as a joke, Simplot suggested that they toss a coin to decide who would own the sorter and dictate the terms of its use. To his astonishment, Maggart agreed. The old man, it seemed, didn't much care what happened to the equipment as long as he could escape the pressure and protests it provoked. The silver dollar fell Simplot's way, and he found himself propelled altogether into the business of sorting and storing potatoes for sale. By 1930, he married Ruby Roseveer, the daughter of a local hardware merchant, auctioned off the twenty acres and farming gear, and moved into a new house in Burley.

For Jack Simplot, the 1920s had been a period of scraping and struggle, but the Great Depression years became the Roaring Thirties. Potatoes, as economists will tell you, are the classic "inferior good": when incomes drop, people buy more of this cheap source of protein. Skittish about banks, he did his business in cash during a period of deflation when banks were crashing and cash was steadily rising in value. He built warehouses in Burley, Declo, Blackfoot, Buhl, Aberdeen, Paul, Eaton, and Murtagh. Then he expanded into onions, another "inferior good," and moved his headquarters to Caldwell, on the western side of the state. In his new region, he opened warehouses in Kings Ferry, Mountain Home, Nampa, Caldwell, Adrien, Marsing, Jameson, and Vail. In 1936, he bought the Bruneau Sheep Company, fulfilling his boyhood dream, and moved into a panoramic irrigated ranch in Grand View, overlooking the Snake. The river still ran green.

By 1940, Simplot was employing nearly 1,000 workers at thirty potato and onion warehouses, with three sorting machines in each, and was shipping some 10,000 boxcars of produce a year. Paying 5 cents a bag for unsorted spuds, he sold the sorted potatoes for 15 cents a bag, or $54.40 for the 360 bags crammed into each boxcar. By the end of the Depression decade, the business was generating annual revenues of over half a million dollars. But it was still a low-margin trade—"only one or two dollars" of profit a car—teaching him well "the value of a dollar." He netted about $15,000 a year.

Then in the spring of 1940, Jack Simplot decided to drive to Berkeley, California, to find out why an onion exporter there had run up a bill of $8,400 for cull (or reject) onions without paying. He wanted his money, but he was equally curious about why the man would bid so much for the onions. Getting up early, he drove all day long down the rough roads from Idaho and along the California coast. Late that night he pulled into a hotel in Berkeley, and at eight the next morning he strode out to the exporter's address. The girl in the office said the boss wasn't in. Fine, said J.R., he would wait until the man arrived. Two hours later, at ten o'clock, a bearded old man walked in. Assuming this was his debtor, Simplot accosted him. But he turned out to be a man named Sokol, inquiring why he was not getting his due deliveries of onion flakes and powder. They sat together until noon, but still the exporter failed to arrive.

As the noon hour passed, Simplot was suddenly struck with an idea. He asked the bewhiskered old trader to a fateful lunch at the Berkeley Hotel. "You want onion powder and flakes," said J.R. "I've got onions. I'll dry 'em and make powder and flakes in Idaho." The two men worked out a contract on the back of an envelope: "On or before October 1, 1940, Mr. J. R. Simplot agrees to commence shipping 300,000 pounds of onion powder at 21 cents a pound F.O.B. Idaho and 200,000 pounds of onion flakes at 31 cents a pound F.O.B. Idaho." Mr. Sokol also agreed to invest $50,000 in Simplot's dehydration facility.

The two men shook hands on the deal and returned to the exporter's office. Mr. J. R. Simplot had entered the food processing business, without any clear notion of how to produce dried onion powder or flakes. Once again he followed his lifelong precept of entrepreneurship: "When the time is right, you got to *do* it." His rationale is written more elegantly in metal on a small plaque that has stood on Simplot's desk—and has greeted him each time he pulls up his chair—for some twenty-five years: *Nothing will ever be attempted if all possible objections must be first overcome.* The objections to signing a contract for delivery of 500,000 pounds of dried, powdered, or flaked onions—without drier, pulverizer, or flaker or any clue of how to build them—seemed altogether prohibitive. But J. R. Simplot struck when the time was right.

Finally, the owner returned to his office and surprised Simplot by agreeing to pay off the debt, albeit on a slow schedule. Simplot then casually asked him where he performed the processing. The man avoided the question, thus heightening the Idahoan's curiosity. Leaving the office, Simplot noticed one of the exporter's trucks pulling out of the driveway. He followed it out to the plant, where he identified the equipment as Nipchild Prune driers from St. Helena, California. Simplot then rushed to his car and drove out through the Napa Valley to St. Helena, arriving just before dark. Before he left Nipchild Prune, he had made a down payment on six tunnel driers, to be delivered in Idaho by July 1, and he had learned from Nipchild how to manufacture a vertical hammer mill and shaker to produce the powder and flakes. It had been a good day's work, Simplot thought as he returned to his car. Little did he know.

Arriving back in Idaho, Simplot focused first on finding a place for his plant which would be easily accessible both to the farmers and to transportation facilities. For the next few months in the fall of 1940, he combed the precincts of Idaho's onion country, along the Boise and Payette rivers, trying to find a landowner and a town which wanted his money more than they abhorred the smell of onions. Even the money was in question, because the agreed $50,000 investment from Sokol failed to arrive. Simplot had to borrow again.

Initially, he settled on Parma and produced his first dried onions in that town. But it was an inconvenient site for shipping. Finally, with the help of the mayor's intervention, he assembled an adequate spread in Caldwell in the midst of southern Idaho's most onion-rich acreage. The land sat next to the railroad tracks two miles west of the town on the road to Wilder. There Jack Simplot built, of gray cinder block, steel, and wood, a stinking factory, locally known, for obvious reasons, as the House of Tears.

Nonetheless with its four oil furnaces, its blowers, slicers, and flakers, its pulverizers and packagers, the building soon became the axis of an onion boom that spread tears of joy among the farmers in the region and on into neighboring Oregon. By providing a rich market for low-grade onions, it allowed the farmers to charge higher average prices for their product, guaranteed to be free of culls; all Idaho onions became top grade. But the benefits did not end with the farmers. One day as Jack perched on a ladder, rewiring a motor, his bookkeeper ran out to him waving some papers. As far as he could figure, the accountant said, they had earned a profit of $50,000 in one month of onion production. Simplot nearly fell off his rung. After the $1 or $2 margins on shipments of potatoes, the yields of his House of Tears seemed a fantasy of wealth. Simplot had been dunning Mr. Sokol for months to get his promised $50,000 investment. But when he finally received Sokol's check for his half of the business, Simplot dispatched it by return mail to California. The old man had not "done it" at the right time. Waiting to see whether the venture would succeed, Sokol lost his share of a business that earned some $600,000 in its first full year and then became "a real moneymaker."

Simplot and his men soon discovered that the process for drying and packing a variety of onion products could also be used—with some key adjustments—for carrots, potatoes, and other vegetables. Simplot himself sketched the design for the first potato drier in chalk on the cement floor of the Caldwell House of Tears. The great virtue of dehydration was shrinkage. A million pounds of product fed into Simplot's machine would emerge about one-seventh the weight, 140,000 pounds. Incomparably cheaper and easier to keep and to ship, dried goods were a key part of the agricultural revolution which would allow America to feed much of the world toward the end of the twentieth century.

This glowing promise, however, began in Simplot's facility only as a series of problems. Potato drying turned out to bring nearly as many tears as onion cutting. They were tears of frustration, as the potential profits wasted away in the tedious and expensive process of peeling. Whether done by hand at exorbitant cost or done by machines that cut away most of the potato, the result was losses. The emerging Simplot empire was about to stumble for the first time, slipping on potato peels. Then Simplot struck on the idea of cooking the potatoes first in a boiler and then stripping off the softened skins by hydraulic pressure.

At that point, coincidentally, the world and the market abruptly and permanently changed. War broke out, both creating a potentially huge demand for dried foods and restricting purchases of boilers only to top-priority weapons producers. Without a powerful boiler, Simplot could not work out his new potato skinning and dehydration process. His problem was solved when a sawmill burned down at McCall in northern Idaho. The young farmer careened at top speed along mountain roads, feeling like an ambulance chaser, to bid on the mill's boiler, which had reportedly escaped the flames. Simplot had acted just in time. By 1942, as American troops spread around the globe, Simplot commanded the world's largest dehydration plant.

Demand for dried potatoes soared far beyond Simplot's expectations. Men from the office of the U.S. Army's Quartermaster General began besieging his facilities with urgent orders for huge deliveries. He began building new plants at a feverish pace, in California as well as Idaho. But he still could not produce nearly enough, and each expansion was choked by a new bottleneck. In a frenzy of entrepreneurial negotiations, financial haggling, and managerial coordination, he managed to overcome each bottleneck in turn. To get more spuds, he bought and cleared several new potato farms. To get more shipping boxes, he bought lumber mills and built box factories. To dispose of the endless potato skins and eyes and sprouts, he built a feedlot for some 3,500 hogs. To get fertilizer for soil wilted by too many potato crops, he bought mineral rights on 2,500 acres of phosphate-rich territory in the Fort Hall Indian Reservation and entered the mining and chemical trade. Each obstacle called forth a new effort of enterprise. But perhaps the worst bottleneck and most difficult challenge of all was the IRS: getting enough investment capital by the tax collectors—and by the 90 percent wartime profits tax—to run his rampantly expanding and diversifying business.

The assumption of the Hoover and Roosevelt administrations of the 1930s that profits were a form of theft had already extended the crash of 1929 into a decade-long depression, during which any sign of revival was summarily extinguished by new taxation. After President Hoover had signed the disastrous Smoot-Hawley Tariff Act, tripling and quadrupling most taxes on imports, he proceeded to compound the damage by doubling income tax rates. Then Roosevelt nearly doubled them again, and in 1935 quashed an incipient recovery by a novel tax on retained earnings. But it was not until the outbreak of World War II that the government, through excess-profits levies and price controls, tried to extirpate profits altogether from the economy.

Profits, however, are the essential fuel of rapid growth. A company can continue to produce at an even pace without them. But it cannot make the vast investments required to respond to the burst of demand which often arises in response to a genuinely new and needed product, a demand which Simplot faced in the early 1940s with the wartime need for dried foods. If he had to send his earnings to the government treasury, he could not send enough potatoes to the government war effort. And if he could not expand, even a 90 percent tax on profits would yield far less revenue to support the Army than a reasonable profits tax on a company in the midst of surging growth. Taxes and controls balked Simplot from either feeding or financing the military.

It is true that by resourceful negotiations with the bureaucracy, larger companies had managed to circumvent this tax and make needed capital outlays. But in his effort to create an entire new industry, Simplot was moving into a new business nearly every month. He had neither the time nor the temperament to explain potato farming, fertilizer production, or box manufacture to bureaucrats. Torn between the law and the profits, and pushed by the Quartermaster General, Simplot, like so many others before and since in the face of confiscatory tax rates, resorted to lawyers and financial finagles for protection.

Thus, while working obsessively throughout the war and living in less luxury than most congressmen, J. R. Simplot managed to gain for himself a reputation as a profiteer and tax evader. To break the bottleneck of 90 percent rates, he created a sprawling complex of kited and cantilevered corporations, all punctiliously designed by Idaho's best legal talent. The company split into some ninety-five partnerships and scores of trusts held variously by Simplot, his family, his friends, his bankers, and his lawyers. It was all so far beyond his own expertise as an untutored trader and spud farmer that it made him nervous. But his lawyers assured him he was within the law, and the financial bottleneck was broken. Simplot was allowed to do his work supplying food for the troops.

Only the Army brass were truly happy. Even the hungriest soldiers never relished the dehydrated spuds. But the men were safely and nutritiously fed, in all climates, throughout the war, and fully a third of all their potatoes came from the dehydration plants intricately owned in the proliferating partnerships of J. R. Simplot and his associates.

Paul Logan, the colonel in charge of procuring this food for the troops, summed up Simplot's achievement after the war:

"The J. R. Simplot Company was born, cradled and thrived because of the patriotism of one man, because of his determination to contribute with all his might to the war effort, and because of his faith in his own ability to overcome obstacles and solve problems. He was asked to build a huge plant for which there was no precedent and when little construction material was available; he was asked to equip the plant with machinery that didn't exist and for which there was no blueprint; and to undertake a food processing procedure on which there was very little technical knowledge. His square jaw moved forward a bit as he replied, 'I'll undertake the assignment!' . . . Working day and night, for most of the war, Simplot and colleagues converted 600,000 pounds of raw potatoes daily into good quality condensed, and extremely useful battlefield food product. . . . For its outstanding contribution to the war effort, this company received a grateful nation's highest award"—the Army-Navy "E" medal, given for excellent industrial performance during the war. Creating a new industry under fire was one of the more impressive feats of recent business history.

Jack Simplot entered the postwar period a bold and happy business warrior, ready to conquer new worlds of enterprise. Instead, his existing world rapidly began to unravel. Simplot seemed destined to repeat the well-worn circuit from rags to riches and back to rags, and there appeared for a while a faint possibility that a grateful nation would fit him with striped pajamas. No longer protected by the Army, he was beset by teams of agents from a newly predatory IRS. Confronted with a bill estimated at $2.5 million, he eventually had to settle for one-fifth that amount. His lawyers had essentially served him well, but even this levy hurt in that difficult period. Sales of dried potatoes plummeted to less than a quarter of their previous level. Unions organized his Caldwell plant, "shut 'er down, and walked off." Simplot chose to fight them and "woke up one morning with 140 unfair labor practice suits." As usual, he learned the hard way.

At the same time, many of his erstwhile paper partners appeared in the flesh, refusing stock in Simplot Corporation and demanding cash for their partnership rights. Even Simplot's father, one of his main partners, predicted that Jack would go bankrupt—"Son, you're going too fast, way too fast"—and required payment of $377,000 on the spot. The elder Simplot promised to keep the money in trust for Jack's family.

Indeed, Simplot might well have gone bankrupt, or lost most of his company, except for one very strange feature of this early postwar period. As most wartime tax rates were lowered, the excess profits tax was rescinded, and millions of able men thronged into the work force; as military spending plummeted and birth rates soared, expert opinion, bemused by Marx, saw these obvious boons for growth as portents of the collapse of capitalism. Nearly all of the world's most prestigious economists, from Alvin Hansen of Harvard to John Maynard Keynes, were predicting a prolonged global depression. Under these circumstances, few people thought Simplot's partnerships were worth much money, and most refused to accept stock in Simplot's reorganized firm.

Though drained to the utmost by the need to raise cash and deep in debt for the only time in his life, Simplot could hardly believe his good luck. As he bought out his partners at bargain rates, he felt the same wide-eyed amazement at the world's blindness to obvious value that had struck him in his youth when he discovered he could pick up healthy lambs and piglets free. "I ain't no economist," he told one of his defecting friends in words that should be inscribed in stone on the portals of the Simplot Corporation's building, "but I got eyes to see." His eyes told him, "This here state is going to boom for a long time to come."

In 1946, a chemist named Ray Dunlap, working on new products for the huge Caldwell facility, suggested to Simplot that they begin freezing potatoes. In the past, this had always seemed impossible; the spuds always turned to mush when defrosted as their very cell structure dissolved. But Dunlap showed that if the potatoes were first cooked and compressed in the right way to eliminate much of the water, they could be efficiently frozen and hold their shape when defrosted. Thus Dunlap created the equipment that contrived the world's first satisfactorily frozen french fry.

Harried by debts and taxes and disgruntled partners—working day and night and stinting on his family—Simplot was then near breakdown for the only time in his life. A man of stern frontier morality, taught at his mother's knee, Simplot was no philanderer. But like many entrepreneurs with strong commitments to family and society (major entrepreneurs are rarely bachelors), Simplot during this period performed an act of violation and adultery: he married his company and its problems. Left too frequently alone, Rosie eventually left Simplot, deepening his sense of guilt and his drive to prove himself in the face of a doubting father and a departing wife. A new crisis of breaking away unleashed in Simplot, as in so many other divorced entrepreneurs, a furious compulsion to rebuild his company and retrieve a family. Although torn by his problems, he still had eyes to see value, and he made a portentous decision.

He brought in his top man, Leon Jones, and told him they were suddenly in the frozen french fry business. But Simplot, though right about Dunlap's freezing gear, underestimated the difficulty of cheaply producing fries without the grease going rancid. He summoned and hired food technicians from Beechnut and other companies and told them to solve the problem. In time, Richard Tobin and Ray Kueneman devised a system by which the potatoes were exposed to no more oil than they could absorb. With no residue, there was no rancidity. The product seemed ready.

By 1947, Simplot's farming, mining, box making, lumbering, and feedlot interests were reviving nicely and he was emerging from his time of trial. Advisers told him to go slowly in french fries. Instead he built the biggest plant in the world, capable of producing three tons of fries an hour, and he deployed several freeze tunnels to preserve them. "Cut costs and prices and go for volume"—the risky and redemptive creed of most successful entrepreneurs—was Simplot's governing creed of commerce. It required him again and again to make huge investments without an assured market. But low prices helped open the market and low costs meant that when demand was created he could achieve greater economies of scale, lower costs, and a larger share of the market than rivals who waited for an assured return.

As Idaho and America recovered during the 1950s, Simplot's empire grew apace. His potash mines turned out to be among the richest in the world, and the chemical businesses he acquired to process the rock into fertilizer also thrived. His farms expanded through Idaho and into Oregon. He launched a series of apartment projects around Boise and Pocatello and bought two of the state's major hotels. But the world was slow to embrace the frozen french fry. For nearly a decade, Simplot's facilities for processing potatoes loomed as cavernous evidence of one of his few errors of timing. Workers employed in his processing division turned to canning and freezing fruits, vegetables, and sweet corn, with an occasional order of dried potatoes and onions from the Army to keep the dehydrators in tune.

The food chains and institutions all still believed, contrary to what Simplot knew, that potatoes could not be efficiently frozen. Raw potatoes were cheap; frozen fries cost twice as much per pound and required expensive refrigeration. Simplot's men would patiently explain that three-quarters of the weight of the raw potato was lost in peeling, cutting, and frying; the frozen fries were actually cheaper and better. Nonetheless, these computations remained beyond the reach of the institutional buyers—restaurants and hotels—and they spurned Simplot's innovation through the 1950s.

The Simplot facilities would have lain entirely fallow except for one surprising development. The American housewife lacked the accountants and computers of the institutions, but she had eyes to see value. Housewives rushed in where the experts demurred; frozen fries began selling unexpectedly in grocery stores. Between 1958 and 1960, sales suddenly doubled, and Simplot began converting his facilities for the last time fully back to potatoes. The company was ready for its most spectacular surge.

Looking up from his work for one of the few times since his father commanded him to milk the cows in Declo, the fifty-year-old J.R. took up skiing and began swooping down the slopes as if he had been born on them. At Sun Valley he befriended the newsman Lowell Thomas, who wrote a memorable column:

"Here at Sun Valley, on famous Mt. Baldy, I've been trying in vain to keep up with a rugged citizen of Idaho. . . . His name is Jack Simplot, from Boise. Built like a Notre Dame fullback, he is one of the outstanding personalities of the West, head of an empire that includes tens of thousands of acres of cattle ranches, gold mines, uranium mines, and deposits of sulphur, iron, manganese. . . . The Idaho potato king, he ships them by the train load. But most important of all he and his people have devised all sorts of new ways of treating potatoes. Dehydration and freezing—baked, mashed, fried, hashed . . . all packaged in a way that cuts down weight and size . . .

"A good natured giant . . . he knows how to pick people and then let them take over. As he goes banging down the Sawtooth Mountains on skis, you can hear him singing and laughing half a mile away."

He does that kind of thing to cynical reporters, who walk from his office groping for similes of great size: They compare him to Li'l Abner, Horatio Alger and the Titans. Upon leaving his presence, it is difficult to remember that he is under six feet tall.

In the late 1950s, when Lowell Thomas wrote his column, Simplot's commercial domains, stretching through most of the Snake River Valley and down to California and Great Salt Lake, were still to experience their phase of fastest expansion. A private company, still fraught with legal fragments and intricacies, trusts and partnerships, affiliates and tributaries: no one could precisely gauge its size in the 1950s and early 1960s. But all observers of the firm agree that its revenues and earnings lurched into their most explosive growth only in the mid-1960s, after Jack Simplot met with Ray

Kroc at his mansion in Solvang, California, and the McDonald's hamburger king told the prince of potatoes: "By golly, boy. Let's get going."

For several years, Simplot had been selling raw potatoes to the rapidly growing chain. But the operation entailed expensive year-round storage and was losing some $300,000 to $400,000 annually. McDonald's couldn't care less, but Simplot needed a better deal. Ushered into the office of a previous McDonald's president, Simplot suggested that he try frozen potatoes and offered to use his own and McDonald's patents to produce them. The executive indignantly lectured him on the unique appeal of McDonald's distinctive homemade fries. They were the firm's most precious selling point. He would never go *frozen*. Never having been harangued so vehemently before except by his father, Simplot was deeply shaken.

Then the president sold out and gave way to Kroc. Simplot struck again and persuaded some McDonald's executives to try out the patented fries in a few stores. They kept coming back for more. Finally, Ray Kroc summoned J. R. Simplot to his ranch near Santa Barbara. They went riding, had dinner, made a deal, and shook hands on it the next morning. On the basis of that handshake of burgers and fries, Simplot rushed home and launched a facility in Heyburn that could produce 30,000 pounds of fries an hour. Simplot has been providing the bulk of McDonald's french fries ever since, building plants on four continents to service the golden arches of the globe. In turn, McDonald's has provided some 40 percent of all the revenues and profits of the Simplot food division.

The trajectory of growth began in 1951, when Simplot bought $62,500 worth of raw potatoes and produced under 2 million pounds of frozen fries. In the late 1950s, raw purchases rose to an annual dollar value of $1.6 million and the company produced 170 million pounds in frozen form. By 1970, the cost of raw material had soared to $11 million to sustain some 400 million pounds of annual processed production. In 1980, Simplot bought almost $100 million worth of potatoes and produced nearly a billion pounds of frozen fries. With the other divisions rising apace, Simplot had grown for twenty years at a compounded rate of close to 20 percent.

On one occasion in 1976, Simplot's luck was simply too good, as he guessed a major move in the potato price and went short 1,400 futures contracts on the Commodities Exchange. As the closing day approached and the price dropped from $17 to $8, hundreds of traders faced ruin. In desperation, some apparently stirred up snarl and panic on Maine's potato markets and train lines to prevent delivery of potatoes that Simplot had contracted to provide. Fifty-five of the losers sued Simplot as the most prosperous available target. The widespread charges that Simplot had manipulated the market were economic nonsense. As the market massively and durably sustained Simplot's position, any theoretical manipulation must have occurred on the other side, among desperate holders of contracts to buy $8 potatoes for $17. But he *had* failed to make a portion of his contracted deliveries, and in the end, to avoid endless fighting in court "against city hall," he had to settle a civil action before the Commodity Futures Trading Commission by agreeing to suspend trading for five years.

It was an embarrassing incident for an upright man, but hardly a ripple in the rising tide of his company's success. In the late 1970s a national upsurge in the fast-food business further spurred the firm's growth. In the recession of 1982, Simplot Corporation for the first time generated revenues of more than $1 billion, some $400 million each from its food and fertilizer operations and some $200 million from its livestock division. But the fundamental source of the success was always the Burbank Russet, nestled in a patch of Idaho sand, arduously cleared and irrigated by Idaho's men and boys.

As late as the mid-1960s, they could still be seen in the fields along the Snake, "railing off" the sagebrush, "grubbing out" the roots and rocks by hand and hoe, digging new ditches and carrying new pipe. Stooped over the rows, with belts around their backs and gunny sacks between their legs, boys still picked potatoes by hand and stacked the heavy bags on trucks for delivery to Simplot's facilities. Working on the farms near the warehouse in Blackfoot were a pair of hardworking black-haired twins named Joe and Ward Parkinson, who would play a crucial role in the next great venture of J. R. Simplot.

As children, they earned 7 cents a sack for picking potatoes and leaving the bags at the end of the row. When a student reached junior high, he would move on to the sweltering work of bucking the sacks onto flatbed trucks and stacking them for delivery to the warehouses. As twins, the Parkinsons, working together, could throw the sacks onto trucks at an earlier age than most of the Blackfoot boys. Later they moved on to the heavier work, carrying and installing irrigation pipes. But throughout their youth, the twins' working life—and working disciplines—revolved around the potato operations of J. R. Simplot, and the town of Blackfoot was largely run by Simplot's man.

In the late 1960s, the Parkinsons left Simplot's domains and went off to distant universities and jobs. But by 1979, they were reunited back in Idaho, ready to lead J. R. Simplot, at age seventy, five years beyond retirement age, into a venture in high technology as challenging as any of the old man's previous enterprises. Simplot's eyes were once again aglow and his voice once again boomed through his executive offices as he hurled himself into this new project on the road to his second billion. In the early 1980s, leading economists were still talking about a new depression, but J. R. Simplot still had eyes to see a booming future on a new technological frontier, a new patch of silicon, for Idaho and America. His new company, led by the Parkinson twins, was called Micron Technology, and its business was not potatoes but semiconductor chips.

Meanwhile, Simplot's father, Charles Richard, the original pioneer in Declo, would probably have disapproved—still thought his whippersnapper son was "moving too fast." Richard Simplot lived well into his nineties and saw Simplot Corporation become one of the world's major businesses. When he died in 1979, his executors found that the old man had indeed kept faith with his Simplot descendants. The $377,000 from his wartime partnership had been safely stored in a large number of savings accounts around the state, each up to the insured maximum and much of it free of interest. A small fortune in 1948, the money had lost much of its purchasing power during the intervening inflation and provided, after taxes, a few thousand dollars apiece for the Simplot grandchildren.

2

THE REAL ECONOMY

J. R. Simplot, who arrived in a covered wagon on the old frontier and grew up to clear the sagebrush along the Snake and launch a business empire into the Great Depression, and made a bet of some $20 million in his seventies on a semiconductor start-up . . . what difference does he make?

It is an old and popular story of rags to riches, but it bears little on the real problems of America, so it would seem to sophisticated men. Indeed, around the faculty clubs and Washington consultancies, the romance of individual wealth seems merely an obstacle to understanding the vast collective problems of the world economy. At best, according to academic observers, what they call the "entrepreneurial myth" can serve as a ballad for the bad times ahead: an anecdote to divert the gullible from their growing personal impotence in a bureaucratic scene of shortages and shared efforts, where we can no longer thrive on the primitive machismo of "cowboy capitalists."

The real economy, according to the best analysts, consists of colliding multinational corporations, national industrial policies, and macroeconomic tides that overwhelm the simple energies and enthusiasms of individual entrepreneurs. These broader trends and developments, economists believe, plunged the United States during the late 1970s and early 1980s into a grave crisis of sinking productivity, marked by actual net decline in output per man-hour, and put the United States well behind European and Asian rivals in industrial prowess and prospects. Long-run energy scarcity assured a rising burden of resource prices. Ever more insidious and intractable problems of pollution would require steadily increasing diversion of scarce capital to industrial hygiene. And an era of sluggish growth, eked out in the face of a maw of debt, many experts predicted, might well swiftly reel and unravel into a new Great Depression.

Within this broad context emerged a set of narrower charges against U.S. corporations. Themselves bogged down in paperwork, they allegedly were bogging down the economy in "paper entre-preneurialism." Overpaid executives, with corporate jets and golden parachutes, mostly trained and gamed in law and finance, responded to the superior engineering, manufacturing, and produc-tivity of foreign rivals by pettifoggery, protectionist lobbying, and financial manipulation. American firms, preoccupied with stock market demands for ever higher quarterly earnings, stinted on cap-ital investment, research, and other long-term projects that were better financed overseas by visionary government banks and guaranteed bonds.

The results were grim. The U.S. standard of living, once the marvel of the world, slipped well behind several European welfare states. U.S. trade plunged into chronic imbalance, chiefly as a result of uncompetitive industry. The U.S. government deficit loomed as a massive and ultimately unmanageable crowd of future claims on the nation's scarce capital. U.S. savings, the indispensable source of investment funds and of finance for the deficit—and long far below the levels maintained by our foreign rivals—fell to an unprece-dented low. Unemployment also stayed high, as did real (inflation-adjusted) interest rates. Bankruptcies continued at record levels even into the cyclical upswing beginning in 1983 and signified the continuation of a deep economic malaise.

Although few economists predicted the strength of the recovery in 1983—and many had foreseen depression ahead—the consensus eventually treated the revival of business as a typical postwar epi-sode. Large deficits and monetary growth had stimulated a surge of consumer spending that retrieved most of 1982's dire losses in pro-duction and employment, but failed to respond to the deeper dis-eases of the system. In general, the economists saw the long stagflation of the mid-1970s as a profound and portentous phenom-enon. But they viewed the recovery as a mere cyclical rise in the statistics—a temporary fever of growth springing from artificial stimuli in fiscal and monetary policy. The long-term prospects of the economy remained grim at best, and possibly catastrophic.

In the world of J. R. Simplot and other entrepreneurs, however, a radically differing view emerged. It registered not in econometric printouts or elegant prose, but in actions and attitudes, intuitions and tacit beliefs that seemed to reflect a different time and a differ-ent land: less the new world of great powers and cartels than the struggles of men and nature on the old frontier. Yet this contrarian vision—this other America—is rapidly changing the very shape and thrust of world development.

It is a country of entrepreneurs who began a profound and far-reaching economic revival in the late 1970s that addressed and resolved many of the problems that the critics cite. It is a country of small firms and new inventions and radical breakthroughs by daring men who are leading the world economy into a new age of growth and prosperity. Indeed, the economy of entrepreneurs can make a plausible claim that it, rather than the world of econometrics, is the real economy. By focusing on this realm, moreover, it is possible to find new meanings and new configurations in some of the conventional statistics.

To close observers of the condition of U.S. entrepreneurship and technology, it has been obvious for a decade that the nation needed only a change in policy to ignite a boom of technological advance, productivity growth, and rising living standards. Entrepreneurs are always preoccupied with capital gains, the increase in value of their companies, and their power to attract investment or secure loans as they launch new goods and services. After the capital gains tax cut of 1978, all the indices of the entrepreneurial economy moved massively up, as a long backlog of innovations at last found significant funding. By the end of the year, new commitments to venture capital funds had risen almost fifteenfold, from $39 million in 1977 to $570 million in 1978. By 1981, actual venture outlays had tripled to some $1.4 billion and the total venture capital pool had doubled to $5.8 billion. The tax cut of 1981, dropping the maximum rate on long-term capital gains to 20 percent, spurred a new surge of investments. By the end of 1983, the pool of venture funds soared to $11.5 billion. During the severe recession of 1982, while many economists spoke of a new Great Depression, actual venture outlays rose to $1.8 billion, more than the five-year total during the slump of the mid-1970s, and in 1983, these outlays approached $3 billion. Over the last five years, investments in biotechnology startups alone totaled some $2.5 billion. The number of major venture capital partnerships soared during the last decade from twenty-five in 1973 to over 200 ten years later.

Lower capital gains taxes can induce investors to put money into new firms. But without a flourishing stock market, especially for new public issues, the investors cannot often get their money back. The sophisticated guesses of elite venture capitalists must be ratified by a broader range of investors before the entrepreneurial engine can bring a wide economic advance.

Beginning in the late 1970s, the stock market began a long move upward. Even though the Dow Jones Industrial Average of the largest firms, as well as Standard & Poor's 500, remained in the doldrums, the Wilshire Index of some 5,000 public companies re-turned to its earlier peaks in real terms and continued its ascent, however erratically, through the early 1980s. The smaller index of 100 venture capital firms, meanwhile, more than tripled between 1978 and 1981.

Of crucial importance to the venture capital industry was the surging market for new public issues. Beginning toward the end of 1978, the number of companies listed on the over-the-counter market rose meteorically, surging 60 percent in two years, from 2,600 to over 4,000. The total amounts raised in new public issues cata-pulted upward from $300 million in the mid-1970s to a peak of some $13 billion reached in 1983.

In 1982, the General Accounting Office measured the impact of the initial surge of venture capital after the 1978 tax cut. The GAO appraised a sample comprising seventy-two companies launched with a total of $209 million in venture funds. These companies directly created 135,000 jobs, generated some $350 million in addi-tional federal tax revenues, and produced some $900 million in in-cremental exports by 1982. By this standard the nearly $7 billion of venture capital outlays in the three years since the tax cut of 1981 will directly generate more than 4 million jobs, over $12 billion in federal tax revenues, and $31 billion in new exports through 1986. Although such estimates seem large, the long-term effect of the technological advances and new wealth engendered by these firms will dwarf these immediate gains.

The institutional structure of the U.S. economy, with its many subsidies and protections for residential construction—enhanced by the rise in depreciation allowances in the new tax act—assured that any U.S. recovery would include a surge in housing. The quotas on imports of Japanese cars helped stimulate Detroit. But contrary to most analyses, this recovery was led not by housing, autos, or consumer goods, but by capital equipment, chiefly elec-tronic, for the entrepreneurial economy. Retail sales actually dropped for the first two months of 1983. But beginning in January 1983, sales of producers' durables rose at an annual rate of over 16 percent, a rise some four times the average pace during the first year of previous recoveries since World War II. Since the new elec-tronic capital equipment was far more efficient than the gear it re-placed, even these record numbers underestimated the formation of capital in U.S. enterprise.

The entrepreneurial boom was not restricted to the elite firms of the stock market and venture capital, or to the sophisticated pro-ducers of high-technology capital goods. Although the broader indices of business starts are complicated to some degree by the increasing tendency of professionals to incorporate for tax purposes, all measures of start-up activity show a strong surge beginning in the late 1970s. While economists and media experts bewailed the evidence that bankruptcies and business failures reached the highest level since the Great Depression, entrepreneurs were starting companies at by far the fastest pace in history, reaching a peak of some 600,000 in 1981 and remaining near that level through the recession of 1982. This rate of entrepreneurial activity was double the rate of the booming 1960s and six times the rate of the 1950s.

The rate of business failures, moreover, is less an index of economic decay than of industrial change. In the United States and around the world, the fastest-growing regions have the highest level of bankruptcies. Japan, for example, maintained a level of business failures double that of the United States throughout the period when its economy grew three times as fast. For most of the 1970s, Houston was a national leader in both bankruptcies and new businesses.

Compounding the obsession with business failure has been an even greater focus on the rate of unemployment. Unemployment data heavily reflect cultural conditions, such as shifts in family structure, demographics, work disciplines, underground economic opportunities, levels of welfare, rates of unemployment compensation, and government subsidies for obsolete work. Employment figures—the actual numbers of jobs—are both more accurate and more revealing of economic conditions.

By that measure, the late 1970s and early 1980s were a period of flourishing economic growth and creativity. In 1981, the employment level crested near a historic peacetime high of 58.7 percent of the adult population. Even at the pit of the worldwide recession of 1982, when a chorus of media pundits and economists spoke of a U.S. depression, employment remained at a level of nearly 57 percent, near the all-time peak, compared to a level that dipped to 55 percent in the late 1960s and a comparable figure of perhaps 42 percent during the Great Depression. By mid-1984, the U.S. economy had produced some 5 million new jobs in two years and the employment rate was just under 60 percent. For years, economists have been telling Americans to look to the welfare states of Europe for lessons in job creation and economic competitiveness. Yet since 1974, the U.S. economy created 23 million net new jobs, and accepted 12 million immigrants, while the EEC countries added no net new employment and sent home millions of overseas workers.

Germany actually lost 1 percent of its jobs. Overall, the U.S. rate of net job creation exceeded Europe's by a factor of five and Japan's by a factor of three.

Even more impressive was the composition of American employment gains. While Fortune 500 firms lost some 3 million jobs, smaller companies have created some 7 million, most of them in the innovative entrepreneurial sector and some 80 percent in companies with fewer than a hundred employees. By far the fastest-growing category of U.S. job growth was technical and professional employment in knowledge and service roles (excluding clerks and secretaries). It rose nearly 60 percent during the 1970s and early 1980s, or by more than 6 million.

Europe meanwhile lavished some $100 billion of government subsidies propping up employment in leviathan corporations, many of them nationalized, and lost some 10 percent of its manufacturing jobs. Japan, with fewer industrial subsidies, lost 11 percent of its manufacturing employment during the 1970s. With 4 percent growth in manufacturing jobs—a net rise of a million—U.S. industry led the developed world in this category so stressed by the critics of U.S. business. And contrary to the theory that U.S. manufactured goods and technology were becoming less competitive while the manufacturing work force expanded, both the U.S. high-technology balance of trade and the U.S. share of world manufactures rose sharply beginning in 1978.

Indeed, 1978 was the watershed year for both the economy of entrepreneurs and the economy of the conventional analysts. But one went up and the other went down. While the usual models showed 1978 as the onset of productivity decline and stagnation—and leading economists predicted depression—entrepreneurs, spurred by the drop in capital gains taxes, launched a broad economic revival. While the leading experts blindly sang a statistical dirge of declining productivity, depleted energy resources, crippling capital shortages, and dangerous and intractable pollution, America's entrepreneurs radically raised productivity, conserved energy, reduced toxic wastes, and enhanced the efficiency of their capital. As Stephen Roach of Morgan Stanley observed: "The pattern of investment changed decisively in 1978, when high-tech spending surpassed basic industrial outlays for the first time."

The problem of the economists is that despite years of effort to predict economic change, they remain nearly oblivious to the vital processes of innovation and new company formation which constitute economic development. Their general posture toward the supply side of the economy is epitomized by the Input-Output tables of Vasily Leontieff, who won a Nobel Prize in 1973 for this alge-braically elegant but static system. These tabulations can compute the interrelated flows of goods and services among industries only by assuming that the underlying relationships are not changing. Designed to aid socialist planning, the Leontieff scheme is still widely regnant in Washington and in economic minds and mathe-matics everywhere. But it is worse than useless in examining a pro-tean economy where entrepreneurs at every moment of every day are transforming not merely inputs and outputs but also the rela-tions among them and the very nature of industries themselves.

An emerging industry like computer software or an exploding one like semiconductors or a rapidly expanding area such as ser-vices will define the future structure and direction of economic ac-tivity. Yet the dropping prices, rising values, and constant changes of inputs and outputs in these entrepreneurial activities—and the dominance of mind over matter in them—conceal them from the statisticians. A leading economist like Charles Schultze, the chair-man of Carter's Council of Economic Advisers, thus can disparage such a catalytic industry as computers as "only 2 percent of GNP," and thus less important than cosmetics or steel.

It is because economists miss the most productive dimensions of the economy that they can assert a dramatic decline in the growth of U.S. productivity. According to the usual statistics, the key sources of the problem have been mining, construction, and utili-ties; finance, insurance, and real estate (FIRE); retail and wholesale trade; and most of all, services, from law and accounting to health care and entertainment. In particular, the services, excluding gov-ernment, FIRE, and communications, have increased their share of total labor hours by about one-third in the last two decades (from 12 percent to 16 percent), but have shown negligible productivity gains.

Such data show an almost uncanny ability to identify as produc-tivity problems the very industries of fastest real productivity in-crease or greatest promise of future gains. For example, the largest productivity drop, of some 4 percent a year, came in mining, chiefly the drilling and production of crude oil and natural gas. This de-cline chiefly reflected a massive rise in oil and gas exploration and drilling, much of it performed by "wildcat" entrepreneurs. As they applied more capital and new technology and more numerous and highly trained personnel in increasingly difficult areas, in pursuit of deeper and less accessible deposits of fuel—from the arctic wastes of the North Slope and the Beaufort Sea through the complex geo-logical formations of the Rocky Mountain overthrust belt to the geopressurized methane deep along the Gulf of Mexico—measurable production per man-hour or unit of capital sharply dropped. Here, according to all the data, we can find a plummeting decline in productivity.

Together with decontrol of prices, however, these efforts broke the demoralizing grip of the energy crisis by discovering potentially unlimited new deposits of available but mostly not "produced" gas and oil. The energy companies developed a series of new seismographic, logging, and extraction technologies of permanent value, relieved the world economy of a ruinous burden of steadily rising fuel costs, released U.S. foreign policy from the clutches of OPEC, and reduced the likelihood of a major energy war. By any reasonable standard, economic or political, the real productivity of mining in America has soared since 1973. Countries such as Japan and Germany, which mostly escaped the burden on statistical productivity growth represented by this dynamic industry, have benefited nonetheless from its achievements in halting the energy price spiral and opening huge vistas of future fuel production.

Most of the other major statistics of productivity stagnation—in retailing and wholesaling, in finance and real estate, in the wide array of personal services—are deceptive and transitory effects of vast and interwoven demographic and structural shifts now under way in U.S. society. The demographic change was the coming of age of the post–World War II baby boom, a bulge of 75 million births that flooded the job force during the 1970s. Nothing comparable happened in Europe. These countries suffered more deeply during World War II, underwent no extended surge of postwar births, and met manpower needs by importing foreign workers during periods of expansion, and deporting them by the millions during the recession of the late 1970s. The United States, by contrast, created relatively settled jobs for some 12 million immigrants and tens of millions of young adults.

Despite the influx of job seekers, male and female, the United States ended the decade with a larger proportion of its adult civilian population employed than ever before in peacetime. More hours worked, by less experienced jobholders, however, swelled the denominator of the productivity index, thus diminishing measured productivity growth. If the U.S. work force had risen at a slower pace—or shrunk, as in Europe—our productivity data would look dramatically better, but we would be a less productive society.

At the same time, the United States poured unprecedented masses of capital into education, giving a larger share of its population more years of schooling than any other country in the history of the world, accommodating more than half its high school graduates in colleges, and almost entirely closing the gap between years of education completed by blacks and whites.

With capital relatively scarce and heavily diverted into housing and schools and with labor relatively ample and in need of training, America's entrepreneurs exploited the opportunity to create a vast array of labor-intensive enterprises that used and trained the baby-boom generation. Launching a large array of new service ventures, from fast-food restaurants and health-food groceries to record vendors and head shops, from convenience stores and barter exchanges to video boutiques and national electronic networks, from law firms and medical clinics to singles bars and jogging equipment chains, from birthing homes and computer centers to private schools and specialized bookstores, from historic-preservation architects and suppliers to surgicare centers and entrepreneurial consultancies, this generation created its own jobs and professions, businesses and styles. The result was a work force and, to a lesser extent, an economy more heavily devoted to the service and information industries that are driving the expansion of the U.S. economy.

Nonetheless, according to the statistics, the offices in which many of these activities occurred were torpid and unproductive. The productivity of offices rose a total of 4 percent during the entire decade of the 1970s, or less than 0.5 percent per year. Since the office is the factory floor of the service sector—and a growing accessory of every manufacturing firm—the near-complete stagnation of office productivity cast a pall over the prospects for the entire economy as the 1980s proceeded. Office costs rose from 20 percent of the average company's expenses to approach 50 percent; the cost of a business letter grew by 40 percent in real terms in a decade; secretaries' salaries mounted by two-thirds.

Many theorists concluded that services, with their requirements of personal contact and exchange, were inherently resistant to the kinds of efficiency improvement that had fueled economic progress during the industrial era. This line of analysis followed the perennial bent of leading social theorists—from Adam Smith and John Stuart Mill to Karl Marx and Joseph Schumpeter—to predict the eventual obsolescence of capitalism and its succession by some form of stationary state. The problem with the theory is that it, like the productivity statistics themselves, overlooks the newest industrial revolution: the industrialization of services, beginning with the automation of offices.

During the very same years that office productivity was so sluggish and offices were expanding their role in manufacturing firms, which in turn were bowing to gluts of paperwork and regulations, the fastest-growing industry in world capitalism was office electronics. Thousands of companies were riding to the rescue of the harried secretary and providing a steadily growing repertory of ingenious and low-priced devices designed to enhance productivity of offices. Pouring out of the factories of America was an ever-rising stream of new equipment, a pastel flood of new machines—cathode ray tubes and other screen technologies, solid-state memories and data-storage disks, intelligent copiers and facsimile consoles, modems, printers, digitizers, smart switchboards, and distributed computer terminals, with ever more "friendly" languages and user-sensitive software, all linked or integrated in ever-changing permutations, with mainframe computers and telecommunications satellites, or fiber-optic cables, and with home computers sharing ever-enlarged databanks and libraries through ever-expanding networks.

With many thousands of entrepreneurs and office marketeers, companies were splitting and merging, seeking niches and creating them, pushing up cubistic headquarters and production lines, mobilizing from Silicon Valley beachheads to outposts in Provo, Utah, and Triangle Park, North Carolina, and Orlando, Florida, swiveling to Phoenix and Colorado Springs, and from Route 128 overflowing with breakaways to 495, north and south. Many were gathered attentively around the secretary's desk, and down at the typing pool, and peering over the shoulders of middle management. Crowding in behind were small throngs of Japanese computer strategists, Taiwanese and Korean parvenus, and urgent German, British, Canadian, and French vendors of office machines.

All together the office-equipment entrepreneurs and their suppliers composed an industrial army unrivaled in the history of the world in technological genius, entrepreneurial daring, and capital clout, and all were obsessively determined to resolve the perplex of office productivity. Is there anyone who imagines they might possibly fail? There is no chance that offices will not succumb to this massive barrage; there is no chance that the next decade will not do for typewriters and secretaries, business letters and stenographers, filing cabinets and filing clerks, red tape and typing pools, what the industrial revolution accomplished for spinning wheels and hand looms and horsedrawn cabs—all dwarfing the gains of mechanization described by Adam Smith in his discourse on the manufacture of pins. The glut of paperwork, largely imposed by government and seen despairingly as a permanent affliction of enterprise, was giving away to practical dreams of a "paperless office."

Meanwhile a similar and equally far-reaching industrial movement, led by entrepreneurs, computer scientists, and manufacturing technicians, was rising up to overcome, for once and all, the dim drudgery of assembly lines, the harsh calculus of Taylor time and motion studies, the continuing sloughs of manufacturing routine. The crucial breakthrough came in computer-aided design (CAD): the actual working out in three-dimensional images on a video screen and testing in a computer simulation all the specifications of a new product or design. Gone are all the tedious sessions on a drafting board, and gone, too, is the need to build and test a long series of intricate prototypes. As one General Motors executive put it, "We fix parts before the car is built." But most important for manufacturing efficiency, the design process creates an exhaustive data base in the computer that can be transmitted to a computer-aided-manufacturing (CAM) operation—whether a fully automated injection molding machine or assembly line or a mere elaboration of numerically controlled machine tools—in a flexible manufacturing system (FMS).

Such operations have already designed, shaped, tested, or processed a wide range of diverse products that is growing rapidly. Among the many are disk-brake rotors and car trunks for GM, welded steel panels for Chrysler, tractor engine blocks for John Deere, dishwashers for GE, prototype nose cones for the Air Force, Cabbage Patch dolls for Coleco, elaborate hydraulic tubing systems for 747s and Northrop fighters, computer-controlled machine tools themselves for Cross and Trecker, even an entire new city plan, with 4,000 digitized three-dimensional buildings on hundreds of streets, for Vancouver, British Columbia, or still more impressive, the design of semiconductor chips, which hold on a tiny sliver of silicon a multiplicity of three-dimensional details comparable less to a single city plan than to the geophysical map of a continent.

This new industrial revolution is heavily based on software created by scores of entrepreneurial American companies. Software is to computers as records are to phonographs: the way to transform a deaf-and-dumb device into a useful machine. More than any other group, the thousands of computer software entrepreneurs epitomize the statistically elusive but explosively creative American economy in the age of information technologies. By changing the computer revolution from a dazzling but largely incomprehensible technical event into a universal force in our most mundane activities, software innovations are central to all the fastest-growing markets, from semiconductor chips to CAD devices, personal computers, credit cards, air travel, financial systems, medical instruments, seismic exploration tools, telecommunications networks, and video games. Yet they use virtually no capital themselves, and the capital equipment they endow is vastly cheaper than what it replaces.

An economic theory that interprets investment as a flow of demand will entirely omit this industry from its catalogs of capital formation. An economic model that measures output in terms of market prices will miss most of the production of these catalytic workers. They are the key to U.S. competitiveness in the world economy. Yet the some 5,000 leading software entrepreneurs pass on their vital contributions to U.S. progress and productivity largely free of charge and statistical recognition.

Here is the answer to the conundrum of how most American economists could describe the U.S. economy as a stagnant system, declining in productivity and innovation, falling rapidly behind its rivals in Europe and Asia, and teetering on the edge of a new Great Depression, during the very period when the United States regained the world lead in productivity growth and industrial progress. As entrepreneurs accelerate the processes of creative destruction that impel all economic advance, the economists measure the destruction, but not the creativity. They see the sinking value of existing capital but neglect the new ideas, hopes, enthusiasms, and plans of entrepreneurs. They count the bankruptcies, but doubt the business starts; they measure the decline of sterile investment in established companies, but miss the smaller flows of creative capital formation; they count the unemployed, but deny the new employment and self-employment; they count sheep, but not software; they overvalue cars and steel and undervalue water quality.

So countries that multiply their production of the well-defined and well-catalogued products of the past—from subsidized steel ingots to protected automobiles—will seem to grow faster than countries that multiply entrepreneurs and innovations. But in due course, if the politicians do not halt the process of creative destruction in the name of a spurious efficiency or demagogic equality, the entrepreneurs will finally prevail. They will establish their companies in the statistical models, standing still at last, ready to be measured, at the very moment they end their most creative phase.

·   ·   ·

For the last decade, the U.S. economy has suffered from a combination of hypochondria and iatrogenic illness. The hypochondria stems from spurious statistics and deceptive anecdotes and erroneous theories of American decline. It results in a period of fear and anxiety, propagated by the media, measured in public opinion polls, and enhanced by alarmist demagoguery. Iatrogenic illnesses are diseases caused by the doctor—in this instance by hundreds of economic Ph.D.s, government planners, and politicians who have responded to the pangs of hypochondria by inflicting thousands of real cuts on the entrepreneurs who make the economy go, as if, like the physicians of the Middle Ages, the experts believe in bleeding the patient as a way of restoring him to productive health.

The government failure, however, was inevitable. For like the medieval physicians, the government experts had scarcely a clue as to the condition of the patient or the sources of its health. The inability to predict, measure, or understand entrepreneurial creativity hobbled nearly all national economic forecasts and proposals. Fortunately the government, in general, failed to impose most of the uninformed plans and fantasies that its experts did offer for the future in which we live.

In the early 1970s, the prevailing wisdom foresaw a cramped and constricted human prospect, blighted by a scarcity of energy, by a structural decline in U.S. productivity as we moved toward a society of services, and by a stagnant economy still dependent on the housing, steel, and auto industries for much of our employment and prosperity. There was no end of vast governmental remedies proposed for these crises: a moral equivalent of war to conserve oil, a regimen of reindustrialization to revive productivity, a special program of guidance and subsidies to promote the new "sunrise industries" of our future, an array of protections and loan guarantees to renew our troubled heavy industry and housing, and new restrictions on immigration to prevent a rising burden on U.S. employment and social services.

Yet energy scarcity has now given way to a glut that, barring major war or price controls, will likely grow for the rest of the century, forcing fuel costs down in real terms and imparting a new impulse of growth. The problem of productivity is about to succumb to a massive technological revolution that will vastly enlarge the productive powers of mankind. The stagnation of housing production will be seen as the effect of a government-fostered glut of housing which left some 60 percent of Americans as homeowners in incomparably the world's best-housed nation. The deep depression suffered by the auto and steel industries will be seen—in the course of time—as easing the shift of resources into the energy, service, and high-technology companies that are leading us into an era of productive possibilities unprecedented in human history. And, most important, few of these entrepreneurial feats would have happened without the crucial contributions of labor, ingenuity, and industrial daring from a new generation of immigrants.

Since experts neither fathomed nor foresaw these changes, the government, however hard it tried, could not plan or promote them. Stultifying every search for the "sunrise" firms of the future was the blinding midday sun of political fashions and settled interests. Washington inevitably taxed the wealth and savings of entrepreneurs and diverted them into efforts to find the future in windmills, and coal, and fusion power, in solar collectors in wilderness areas, in giant centralized computer systems, in subsidized trains, in new and ingenious ways of further fixating capital in housing, autos, and steel, in all the usual, elaborate schemes for propping up the past in the name of progress.

The central reason that the "sunrise" industries were ignored, however, is simpler than power or fashion: Most of the companies which played the decisive role in overcoming the trials of the 1970s hardly existed when the decade began; they were merely ideas in the heads of entrepreneurs, or tiny firms scarcely discernible in the throng of many millions.

The energy crisis, for example, was not resolved chiefly by the large oil companies or by the leviathan vendors of nuclear power and subsidized synfuels. Rather it was overcome by thousands of wildcatters around the world and by a few entrepreneurs who recognized—against all the counsels of geological expertise in the Department of Energy—that the fuel of the future would be natural gas, and that it is virtually inexhaustible. Bringing further relief were thousands of firms—and millions of individuals—increasing the fuel efficiency of virtually every mechanical process in the economy and conserving energy at a pace far exceeding the prognosis of those urging an era of draconian controls.

Solving the productivity problem as well were firms unformed or too small to be found in 1970 and thus sure to have missed all subsidies for the sunrise. In particular, new companies selling personal computers are giving small business the capability for financial planning, inventory management, and accounting controls once available only to large corporations with whole departments devoted to these tasks.

The projects that these entrepreneurs initiated and carried through during the 1970s—the technical and marketing problems they confronted and overcame—had one essential quality in common. All had been thoroughly contemplated by the regnant experts and dominant companies, with their large research staffs and financial resources, and had been judged too difficult, untimely, risky, expensive, and unprofitable. These breakthroughs, which sometimes appear inevitable in retrospect, in prospect seemed uninviting to the leading experts in the field.

The universal marketing of personal computers appeared irresistible to Stephen Jobs of Apple in his Cupertino garage. But it seemed altogether too risky or costly to authorities at Hewlett-Packard. The immense treasure of natural-gas reserves that loomed in the mind of John Masters as he pondered oil company log books in western Alberta—or that struck the imagination of independent engineers probing the possibilities of geopressurized methane near Louisiana's coast—seemed a ridiculous exaggeration to the experts of Exxon or the Department of Energy as they explored the greater promise of synfuels. The early production of computer systems for widespread use in design and manufacturing struck Martin Allen and Philippe Villiers at the small offices of Computervision in Bedford, Massachusetts, as the birth of a new industrial era. But it seemed a farfetched and low-priority idea for several years to the corporate leaders at IBM.

The entrepreneurial achievements of the 1970s and early 1980s came in the face of a hostile press, a resistant culture, and a stagnant "economy." The most popular literature of enterprise was devoted to the contemplation of industrial crimes, the prophecy of doom, and the talismanic protections of gold and land, and much of the activity of government was channeled into choking small business with new taxes and regulations. The breakthroughs of these entrepreneurs are an amazing testimony to human will and ingenuity, vision and tenacity in defiance of the odds.

It is the very essence of human creativity, however, as Albert Hirschman has written, that it *always* comes as a surprise to us. If it didn't defy the odds, we could plan it and it would not be necessary. The unexpected boon, the industrial miracle, has become the predictable and providential surprise of capitalism. Entrepreneurs do not succeed through marginal increments. They succeed by shooting for the moon and hitting natural gas under the blast-off site. They head for India and hit the Caribbean. If one follows their activity closely—keeping an eye on the J. R. Simplots of the world—it is still even possible to discover the unknown continents of the real economy.

3

THE EXPLORER

The prophesied depressions of the period were not merely economic. The late 1960s and early 1970s launched a new religion of disaster as the opiate of the publishing classes. For a decade, like doomsday adventists, they gathered at the tops of glass towers in mid-Manhattan and gazed into the lowering clouds for glimpses and portents of profitable gloom. Remember *The Closing Circle?* The greenhouse effect? The death of Lake Erie? The coming ice age? *The Limits to Growth?* The end of the family? *The Day We Almost Lost Detroit?* It was a time when intellectuals thronged every new theory of catastrophe and shunned only a solvable problem, a reasonable remedy, a market solution.

By 1973, it seemed, much of America was awaiting retribution for guilt-ridden riches—listening for an avenging word. First it came from the desert, as if from men high on camels and hashish: Colonel Qaddafi, Sheik Yamani, and the Shah of Iran, posturing as nemeses for the prodigal and oil-addled West. Then it echoed at the White House in Washington, on Capitol Hill, and at conferences of scholars at MIT, Berkeley, and Harvard. A demoralized science of economics mated with a series of other dismal disciplines to produce a geology, an ecology, even a physics of despair. The word was "crisis," and the crisis was energy: entropy, scarcity, exhaustion.

In any such crisis, the people turn anxiously to experts, for understanding and consolation, for explanations and remedies. The experts on energy soon came forth in numbers, from the Federal Energy Administration, the Ford Foundation, the Harvard Business School, the Committee on Economic Development, the National Academy of Engineering, the White House Energy Policy and Planning staff, the National Academy of Sciences, the Carnegie

Foundation, the Club of Rome, the National Research Council. All consulted the most eminent men of special knowledge from Bell Laboratories, Livermore, Argonne, and the U.S. Geological Survey, from the paramount technological businesses and even the White House: such men as Gordon Moore of Intel, Ralph Gomory of IBM, and Frank Press of the President's Office of Science and Technology Policy.

These peers of American science offered a statistical vision of the future hardly more inviting than the imprecations of the sheiks. The consensus projection of American oil and gas reserves set a sentence of seventeen years, followed by life at hard labor, probably mining coal. In its report published in September 1974, *Energy Resources for the Year 2000 and Beyond*, Mitre Corporation predicted a rapid decline in the availability of fossil fuels beginning in 1990. Even the giant oil companies with their command of all the most expensive geological expertise accepted this scenario, and Exxon boldly proceeded to commit $30 billion for synthetic fuels production—largely without government aid—even though the project would fail unless conventional reserves ran low.

The experts acknowledged that by the use of coal, nuclear power, and shale, the crisis might be deferred. But the risk and expense of these solutions seemed only to add new problems to the old scarcities. Coal posed dire threats of pollution and of overheating the biosphere; nuclear power was regarded as politically and technologically perilous; synthetic fuels production entailed not only vast wastage of water but also huge new capital investments that would be difficult to sustain during a period when some $60 billion was shipped to the Middle East annually and the economy faced an alleged need for reindustrialization.

Following the paradigm of *The Limits to Growth*, issued by the Club of Rome in 1972, the established wisdom of the time saw a new age of austerity in store for the West. The eminent gnome of New York's international bankers, Robert Roosa, and energy guru Walter Levy contributed ominous articles to *Foreign Affairs*. Professor Charles Lindblom of Yale summed up the mood in the opening paragraph of his magisterial *Politics and Markets*, published in 1977: "Relentlessly accumulating evidence suggests that human life on the planet is headed for catastrophe." The only way to avert it, he maintained, was through imposition of central planning.

The politicians and bureaucrats took it from there. A Department of Energy was established; a synfuels corporation was set up; and Congress promulgated a new national speed limit, a seven-volume set of home appliance efficiency standards, and an array of conservation tax incentives. It enacted a law against the use of natural gas in new utility boilers and a complex scheme of price controls and entitlements on both oil and gas. Washington began subsidizing windmills, solar cells, insulation, and "gasohol," while penalizing the use of petroleum. Yet year by year, as the 1970s proceeded—from gunfights in gas lines, bicycle lanes on Fifth Avenue, and great hovering clouds of woodsmoke pollution in rural New England, toward President Carter's climatically impotent declaration of "a moral equivalent of war" in 1979—the problem grew worse and worse: Imports increased, scientific projections grew gloomier, and OPEC tightened its noose. In 1979, it again doubled its prices, and the economy gasped.

A similar drama, with similar roles for the experts and the politicians, was being played out in Canada, the principal non-OPEC source of American energy supplies and a belated oil producer believed to have huge reserves in the mountains of the west. Like the United States, Canada imported half its fuel, mostly from Venezuela, to the eastern provinces; but its exports were rapidly expanding from the oil fields of western Canada to the west and central American states.

In the fall of 1972, however, the National Energy Board of Canada issued a stark warning that oil and gas production was pushing near its limits and could no longer keep up with rising domestic and foreign demand. In 1973, after reports of dwindling reserves in the "oil patch" of Alberta and protests of an "energy sellout" to the United States, Canada imposed controls on its exports. The long oil boom in the West was apparently coming to a close. Imperial Oil, Exxon's affiliate in Canada, dominant in the area since 1947, began withdrawing to focus on costly and perilous exploration in arctic oceans and remote foreign frontiers. And while the established petroleum industry in Canada began to cut back, the government sharply increased energy taxes. Both sides explained their actions by arguing that there was no more oil to find anyway. Production in the oil patch reached a peak in 1972 and briskly declined in the years that followed. As in the United States, natural gas in particular was seen as a dwindling asset. Canada's resource was assayed by the experts as enough to last some twenty years at current rates of usage, far too little to satisfy the growing gargantuan thirst below the border.

To this situation came John Masters, a 1948 Yale graduate, then an unemployed explorer from Tulsa, Oklahoma. He had no money and owned no oil reserves, but he did have a few ideas and some brilliant friends. Over the following seven years, he would build a company. He would go into the mountains of Alberta in 1973 when all the other companies were coming out, and would find, and in a sense embody, the solution to the energy crisis. His insights would spark large new discoveries in the overthrust belts of the Rockies and Appalachians in the United States, and in foreign ventures from Colombia to Spain. But it is less his ideas than the spirit he epitomizes and the phenomenon he embodies that are now dissipating the pall of the Arab East and providing the answer to the larger crisis of enterprise in the West.

In 1973, though, he was at a nadir, aged forty-seven, without a job, without capital, working out of a borrowed one-room office in Calgary, pursuing a concept that all the experts perceived as foolish. Some twenty years before, as a precocious prospector for Kerr-McGee, hired away from the Atomic Energy Commission by Dean McGee himself, he had been a rising star. At twenty-eight, he led the team that discovered Ambrosia Lake in New Mexico, the largest uranium deposit in America. Later, as the company's chief geologist, he had made the first discovery of oil in Arizona and two finds in the Gulf of Mexico. But that was long ago. During the previous twelve years, as the company's chief geologist, working everywhere from the Gulf Coast through Texas and to the Rockies, and as head of the Kerr-McGee exploration effort in Canada, he had made no substantial finds of oil or gas. There were reports of mental instability—a nervous breakdown during an earlier stay in Canada—and rumors that he had lost his touch. The word was that he had become obsessive about the large potential of possibly huge but thinly spread reserves in the Alberta foothills: gas fields already drilled and abandoned and certified worthless by their oil company owners. At best, it was believed, these fields could offer some small but steady yield if energy prices doubled, a doubtful prospect.

Finally Kerr-McGee summoned Masters back to the United States for another assignment, some capacious desk in Oklahoma City. Dean McGee's patience with his protégé was running low. Rather than leave Alberta a failure and give up his dream of a bonanza in natural gas, Masters told Dean McGee he was quitting. In a lifesaving coup (by announcing "You quit too"), he also induced a Canadian friend and colleague, Jim Gray, to join him. Together they formed what was to become the legendary Canadian Hunter Corporation. They were leaving the precincts of expertise and entering the realm of exploration. No longer "company geologists," they were becoming a company—without assets, but with ideas.

Their central ideas were expressed in a fund-raising memo they presented early in 1973, some six months before the oil price hike, to the major oil and financial firms of Canada: "No matter what various politicians do to impede these changes, supply and demand, with a big assist from OPEC with regard to oil, will force these prices to levels that are difficult for us to conceive of today. These price factors make it possible to review old well information and reinterpret fields that were discovered and discarded years ago."

Masters believed in particular that new technologies and higher prices would make it profitable to exploit natural gas in low-porosity "tight sands." Tight gas—like the gold flakes in ocean water or the oil in shale—had never been seen as a valuable resource in the past. But Masters knew that Amoco scientists had developed new methods of fracturing sandstone—using a variety of pumped chemical foams, hydraulic pressures, and even nuclear explosions—to pummel tight sands into a relatively loose and fissured form. A Texan professor named Steven Holditch, "the father of mass frac," had invented a method of splitting tough underground rock formations into fracture patterns two thousand feet long. Masters asserted that this technique could transform the barren wastes of Alberta's tight sandstone—already perforated with dry or exhausted holes—into a treasure trove of natural gas. Moreover, the log books, giving the geological details from some 100,000 wells and all available for free inspection in the files of the Energy Board in Calgary, would reveal the location of this resource without further drilling. Masters also had the notion, which he did not stress, that huge *new* deposits could be found through a search informed by the new economics and technologies of gas.

Masters readily acknowledged that these propositions were difficult, uncertain, and expensive to apply. Mass frac, for example, cost nearly $500,000 a well, justifiable only for lucrative finds. But he saw 1973 as a year of unique opportunity to acquire huge potential resources at costs that would seem negligible as the world moved into what he was sure would be an era of much higher energy prices. "Once an opportunity is generally known," as Masters put it, "it is pretty well gone."

Masters had identified an entrepreneurial moment: when risks are high and calculable (at more than $1 million for every dry hole), while rewards glimmer in the misty distance, dim and deceptive to the naked eye, looming in nebulous magnificence only in the conceptual glimpse of the entrepreneur. "You have to recognize," he wrote later, "that every 'out front' maneuver you make is going to be lonely. But if you feel entirely comfortable then you're not far enough ahead to do any good. That warm sense of everything going well is usually the body temperature at the center of the herd."

It was not Masters who was "out front" at that point, however.

Masters was to be the chief finder of gas and oil, but it was Gray who led the effort to find capital, a more important early objective. Masters's grandiose visions were readily dismissed as a mirage by all the major companies.

"The response was always the same," Gray remembers. "The president would be all enthused with my pitch. Then later he'd arrange dinner with some so-called expert. The guy would tell him we were wingy and anyway gas was something everyone was piling out of. We always had several CEOs on a string, adding more while the earlier ones dropped away."

Perhaps one of the problems was their focus on companies with large experience in oil and gas. As Chesterton has observed, "The argument of the expert, that the man who is trained should be the man who is trusted, would be absolutely unanswerable if it were really true that the man who studied a thing and practiced it every day went on seeing more and more of its significance. But he does not. He goes on seeing less and less of its significance." For whatever reason, the expert-ridden companies already dominant in a field rarely produce the breakthroughs that transform it. From the failure of most carriage makers to produce a workable automobile to the failure of Kodak to make an instant camera, established firms have usually stood aside while new companies, or firms in other fields, have introduced the radical innovations.

In this case it would be copper executives, happily free of success or certified knowledge in natural gas, who first comprehended the promise of Canadian Hunter. In the copper business they were familiar with the vistas of profitability that had opened in low-grade ores after the nationalization of mines in Chile in the 1960s raised the world copper price. In the end, slag heaps and other highly diluted deposits in Canada yielded profits comparable to the world's best mines of the past. But the most unexpected profit from these low-grade ores was the minds capable of identifying similar patterns in other fields and the confidence to exploit them.

The copper executives were Bill Row and Alf Powis, Noranda's executive vice-president and president, and their own entrepreneurial courage can be measured by their willingness, beginning with a $5 million outlay, to pour a total of some $300 million into a tiny company in another field over the next five years—in the face of dogged skepticism of Toronto establishment figures such as Jack Armstrong, president of Imperial Oil. These funds, moreover, were expended on the basis not of proved reserves but of a visionary idea that emerged in the mind of John Masters as he and his team of geologists pored through old logs in the light of new findings from Hunter's first series of successful wells.

Oil and gas exploration is largely a search for primeval seashores. Just as coal represents the compacted remains of millions of years of vegetable matter piled up in freshwater swamps, oil and gas are the residue of similar eons of marine animal life, decaying near the mouths and deltas of long-forgotten tropical rivers or in the reefs and channels of long-annihilated seas. The smaller strikes tend to be in the reefs and channels, but occasionally it is possible to discover the vast beach of a paleolithic ocean, buried, twisted, and compressed under a many-layered welter of hidden continents that have been shifting and turning their maws and masses and mysteriously secreting their treasures over immemorial time. Sometimes the beaches are buckled and trapped by evulsed mountains thrusting up and over porous stone reservoirs, the *overthrust* belts of oil and gas; sometimes they are caught in great salt domes, or under hulking folds of shale and clay, the geologists' *anticlines*, that capture the gases and fluids as they are pressed upward from the beaches below. Over the eons of geological time, western Canada had several times succumbed to such seas, had erupted in sheer ranges of Rockies that shouldered the sandy beds aside, shedding their sediments down toward the west, to be submerged and sealed in many-layered avalanches of impermeable rock.

Masters summed up the problem: "The process of finding oil is essentially the analytic reconstruction of geologic history in order to determine the probable hiding place of oil and gas accumulations that are buoyant, mobile, and constantly seeking upward escape. . . . It has elements of a detective story, a spy mystery, the search for a hidden tomb. . . ."

It was this labyrinthine puzzle, this fathomless stratigraphic maze, buried beneath the silent and scintillating scenery, the luminous mountain topography of Alberta, that John Masters—after many setbacks over fifteen years and with much help summoned from afar—finally solved.

His technique, integrating the knowledge acquired by fresh drilling with the enormous body of data from scores of thousands of old electric log books, was not new. What was new was the creative interplay between new and old data, as the logs were used as a tool for geophysical reconnaissance, leading to immediate siting of new wells, and the projection of new theory.

As Masters explained in technical prose that nonetheless fairly bursts with excitement and pride, in the manner of its author:

"Soon we had contour maps which defined the areas of best permeability. . . . We were contour-mapping detailed reservoir quality on an exploration scale from electric log measurements! We had big, one inch to one mile maps of the Halfway formation, seven feet

by four feet, showing all the land ownership, all wells, all tests. . . .
We were mapping trillions of cubic feet of 'undiscovered' but actually already indicated gas. . . ."

The combination of a strong and far-reaching concept with the persistent and ingenious detailed log analysis in the end suggested the tantalizing possibility that Canadian Hunter had found, in the deepest part of the Alberta basin, a gigantic sedimentary beach. Conceivably stretching for hundreds of miles across Alberta and into British Columbia, it perhaps contained trillions of cubic feet of natural gas: a possible new field which could substantially increase the natural-gas reserves of North America.

The theory gained some ground as rock samples from startlingly productive new wells—much more permeable than the usual tight sands—were tested in Calgary. Dave Smith, Hunter's chief geologist, and Bob Sneider, one of a brilliant team of consultants from Houston, joined Masters in the core lab one day in September 1976 to appraise the materials. Pondering the heavy sandstone cylinders of rock chiseled from the new well, they marveled at their visible porosity, the spaces between the conglomerate pebbles. They exclaimed with delight at this sign that at least some of the wells in the region could hit sweet permeable patches which would more cheaply and rapidly yield their fuel. But Sneider was silent, contemplating not the immediate flows of cash, but the larger meanings of an anomaly.

He gazed for several minutes in perplexity at the gray samples. His mind wandered back to a trip to the Gulf of Mexico with Masters and his Houston colleague Larry Meckel. They had visited "bays and estuaries, channels and deltas and bars, lagoons, swamps, growth faults, and salt domes": a visible current replication of all the ancient formations, now lost and scrambled deep in the earth, that were the goal of their quest. Masters wrote: "We jumped in the water and felt with our toes the sand of a transgressive overlap. . . ." What was it about those gray stone cores? Sneider wondered.

Then he snapped his fingers and burst out with the answer: "By God, that's beach conglomerate! Pebble beaches. Look how well sorted it is. Look how it coarsens upward!" A wide blanket rather than a narrow riverine channel, the reservoir could possibly fit into an extended littoral "trend" of deltaic plain, coal swamp, and offshore accretions that would make up, as it transpired, the Elmworth Deep Basin.

But first there would be many more dry holes, at a cost of $1 million apiece. There would be many misgivings, after their first gusher, as they moved deeper into the suspected trend toward British Columbia, into what seemed, by all odds, a graveyard of 5,000 square miles, punctuated only by forty abandoned dry holes, without the usually revealing logs from which to map potential reserves. Even Noranda could not imagine a large gas discovery in an area which had been explored by several multinational giants and, after a multimillion-dollar investment, been written off for good. Hunter hit another strong well, however, twelve miles farther down the trend. It was a lot better than another dry hole, but it offered no proof of a grander design.

By July of 1978 Hunter had spent $82 million on these intriguing and occasionally successful, but still inconclusive, explorations pointing to what Trans-Canada Pipelines called "a temporary gas bubble." But Dave Smith then decided to accelerate things with a $500 million idea, and a short but now legendary flight in an Okanagan helicopter. If, as Masters believed, the Alberta trend ran northwest through undrilled wilderness into British Columbia, one might be able to find outcrops of beach conglomerate in the foothills of British Columbia. These outcrops would then allow them to map more clearly the precise direction of the trend and focus their land purchases more accurately. In pursuit of this idea, Smith, Meckel, and another Hunter geologist took off on their famous northwest flight from the heliport at Fort St. John. Even though he did not make the trip, John Masters, as usual, tells the story best:

"A half hour later they were skimming over the southern end of the outcrops. They touched down once, then again, and again, as they worked their way northward. Each outcrop showed rocks that were clearly of continental origin—delta, plain, swamp, river channel. No sign of the coastal beaches. Then at Bullmoose Mountain, they found massive cliffs of pebble conglomerate. It had the sorting and grading of a beach. They had found the needle in the haystack."

They had found the key piece of information that told Hunter how to locate the trend across fifty miles of undrilled, unleased acreage. As soon as they got back to Fort St. John, Larry Meckel rushed to a phone and announced to Masters their discovery: "You could hear the goddamn sea gulls!" Masters adds, "They were screaming across a hundred million years of time."

This was the clue they needed to confirm Masters's theory of an immense basin of gas, in total resource one of the largest reserves in the world.

Now they needed big money. "An oil finder will usually see only a flicker, a momentary opening," Masters wrote, "but he must blast through it like a panzer general, committing men and material and assets to pry it open and hold it open. If he flinches, he is lost. If he is wrong, he is lost. If all goes well—he has the luck of the gods." It was this willingness to strike with force from a redoubt of mere faith that built Hunter into a multibillion-dollar company in 1979.

Up to this point, Hunter had depended chiefly on Noranda. But Noranda had run into trouble in the copper business and could help no further. Jim Gray's frantic calls to other companies bore little fruit. The banks and big industrial firms still balked, and the leading geologists dismissed Masters's claims of a large basin. Hunter had been able to take command of the Alberta portion of the basin chiefly by virtue of the faith of Gus Van Wielingen of Sulpetro, who committed $24 million in exchange for 50 percent of the rights in any acreage purchased with the money, but without any further collateral or commitment. This deal financed the first panzer campaign. Then rumors of a large strike began circulating and other money began to come in—from Blue Sky and Petromark, backed by German tax shelter funds, and from the increasing flow of income from operating wells. After the sea gull revelation, Hunter purchased rights on 334,000 acres in British Columbia for $47 million. Other firms began to realize that something important was happening and they started buying into the company.

Finally, on July 3, 1979, Cal Evans, the vice-president of exploration for Imperial Oil Company, Exxon's Canadian subsidiary, called on John Masters, the president of Canadian Hunter, at his office in Calgary, to propose a deal. Jack Armstrong had changed his mind. Imperial would offer $60 million worth of drilling in exchange for a range of complex interests in the Elmworth Basin. After conferring with Jim Gray, Hunter offered a simpler plan, 15 percent of the company for $150 million, and that was the eventual deal.

On August 12, the *Financial Post* of Canada reported: "Imperial Oil Ltd., Canada's largest oil company, is now in the final stages of negotiations with Noranda Mines Ltd. to buy its way into the extensive land holding of Noranda's 75 percent owned subsidiary Canadian Hunter Exploration Ltd. . . . For Noranda, the deal establishes its funding of Canadian Hunter as its shrewdest investment in recent years."

Masters wrote in his diary: "We are living through a period of momentous oil and gas discoveries, yet a large segment of opinion in our industry and in the regulatory bodies seems oblivious to them. They seem to be entirely satisfied with projections of Canadian hydrocarbon supplies made several years ago in an entirely different economic and psychological climate.

"What predictive index gave the slightest indication that in 1967 we would find at Prudhoe Bay the largest oil field in the history of the U.S., or that in 1976 we would find in the Deep Basin the largest gas basin in the history of both the U.S. and Canada? And can you name a single geologist in the entire world five years ago who would have bet 25 cents that a new Middle East would be recognized in Mexico?" By 1984, 17 trillion cubic feet had been ascertained at Elmworth, giving it the fourth-largest available reserves on the continent, and suggesting a still-larger long-term prospect: a total possible resource of some 400 trillion cubic feet, or six times the know reserves of Canada.

• • •

Some 80 percent of all the wells drilled in the history of the petroleum industry have been drilled in just four American states. Yet vast new finds, particularly of natural gas, continue to be made in the United States, from the overthrust belt in the Rockies to the Tuscaloosa Trend in Louisiana. But the fact is that equally capacious and more easily accessible reserves are likely to be found anywhere in the world where men like John Masters and his associates are allowed to explore.

The essential problem of energy scarcity recapitulates the problem of all economic progress. The limits to growth are found not in God or nature, but in failures of faith and restrictions of law: all the doom-laden extrapolations of expertise that deny the infinite possibilities of creative men as they penetrate the frontiers of the darkness that is always closing in on mortal minds, and reach—in risk and worship—for the inestimable treasures of light beyond.

The importance of John Masters is measured not chiefly in the still-debated indices of trillion cubic feet of natural gas at Elmworth but in his continuing command of the crucial underlying source of most business triumph: dedication to technological and scientific learning that does not eclipse an overarching knowledge of more profound truths. It was the spirit of enterprise—the mysterious workings of creativity and faith—that moved the mountains of human sloth and uncertainty which had gathered for centuries over the deep basins of energy treasure in Canada and the United States. It is this spirit of enterprise that can surmount all the material scarcities of human life.

Canadian Hunter Corporation ran into trouble in the years 1981 and 1982. Not only did the firm find the essential exploratory solution to the energy crisis, it also, unfortunately, rediscovered the perpetual cause. Still believing in the calculus of scarcity, the Canadian government has resolved to restrict drastically its exports of natural gas and hoard Canada's energy reserves as if they were running out. The energy experts in Ottawa are still preparing for some doom scenario in coming decades and in the process are depleting the reserves of enterprise which are always indispensable in overcoming the real crises.

So while Hunter's wells still pump a steady stream of gas into the Trans-Canada Pipelines, Masters and Gray are turning south, to the United States, to drill their new wells, through a subsidiary entitled American Hunter. Together with the disbanding of the battalions of experts at the Department of Energy, this flow of human capital—the Hunters, themselves—south from the Elmworth Basin will probably be more valuable than any increase in its southward flows of natural gas might have been. Governments that attempt to hoard wealth in the form of matter or heavily redistribute it in the form of money often will find its crucial essence then slips away.

Through all the centuries of man, there has recurred this same morbid misunderstanding of the nature of wealth and the wealth of nations. Always wealth is seen as something solid and calculable: to be seized and held, clutched and hoarded, measured and inventoried, amassed and monopolized. In the age of imperialism, it was imagined to consist in land and the armies which could acquire it; in the mercantilist era, it was recognized as bullion, gained through a favorable balance of trade; in every period, men have fawned over gems and glitter; in the modern age, fossil fuels and strategic minerals have seemed to be the open sesame, but seekers of wealth still fumble for gold and baubles, and real estate as well.

All bespeak the materialistic fallacy, a fixation of leftists, but a shibboleth also for much of the intelligentsia of capitalism: the idea that wealth is material and collectible, finite and definable, subject to measurement and inventory, to entropy and exhaustion. The way to get rich is to find some precious substance and hold it. Its price will inevitably rise in time as its quantity declines with use. This is the fantasy through which Pierre Trudeau was bankrupting Canada in the early 1980s and the Arab leaders were impoverishing the world and destroying their own future.

Wealth consists not chiefly in things but in thought: in the ideas and applications which confer value to what seems useless to the uninformed. The Arab leaders should learn that they can best enhance the value of oil—and the wealth of oil-producing nations—by lowering its price and enlarging its uses. This is the central rule of riches, understood by every major titan of wealth, from John D. Rockefeller and Henry Ford to the entrepreneurs of modern computers and the industrialists of contemporary Japan. Each gained his fortune not by increasing the price of his product but by drastically dropping it, bringing it within the reach of the creative uses and ideas of millions, and thus vastly enlarging its total value and market. John Masters did not find value in the Alberta mountains; he brought it there. Its value ultimately sprang from his own values: his courage, ingenuity, diligence, and faith.

The strange effort to subject the mind to the laws of matter—life to the laws of death—ironically comes at a time when physicists are emancipating matter from its Newtonian constraints. While economists discover new limits to economic growth in the supposedly immutable laws of physics, scientists are discovering a vast prodigal arena of life and freedom in the realm of the infinitesimal. Penetrating beyond the opaque and paltry surface of things, they are learning to move and work in a labyrinthine world as intricate and variable as a city and as fertile as a deltaic plain, all encompassed in such seemingly inert forms as the silicon in a grain of sand or the DNA in a germ. When a microprocessor system the size of a moth can hold the contents of *War and Peace*—and read it to find all passages in which Natasha talks to Andrei, or Pierre talks to God—the ostensibly remorseless constraints of matter fall hopelessly away. The "limits" to growth become merely its frontiers. From the awesome reaches of the universe to the microelectronic galaxies of inner space, from microbiology to petroleum geology, the world opens its portals, sloughs off limits and boundaries, and overcomes the "closing circles" of ecological expertise with ever-widening spirals of possibility.

But at the Ford Foundation and the Harvard Faculty Club, the world seems bleak and forbidding. Brows are furrowed, hands kneaded, voices quake over an expert report, false like so many others, that we are losing our farmland, our forests, our wilderness retreats (and no one can see the forest for the trees sprouting in New England fields). We are *dependent*, moreover, it is so truly seen, with a full sense of the endless betrayals of life beyond the womb, on unreliable strangers, for food, and minerals, and nuclear forbearance.

There is another report, entirely true, that people in America, in all walks of life, are actually *dying of cancer* (another way of putting it is that they are living longer and avoiding death by other diseases). The professors are concerned. They know they are living in an era—they dare to say it—of unprecedented perils: of scarcity, pollution, famine, and plague. In fact, these contemporary crises are unprecedented chiefly in their possibility of being overcome.

Why is it that as real human possibilities expand almost boundlessly, many intellectuals feel only new pangs of claustrophobia? While science and enterprise open vast new panoramas of opportunity, our established experts flee in horror to all available caves and cages, like so many aborigines, terrified by freedom and change. From the statistical and ecological penitentiaries in which they have confined themselves, and wish to incarcerate mankind, they can find hope only in halting progress, possibility only in limiting population, gaiety and freedom chiefly in glum sweats and sterilities of "liberated" sensuality.

These intellectuals, of course, are absolutely sincere in their claustrophobic testimonies. Their morbid anxieties about "nonrenewable" resources, "finite" reserves, limits of growth, closing circles of nature, all bespeak the predicament of any mortal worshiper of matter and flesh. Matter is "nonrenewable," flesh is finite and exhaustible, co-eds flee the withered touch, youth is fleeting and beset by natural laws and depletions of energy. The contemporary intellectual, denying God, is in a trap, and he projects his entrapment onto the world. But the world is not entrapped; man is not finite; the human mind is not bound in material brain.

Like most of the hype and hysterics of modern intellectuals, the energy crisis is most essentially a religious disorder, a failure of faith. It can be overcome chiefly by worship: by a recognition that beyond the darkness and opacity of our material entrapment is a realm of redemptive spirit, reachable through that interplay of faith and fact which some call science, others poetry, but which is most luminously comprehended as forms of prayer.

The exploration of matter is always a crucial preliminary phase, pursued through the scrupulous collection and manipulation of empirical data in the light of physical laws. But matter obeys these laws only to the extent that it is dead. Any creative breakthrough, in science or art, enterprise or love, depends on glimpsing and engaging some higher realm of life. Beyond the long labyrinths of things, the multifarious carrels of fact, the inspired explorer can finally break out into the mansions of providential mind. He then sees the limits of the culture of thanatopsis: the dismal mazes of entropy and death, the grim aporias of sense and flesh, the vain hoards of sterile wealth. He can stand at last with wild surmise on the frontiers of matter where life and God again begin, and see a world renewed and shining with possibility.

4

THE MAN WHO WANTED TO CLEAN THE WATER

"There was water everywhere," Milos Krofta remembers. It was 1935 in Ljubljana, Yugoslavia, at the country's largest and most advanced papermaking factory. It was always wet; water was always spraying from some pipe or dripping from a vat or leaking from a valve. It bothered him. A blond, erect, fastidious young man who had been the youngest engineering graduate in the history of the local university, he was now studying for his doctorate in paper manufacture at a leading technical university of the day, Darmstadt in Germany. Between his trips north to the school, he was also working as an assistant technical manager in the plant, assigned to find ways of reducing the costs of production. The son of one of the owners of the company, he expected soon to play a still more significant role. And he kept slipping on water.

It was perfectly natural for a paper mill to be wet. Papermaking is mainly a matter of processing an array of fluids. Although the final product is a tissue of dry cellulosic fibers, for most of the productive steps the moving pulp, the so-called "half-stuff," is a slurry of between 95 and 99 percent water. This flux of intact and freely flowing cellulose fibers is beaten into a cohesive pulp. Then the so-called "white water" residue left over from the pulping process is recirculated to dilute the mixture and speed its flow. Spread into a thin homogeneous film or web, it runs down a wire-mesh screen that finally strains away the water, leaving the fibers and fillers to be shaped, dried, heated, treated, and gently rocked and rolled into paper, while the wastes are flushed away and forgotten.

Krofta, though, did not forget the wastes. He would sometimes go down to the river, the Ljubljanica, which swept by the mill, and watch the tons of effluent tumble from sluices into the stream. It didn't look very different from the waters passing through the plant. Except that it was officially designated "waste," it might well have been another flow of paper fibers. He wondered what was in those frothy cataracts. He asked questions of the workers; he tightened valves; he inquired persistently about the chemistry of the wastes; and he refused to accept the usual dismissive replies.

Krofta was groping his way toward the mode of thinking that we now term ecological. His first step was to see that the wastes were a crucial part of the process—white water that was getting away. He decided to write his thesis on the problem of how to measure the contents of these wastes. He concluded that they offered the key to reducing further the costs of production.

As he pored over the accounts of his father's firm, he saw that most of the costs were relatively fixed. The capital equipment was in place, its rate of depreciation set; labor could not be paid less or forced to work much harder; financing costs were determined outside. Fully half the expense of papermaking came in raw materials, the fibers and fillers: the wood pulps, espartos, rags, and chemicals mixed in the fluid slurry pouring through the plant.

This slurry, he believed, bore a secret of hidden losses, never measured or considered by the management but crucial to improvement of the profitability of the firm. If as little as 10 percent of the fibers and fillers were lost in the wastes leaking about the plant or flushed into the Ljubljanica, they constituted a major cost of production.

Such a hidden cost would amount to 5 percent of the total expenses of the factory, or about one-fifth of the entire amount spent on labor, one-half the cost of power, or, more significant, one-fifth of the gross profits. The hidden expense of waste would also represent a significant part of inventory and thus of financing costs. It afforded a major opportunity for improving both the mechanical efficiency and the financial performance of the mill. The plant already recycled its inside white water; perhaps more of the outside effluent could be recaptured.

In part the problem lay in the existing technology for purifying water. Based on sedimentation, it required large tanks and long periods of time for the "dirt" or other contents to sink to the bottom, and this saturation damaged the fibers. Then it entailed removal or treatment of the sludge. Additional filters demanded additional channels for fluids to flow through the plant. All such methods of further purification or recycling were far more costly than they were worth. Since Krofta could not solve these problems, his queries became more and more irritating to the factory staff.

Finally the factory manager summoned him. A bewhiskered Austrian, he had run the plant since the years of the Austro-Hungarian Empire that had ended after World War I some seventeen years before. He was skeptical of this young Slovenian engineer with his proud bearing and his advanced degrees, his assumed ascendancy and his impertinent prying. "What's the matter with you?" the Austrian demanded. "Do you have water on the brain?"

Krofta didn't answer. The manager pressed on with what in that simpler era seemed a conclusive argument: "Don't you know that water is free? It's the only thing in the whole plant that we don't have to pay for. If you want to reduce costs in the mill, you'll do better if you worry about the things we pay for rather than the things we get for nothing." But Krofta continued to worry about the water.

Indeed, nearly fifty years later and on the other side of the globe in Lenox, Massachusetts, Milos Krofta was still worrying about the water. At seventy-one years of age still an erect and handsome man of courtly European bearing, he ran his own engineering firm designing and installing proprietary equipment for water clarification and sewage treatment in paper mills around the world. With offices in thirteen countries and annual revenues of some $6 million and gross profits close to $1 million in his increasingly frequent good years, he lived comfortably amid the Berkshire hills. From his Lenox headquarters in a half-timbered villa, he could look out through wide windows at a rolling sylvan panorama, sparkling with freshwater lakes and streams, a vista of less vertiginous alpine glory but in its way no less beautiful than the Ljubljana of his youth.

But ugh—what's this? Does one flee halfway around the globe to drink dirty water? There was something definitely wrong with the local water supply. Provided from clear reservoirs on the top of a nearby mountain, the water of Lenox was mysteriously turning sour and brown in the taps of the town. The year before, Krofta had attempted to solve the town's sewage problem. Now Krofta's water worries were moving into a new phase, toward a new company—Krofta Waters, Inc.—which would decisively enter the public realm and address the ubiquitous problems of water purification for cities and towns.

Water pollution was part of a larger problem of capitalism that commanded increasing public attention as the 1960s and 1970s progressed. Beyond the crisis of fossil fuels, the American economy was seen to face a further nemesis, deeper and ultimately more menacing. This time it was not the Third World but the world itself: nature personified as a new proletariat gagging on the effluents and effects of industry. Every sign of commerce began to signify a rising residue of environmental burdens: additives and surfactants, plastics and phosphates, X-rays and electromagnetic waves, PCBs and EDB, nuclear leaks and toxic wastes. Seeping into the aquifers and the oceans, infecting our soils and grasses, accumulating in our meats and fruits and greens, building up in our bodily fats and tissues, measurably defiling the very milk of the mother's breast, unseen acids etched an environmental portrait of Dorian Gray, a long-unnoticed ledger of decline and decay, behind the ever radiant and smiling public face of capital.

Pollution was what is called an externality: an effect of market transactions that the market necessarily missed. Economists since Adam Smith had known about externalities and seen them as a manageable problem of free markets. In the new vision, however, externalities became the essence of capitalism. As economic growth proceeded beyond the level of subsistence, and populations proliferated everywhere, the market, it appeared to many conscientious and insightful observers, missed virtually everything important: from air and water to the moral order and the very survival of the race.

The problem was termed in the literature "the tragedy of the commons": the English discovery that "commons"—pastures open to all townsmen—would invariably be overgrazed. Each herdsman or entrepreneur would benefit nearly full measure by adding to his herd as quickly as possible, beating his rivals to the remaining grass, but the cost of overgrazing would be paid by all.

Applying to all commonly held resources, from water to wilderness, the logic of the commons evokes no corrective feedback or invisible hand. The most cherished virtues of the entrepreneur—his classic bias for action, eye for opportunity, bent for competition, drive to efficiency—remorselessly betray him even as they make him rich. His very system of accounts drives him to shift costs whenever possible from his own corporation to the commonwealth. Even what he proudly calls goods and services—from beachfront hotels and sugar-free bubble gum to all the voluminous paper and plastic packaging of our lives—seemed mere externalities: bads. The faster the individual profits of growth accrue, the more massively the unledgered losses of society accumulate.

On the most basic level, the logic of the commons creates a dire predicament of population. Conscience cannot stay it. If conscience leads some to forgo children, for example, the unconscionably prolific will dominate the world and the tragedy of the commons will end by destroying conscience itself as well as the world. Gresham's law rules; the bad finally chases out the good. There is no way out;

even soap, it turns out, is merely a new form of dirt. As the people of Lenox would soon discover, ordinary chlorine, the key to a miraculous breakthrough in water treatment that banished most waterborne diseases, now emerges as a dangerous pollutant itself, combining with humic acid from decaying organic matter to form carcinogenic trihalomethanes. The manufacture of filters and scrubbers itself produces new pollutants; so does their operation.

Even the moral inheritance of the society falls before the remorseless logic. Entrepreneurs can gain great individual profit from exploiting the social and sexual constraints of the community: selling violent shocks and pandering to prurient interests. The community as a whole pays in violent crime, illegitimacy, family disorder, and the breakdown of commercial disciplines, but Larry Flynt of *Hustler* and the producers of *The Texas Chainsaw Massacre* become millionaires.

Since there is no invisible hand to intervene, the tragedy of the commons appears to be the final contradiction of capitalism. For nearly every company uses air, water, roads, airlanes, rivers, sealanes; nearly every firm charges the atmosphere with noises, obtrudes on the common consciousness with advertising and other cultural affronts, and benefits by addicting its customers. The self-interested entrepreneur will debauch the common pool of resources and the heritage of bourgeois morals and working disciplines on which he finally depends.

Freedom, so this analysis suggests, is ultimately self-destructive. Entrepreneurship leads to social degeneration. Garrett Hardin, the author of the seminal essay "The Tragedy of the Commons," concludes that even the "freedom to breed is intolerable," that the only acceptable way of life is "mutual coercion, mutually agreed upon." Even immigration must be prohibited. Because each immigrant gains nearly the full benefit of his move and pays little of the cost in congestion and resource usage, or in the loss of the human capital of his birthplace, immigration too partakes of the logic of the commons. The tragedy of the commons can be overcome only by demographic and economic stasis: socialism.

The Congress discovered the new need for police powers over entrepreneurs with high fervor. Abolitionism ruled the day. Senator Edmund Muskie in 1971 introduced the Water Pollution Control Act, which ruled that no effluent of any sort could pass into an American body of water after 1985 without a permit.

As an act of law, voted in the Senate 86 to 0, it declared that no limits of wealth or convenience could stand between the assigned regulators and the purity of our streams, rivers, and aquifers. The view arose that governments could clean the water by issuing orders. Environmentalists angrily rejected pollution entitlements and taxes that would allow markets to regulate and reduce the flow in an economical way. How, after all, it was asked, could you put a price on clean water? The entitlement approach, it was agreed by the solons, would fail because the entrepreneurs would pay the tax like any bribe and continue their revels. Congress determined to act by a sweeping prohibition.

One problem immediately arose from this passion to avoid tainting the rites of purgation with any hint of commerce. It meant that only the cleaners incurred the costs. If you rushed to buy the best new filters and scrubbers, you lost to the companies that rushed to hire lawyers and lobbyists and persisted in polluting the commons. But this evasive action only confirmed in the minds of environmentalists the need for fiercer enforcement, which in turn would evoke yet more ingenious evasion.

Corporate resistance, moreover, made cleaning the water an increasingly expensive activity, devouring an ever-greater portion of the nation's wealth and jeopardizing other social goals, even in the environment itself. The state-of-the-art treatment plant at South Lake Tahoe, cited as "best available technology" by EPA in the mid-1970s and prescribed for copy elsewhere, exemplified the problem. The facility removed nitrogen from the water as ammonia and puffed it into the atmosphere. It emitted gases in burning its copious sludge and in cleaning its filters. It gorged energy, lime, alum, and activated carbon, all of which were produced in pollutant plants in other places. In the end, the water was cleaner but the air was more polluted and the costs prohibitive. Many observers concluded that industrial society itself was the culprit. Treatment plants, as industrial facilities themselves, were less the solution than part of the problem.

Such concerns about capitalism increasingly pervaded America's rulers of opinion: the universities, the media, the churches, the poets, the established rich and their foundations, even the middle and lower classes and their elected representatives. What was not widely seen by the social critics, moral prophets, and media leaders was their own crucial role in defining the opportunities of capital, setting the scene for entrepreneurs.

If the opinion leaders of society prescribe the unhindered pursuit of individual pleasures as the goal of life—if they celebrate in their literature and their liturgies an essentially hedonist ideal—capitalists will rush forward to serve this public mood and will generate the externalities it entails. But if the public consensus changes, as in the 1970s it massively turned in favor of environmental concerns, entrepreneurs will eagerly move to fulfill the new mandate, the new market.

At this point, though, regardless of its professed intentions, government will usually become a major defender of the old values and the corporate bodies that benefited from them. Social change is not simple; it demands a vast train of economic adjustments, educational adaptations, distributional effects, technological innovations, corporate rearrangements. There is no possible way for such changes to be effected through politics, where every cost will create a constituency for the past. Entrepreneurs, as the engineers of change, are indispensable to the social enactment of a shift in values.

Not all societies, however, produce entrepreneurs; not all societies therefore can achieve rapid and salutory growth and change. U.S. society took the lead in moving to a new era of environmentalism, with all the technological and social shifts it entailed, because it liberated entrepreneurs. They came from around the world to carry forth the banners of conservationist technology, transforming the focus of the U.S. economy, moving toward ever more efficient and clean forms of growth in recreation, information, and service industries and reducing the externalities of manufacturing. Predictably, however, the defenders of the old order mobilized their forces and entered the realms of politics in a variety of deceptive and seductive guises.

Milos Krofta was one of the entrepreneurs who emerged to develop the new markets, to internalize the externalities of the industrial expansion that dominated the previous consensus. He found himself confronted by the usual coalitions of the past.

By that time, he was ready. His life as an entrepreneur had trained him in the dynamics of change and prepared him for his role. America too was ready, because it had grown or attracted many such architects of changes. But both Krofta and the United States came to their entrepreneurial opportunity through a long gauntlet of global crises.

• • •

Amid alpine mountains plummeting to rocky green valleys and among the tangled roots and mingled tongues of aborted Balkan nations, Milos Krofta was born to the life of a twentieth-century entrepreneur. The year was 1912, the city Laibach, and the country Austria. His father was a Czech banker, his mother the daughter of a wholesale grocer. The region would be better known as Slovenia, but that too would pass, along with the Austro-Hungarian Empire that ruled it. Later the city would become Ljubljana, in the north-west corner of Yugoslavia. But Ljubljana was always in easy reach of Austrians, Italians, Hungarians, Serbs, and Croats. To live there, as Krofta remembers, was to know from childhood that one was wrong, and to learn from early youth that one would soon be corrected by a man with a gun and a bloody new map.

Krofta thus learned in his early life a prime lesson of entrepreneurship in this or any century. The current maps, the established charts, the regnant regimes, are wrong, and will change. The riches will go to the contrarians—the men who keep their minds on the thing rather than on the names or party lines. Always beleaguered, beset by Damoclean governments, they rule the only world that endures: the world of knowledge and nature, mind and art, inspiration and industry, the world that sustains the life of man as he struggles within the nets and maps of power and the past.

Milos Krofta gathered this truth of creative destruction as a small boy on his grandmother's lap, when he heard the tale of his great-grandfather's career. He had reigned as titan of the carriage trade between Trieste and Vienna, the coachman of stately Lippizaner steeds, a man of means, on the lifeline of Austrian commerce . . . until the coming of the steam locomotive made him a grocer.

To avoid such a fate, Krofta resolved to learn mechanical engineering and to go to work in one of the area's three major factories, the largest paper mills in Yugoslavia, which his father and uncle, through their bank, had taken over after World War I. At twenty the youngest engineering graduate in the history of the local university and already conversant in five modern languages—Slovenian, Croatian, Czech, French, and German—he left for Prague for further study. There he learned English and met his future bride, Maria Hybler, also bright and blond and Catholic, the daughter of a textile manufacturer. The next year he went to the University of Darmstadt, which commanded Europe's leading department in papermaking technique. In 1935, at age twenty-three, he won his master's degree and began his doctoral studies. Each year he would visit the leading paper mills of Europe as part of his training.

In 1937, he married Maria and gained his doctorate just as the Nazis marched into Austria and cut off his normal route home. When he arrived circuitously back in Ljubljana, he found that all the Austrians then in managerial positions in the mill had fled, and he himself became manager of all three mills. Thus, at age twenty-five he was running a papermaking complex that employed some 1,000 workers and produced 150 tons a day, or more than half the total supply of the country.

He would not have much time to worry about water, however. In

1941, the war reached Yugoslavia, and after a brief bombardment of Belgrade the precarious polyglot nation fell to the Axis powers. They split Ljubljana in two, with the Germans taking the north, including two of the Krofta factories, and the Italians capturing the south, including the largest mill, at a town called Vevce, where Krofta actually lived and worked. As part of their Germanization program, the Germans removed most equipment from the two mills, loaded the managers and workers into boxcars, and shipped them north to labor camps.

The Italians, meanwhile, grandly surrounded the unarmed Vevce complex with tanks, troops, and artillery, captured the plant in a ferocious charge, and moved some 200 soldiers in to stay. Krofta went out and negotiated with the Italian officer in what turned out to be their only common language: Latin.

Nonetheless, he was jailed with the rest of Vevce management and union leaders in a prison so crowded that no one had room to sit down, while the invaders settled in to contemplate the huge vats and sluices, pulpers and rollers, grinders and cutters of the factory. After three days, they made a decision to live off the mill, and brought Krofta and his men, stiff and sleepless, back in to run it.

Krofta's was a thankless managerial task, attempting to continue production in the heat of a many-sided conflict. But he embraced his conservative role with full fervor and resourcefulness. When Italy fell in 1943, the Germans took Vevce and carted away anyone not firmly employed. As one of the largest employers in the country, Krofta fought to preserve jobs. Preserving jobs, he was saving his workers from the camps. As a Yugoslav patriot, he was salvaging the industrial base of his country. If the mill stopped production, the occupying forces would dismantle it for war material. In a world of revolution and turmoil, he towered as a force of preservation.

But to rising guerrilla forces, dominated by communist cadres, Krofta appeared a capitalist in charge of the means of production, and thus the true enemy. Although the factory produced no significant military supplies, one night the communists burned down part of it; later they attempted unsuccessfully to blow up the central chimney with defective dynamite; on one occasion, they sneaked in at two in the morning, past the sleeping encampment of Italian troops, and murdered the manager of the mill with a bullet in the brow. Krofta leaped from his bed and rushed toward the sound of gunshot. The man died in his arms on the factory floor, under a newly erected banner that threatened "all traitors" to the nihilist mandate of terror with a similar fate of sudden death.

Living from day to day, maintaining a residual process of production, listening furtively to Radio Free Europe, hoping for peace and democracy, Krofta became increasingly optimistic about the future course of his country as the war turned against the Nazis. Then strange and shocking reports began coming in from unexpected quarters: namely the regimes of the victorious Allies. First, after a visit by Randolph Churchill, the British decided to recognize the Tito government, thus making all anticommunists in essence enemies of the West. Then under the Yalta agreement, the Allies surrendered the country altogether to the communists.

"Always an optimist," as Maria says, Krofta still believed he might continue to produce paper under the new regime. But in May 1945, the new government confiscated the banks and jailed his father and uncle. Finally, early in July, an elderly communist worker confronted Krofta on a morning inspection of the plant and asked to speak to him privately. The next day, so Krofta was told, the police would present him a document confiscating the mill and authorizing his arrest as a capitalist enemy of the people. He returned to his apartment and quietly packed to leave. He told Maria, now with two daughters, Tjasa, five, and Hanka, six months, that he would have to "go away for a few days." She would not see him again for six months.

He decided to leave in their only operational vehicle, the mill automobile. It was a dark-green Steyer, propelled, in the wartime requirement, by a stove in back and fueled by hand from a large bag of charcoal on the roof. His goal was Trieste, a city some sixty miles down a hilly road to the sea. Claimed by Yugoslavia and thus reachable on Slovenian documents, the city was occupied by British forces and thus allowed access to the West. He asked a trusted older worker to accompany him, drive the car back, and report the outcome to Maria.

The auto started dramatically, belching fiery fumes and issuing explosive reports. Still, they barged off unhindered and made it away toward Trieste, provoking surprise and alarm along the road but no resistance. Purporting to be on an errand for the mill, they passed first through the Yugoslav checkpoint, choking with fear and fumes as the communist soldiers parsed the documents. Then they passed through the British lines, equally tense, because the British were fully cooperating with the communists and had been routinely remitting Catholics, Jews, and other presumed enemies of the regime to communist jails and firing squads. But Krofta made it into the city, with a small bag, and the driver returned to the mill in his stertorous auto.

In Trieste, Krofta moved in with friends and suffered the agonies of an entrepreneurial transformation. He seemed in every way a failure. A noncombatant in a world at war, he had failed, for whatever good reasons, the primal warrior test of manhood. Leaving his wife and two young girls behind, in danger and distress, he had failed, for whatever good reasons, the husband's role of provider and protector. As a manager, he had lost his mill; as a citizen, he had lost his country. As an able-bodied man, he was dependent on friends for food and lodging. At first, it was all too much. He retreated into an irresponsible diversion, writing a philosophical essay on the sources of beauty. Then he contemplated returning, but there was no way back. He resolved to press on to Italy, where he could begin an entrepreneurial life.

Meanwhile, back in Ljubljana, troops arrived at the plant and formally arrested him *in absentia* and confiscated all his property, including all Maria's family books and heirlooms. They locked up hundreds of Ljubljana's businessmen and entrepreneurs, many never to be seen again. KGB agents repeatedly interrogated Maria, but she refused to divulge what little she knew of her husband's whereabouts, and then absconded with her daughters to the apartment of friends to work out her escape.

For nearly six months, she waited and failed to find a way. Finally she placed her bet on a sinister underworld figure who promised to drive her safely past the checkpoints on the bridge between Susak and Fiume. Instead he left her on the wrong side, at two o'clock on a wintry December night, to make her own way across, with her infant daughter in one arm and five-year-old Tjasa walking beside her, and with long-expired documents in her hand. Fate and the Christmas season were on her side. Handing her papers to the lone soldier on duty and watching him peruse them, she realized, with sudden elation, that they were upside down. A South Serbian drafted into the army, so she thought, he apparently could not read Slovenian. Embarrassed, he waved them by.

She eventually found a bus stop and got a ride to Trieste, where she learned from friends that Milos was in Milan. On New Year's Eve, she managed to reach him by telephone. After a week in Trieste acquiring more timely documents, she took a seven-hour bus ride to Milan, where Milos awaited her at the station. Dispossessed, official traitors in their homeland, with no sure future anywhere, the Kroftas were among the lucky ones, the few chance survivors who bore in their minds the crucial, transportable capital that would rebuild the world. Milos Krofta had left the realm of management and preservation and entered the realm of the entrepreneur.

Through Italians who had previously sold him papermaking gear and purchased his paper, Milos had managed to set himself up as a consultant to the industry even before Maria arrived. Moving into the office of the Vevce mills' sales agents in Italy, sleeping on the floor and eating macaroni among the destitute in public kitchens, he contacted every commercial connection he had made during his years of study and travel. He also began to follow up on an interesting discovery he had made in a trip to Sweden just before the war.

In Sweden, he had found a firm called Adka that was manufacturing a different kind of water purification gear based not on sedimentation but on flotation of the pollutants. The devices were too small and inefficient for widespread use in paper mills, but at once he saw their potential. Although the war had prevented him from applying the principle in Vevce, he immediately recognized that it offered a way of solving the problems of the Ljubljanica effluents.

Flotation was the original foaming cleanser. Rather than waiting for the particles of extraneous matter to sink by gravity in motionless water and collect on the bottom of the tank, flotation would bring them swiftly and effervescently to the surface, even of moving water, to be scooped or poured away. Theoretically this process would operate ten times as fast as sedimentation and thus require much smaller clarification bins and much cheaper equipment. Krofta decided to start a company to design and sell appropriate gear.

His first client was a young paper mill owner whose father had just died, leaving him in charge, to contemplate, like the Italians in Vevce, the inscrutable means of production: masses of papermaking machinery all wasting away in want of an entrepreneur to give it life. Krofta guided the company back into production and found customers for it in many countries. More important to him, though, he also built his first fully operational flotation water clarifier for the plant. He called it the Krofta Unifloat, and it could process 2,500 gallons per minute, or more than four times as much as the Adka he had seen in Sweden.

For five years, using his reputation as manager at Vevce, Krofta operated successfully as a consultant in Milan. Once again his business took him away from his family. He made long trips to Switzerland and Austria, Canada and the United States, and even to India, where his five months making plans for a pulp mill ended abruptly with the outbreak of civil war. As time passed, though, he became apprehensive about the politics of Italy. As in Yugoslavia during the war, the communists commanded a powerful minority position in the country's affairs. They dominated the unions around

Milan and elected many municipal officials in northern Italy. They began random disruptions and strikes that made business increasingly difficult in the short run and threatened to make it impossible in the long run. When war erupted in Korea, tensions rose to a higher pitch. Krofta resolved to make another move, this time to Argentina or the United States.

Because he had heard that it was difficult to get into the United States or into its paper business, allegedly dominated by a few giant firms, the Kroftas' first efforts focused on Argentina and its large Slovenian community. But the Argentines rejected their application. To his surprise, the United States accepted them as one of the last families qualified under the displaced persons program begun after the war for political refugees. An effort begun in compassion, it brought to America many of the men who made its economy work for the next three decades.

Krofta would not arrive in the United States, like so many other immigrants, bereft of work or connections. Before he left Italy he had reached an agreement with an American executive whom he had represented in Europe to purchase a paper mill in Ancram, New York. With Krofta's experience and the executive's financial and administrative skills, they planned to create an important new paper firm. It was not to be. The firm was manufacturing a luxurious 50 percent rag bond, supposedly for legal forms, on a military contract at what seemed to Krofta the exorbitant price of 22 cents a pound. But the obsolete equipment in this low-volume facility could not produce the stuff any more cheaply.

Krofta decided to keep the plant running as well as possible and return to his deeper interest, worrying about the water. He created a small prototype of a new system, both simpler and more efficient than his Italian Unifloat. This new device he called the Flotator, and he set out to sell it from Ancram. This decision turned out to be just as well, because with the end of the Korean War, the government canceled its contract to pay 22 cents for 8-cent paper and the mill had to be sold. Krofta and his family moved to Lenox, Massachusetts, a small town in the midst of the Berkshire papermaking center that arose next to the Housatonic River a century ago.

The first customer for the Flotator turned out to be Byron & Weston, now Crane & Company, the Dalton, Massachusetts, firm most famous for producing the paper for U.S. Federal Reserve Notes (i.e., money). Krofta got the deal by offering to return his advance and remove the device for nothing if it failed to work. For the next twenty-five years he introduced a major new version of his device every four years, obtained some twenty patents, and created company offices in eleven countries and three American states. In the mid-1960s the Yugoslav communists quietly purchased three flotators for the Ljubljana plants. By 1970 he had driven Adka out of the business and became the world's leading producer of Dissolved Air Flotation clarifiers. In most new papermaking facilities, his approach has displaced the settling cones that used to loom up decoratively outside all paper mills with indoor flotators over thirty times as fast and far more efficient in recycling fiber.

Entrepreneurship entails a sense of limits as well as a vision of possibilities. Krofta could achieve his breakthrough in providing capital equipment for paper mills around the world—and stay ahead for twenty years—chiefly because he knew enough to concentrate on what he knew. He did not diversify. Both in technology and in marketing, he exploited his proven assets. Moving down a learning curve to produce ever more effective sewage treatment gear for paper mills at ever lower cost, he was always a target in motion. Small as a company, he was always large, and usually dominant, in the markets he chose.

Crucial was his decision to specialize in devices that cost under $200,000 and could be purchased, without ado, by plant managers and engineers. Krofta was an expert at talking to paper mill operators, men who shared his experience and knowledge and respected his work. He eschewed huge projects dependent on committee decisions, political processes, and large financial leverage: seductive routes to riches that could bankrupt his small company if they went wrong.

Such strategic limits succeed not by restricting vision or aggressiveness but by focusing it. Just as important as Krofta's sense of limits was his exhaustive vision of the full dimensions of the limited market he chose. Unlike many American entrepreneurs who achieve a similarly limited success and then are blindsided from abroad, Krofta from the beginning understood that he was competing in a global economy.

His aggressive international posture was as important to his lead in U.S. industry as his strong patent position. Even losing money in a particular country, Krofta International was valuable in preventing foreign rivals from gaining dominant shares in their home markets and using them as a base for attacking his U.S. stronghold.

When he chose to move into large systems, though, treating sewage for entire towns, and again when he decided to diversify into purifying tapwater, he lost his advantages of international reach and industrial repute. Even his keen eye for the low-cost solution only aroused suspicions about the degree of his commitment to water purity, to many of its advocates less a technical and economic problem than a moral issue.

Nonetheless, Krofta in his seventieth year proposed a $73,000 sewage treatment system for the town of Lenox that was both cheaper to run and more effective than the $400,000 system, later expanded to $600,000, proposed by expert consultants. He was still naive enough to imagine that the $327,000 difference would give him a significant edge. He was wrong.

The town turned him down flat. The Environmental Protection Agency and the state together defrayed 95 percent of the price of the expensive plant, thus reducing its effective cost to less than Krofta's. The state would even throw in a dump truck needed to remove sludge that Krofta's device would have recycled. Who would care if the town also used the truck to sand the roads? As long as the selectmen did not try anything so novel or provocative as a new and cheaper system, higher government bodies were willing to shower the community with treats.

Even Krofta profited in this feast of his failure. Not only did he get the role of testing the output of the plant, he also learned to try a different approach next time he wanted a major municipal contract. When two years later alien tastes and colors began to infect Lenox's mountain water supply, he resorted to the primal act of entrepreneurship, the quintessential start-up strategy from the time of the earliest caveman capitalist.

In all likelihood, capitalism began when some paleolithic trader finally rebelled against the intricate demands and negotiations of multisided barter and abruptly decided to take a chance: simply present his skins free and hope for the best. This would likely prompt the recipient to reciprocate with a still more valuable offering, thus initiating the endless rounds of gifts, presentations and ritual exchanges common in primitive societies with barter economies. As Claude Lévi-Strauss has written, "Reciprocity is the fundamental law of social life."

By denying this fundamental law, bureaucratic politics—with its prohibition of bribery, its ideal of altruistic service, its assumption of a public interest beyond mercenary concerns—recreates the same kind of labyrinthine snarl as a nonmonetary tribal system. In the same way, the logjam may sometimes be broken with a gift. Gifts invoke a group of proprieties and expectations quite different from contracts. Krofta simply gave his Sandfloat water purifiers to the town together with servicing and training for town workers, for a one-year demonstration without charge. If after a year the town wanted to buy it, Krofta would ask $350,000, to be paid off over a ten-year period, all contingent on eventual certification by the state Department of Environmental Quality Engineering.

Because the DEQE normally could accept no installation that did not meet the existing EPA specifications, certification posed an apparent problem for Krofta. As Krofta described the approval paradox, the state could approve anything as long as it was already approved. But Krofta's entrepreneurial gift had overcome the approval paradox; the state allowed Lenox to use Krofta's device. His new Sandfloat was already legally cleaning the water of Lenox when at age seventy-one he moved on to the larger challenge of water purification in Pittsfield, a nearby city of 50,000, ten times larger than Lenox and under an order from EPA to purify its turbid tapwater.

To the Pittsfield mayor and city council, Krofta made the improbable claim that he could solve their problem with his Sandfloat process for just one-fourth the cost of the system proposed by the leading experts in the field and certified by EPA as the "best available technology." Without his success in an adjacent town, this proposal for the larger city could not even have been considered. As it was, his plan was not even noticed by any of the relevant city officials until a reporter seeking scandal in Pittsfield's dirty water instead discovered this strange courtly gentleman with his bubble machine.

For all his innocence of the new market he had entered, he continued to focus on two things he knew better than any of his gathering competition: the place where he lived and the technology that he had invented. His new venture thus seemed to him a measured and organic extension of his previous industrial business. He was quite wrong. He was in fact proposing a revolution in the field of public health.

On the surface, there appeared to be no way he could prevail. Public health has become a virtual religion in the United States. Indeed, the phenomenal achievements of public health professionals in preventing disease and extending human life commanded a due measure of reverence. Early in this century, public health measures, focused on water, had transformed the very conditions of human life by abolishing its most lethal nemesis over all the millennia: the regular and pandemic eruption of plagues.

Defending public health in the crucial matter of water cleanliness was a complex of expert bodies that upheld a principle of purity at any price. Since the cost of failure was epidemic disease, it seemed a reasonable principle. Perhaps most important in upholding it were the great national consultant firms that advise multinational corporations and great municipalities alike on all their major procurements in the field.

Of these firms none was more prestigious than Metcalf & Eddy, and in the matter of Pittsfield's new water purification plant, Metcalf & Eddy had already made its finding. Pittsfield needed a $29 million facility in Dalton, Massachusetts. It should be built of brick, contain a laboratory and office space, and be manned twenty-four hours a day. It should be served by expensive new water mains into the city. It should include every possible kind of redundancy. It should be capable of meeting, with water suitable for a baby to drink, the demands of extinguishing a conflagration sweeping through the entire town. It should be prepared to weather for weeks a transportation strike that barred its access to necessary chemicals. It should employ only the most venerably tested and approved technologies.

In short, it should be a cathedral, like all the other cathedrals built by towns and cities across the country and devoted to the national ablutions of public health. It did not occur to Metcalf & Eddy that anyone in the small city of Pittsfield, Massachusetts, could take a different view of the matter. It did not seem possible that elected officials in Pittsfield would reject the findings of Metcalf & Eddy in favor of the bizarre idea of applying a paper mill sewage treatment technology to the purification of drinking water.

The eminent consultants regarded Krofta and his chief lieutenant, Dr. Lawrence Wong, essentially as a comedy team. Both men spoke with thick foreign accents, easily mimicked, lending a still more exotic air to their already outlandish pronouncements. It was exactly as if, in the midst of the stately and liturgical rites of preparing to erect a cathedral, some bozo had stood up and declared that all they really needed was some shelter (an insulated Butler building would do), a few hundred folding chairs for the congregation, a podium, and a Formica table for the cross and the wine.

The consultants believed that if some of the Pittsfield politicians were not laughing at Krofta, it could only be because they could not understand what he was saying. An authoritative presentation by a Metcalf & Eddy vice-president, with slides and charts and with cogent, faintly derisive dismissal of Krofta's sewage equipment, would easily save the day.

Conditions had changed, however. Just as water pollution laws had earlier expanded Krofta's market for paper mill gear, public sentiment was now shifting to give him opportunities in providing cities and towns with cheaper and more efficient water clarifiers. Environmentalism had lost none of its favor, but tax cutting had also gained popularity in what had become widely and justly known as the Commonwealth of Taxachusetts. In 1980 the voters had approved Proposition 2½, which drastically lowered property taxes in most of the state and suddenly instilled a spirit of austerity in the state's affairs. A new mayor named Charles L. Smith had unexpectedly won office in Pittsfield after a campaign attacking the wastefulness of the incumbent administration.

Nonetheless, there was no existing market for flotation purifiers for drinking water, and without Krofta there is little evidence that any such market would have emerged. Like most innovative projects it was an entrepreneurial opportunity created by the act of attempting to fulfill it.

The climax came on January 22, 1982, when the mayor and city council finally held a public meeting with Metcalf & Eddy officials and Krofta both making presentations. Officially a session of the Pittsfield Water Commission, the hearing brought together nearly all the principals in the dispute. Mayor Smith stayed for two and a half hours. The city council participated vigorously. The vice-president of Metcalf & Eddy appeared with his Pittsfield deputy and with impressive audiovisual aids. A still-higher executive in the company came to observe. A further consultant from the Hartford Center for the Environment and Man, a comparatively tiny firm invited by the mayor two days before, came to help appraise the work of Metcalf & Eddy.

The representative of Metcalf & Eddy, however, did not understand the change in public sentiment or political attitudes. In an hour-long slide presentation, the smoothly authoritative and articulate vice-president attacked the Krofta system's durability, dependability, performance, and ability to meet the city's long-term needs. He charged that it would gorge energy. He wrongly said it could not eliminate the crucial trihalomethanes recently discovered to be a possibly carcinogenic by-product of chlorine. He even claimed that in the end, assuming heavy state aid, it would be "basically a total washout in costs."

Krofta's firm was accustomed to dealing with industry, he said, and industry wanted the least expensive equipment that would do the job. "You're looking at it from a sales point of view," he said, addressing Krofta. "You're a manufacturer. We're looking at it from a public health point of view and from the long-term best interests of the city. . . . Cost is not a primary consideration."

His, however, was a voice from the past. Since enactment of Proposition 2½ the state had been so inundated with local demands for support that it could no longer promise generous aid for overpriced projects. Other municipalities had already all but exhausted the state's $75 million fund for construction of water treatment plants. The mayor interrupted the meeting and told the water commission to leave the question of state aid out of its decision. "I will proceed without expecting any help from the state," he declared.

The consultant continued, citing the virtues of his brick structure, the new pipes and water mains it entailed, the endless redundancy it provided. He pointed to the employment it would create both in construction and in maintenance compared with Krofta's simpler automated facilities. Then, in a major tactical error, he said that if the city really wanted to cut costs, Metcalf & Eddy would recommend not Krofta's flotation gear but rather a system using old-fashioned direct filtration through anthracite, sand, and gravel. It would cost no more than Krofta's plan, and it had been approved for decades by the government.

This was bureaucracy speaking in its clearest tones. The consultants with straight faces could call for an obsolete system for the same price, as long as it was technically approved. The people could drink somewhat dirty water and it would be fine as long as the dirt was certified by the EPA.

From then on, Krofta was on his way. In response to the charge of excessive energy use, the next week he added a new cost-saving frill to his plan. He proposed installing a 100-kilowatt water turbine electric generator on a gravity pipeline below his facility, allowing the plant to produce its own power, saving another $60,000 per year for the city. The city authorities gratefully accepted the change. The mayor's consultants, the Center for the Environment and Man, followed with an approval of the Krofta system. Though there were voices in the city government demanding yet a new set of consultants to scrutinize the work of the Center for the Environment and Man, the mayor decided to call the game short before the advisory fees exceeded the cost of the facility.

Finally Governor Michael Dukakis came by for a presentation and tour of the Lenox plant and expressed his enthusiasm for Krofta's money-saving ideas. Krofta reciprocated by proposing the creation of an air flotation barge to clean the waters of Boston Harbor, the first truly floating flotation facility. The New York State government readily approved tests of Krofta's flotation gear for that state's cities and towns. The pariah of public health was becoming a symbol of water purity, and state politicians gathered to receive the reflected glow.

After a year's trouble-free operation in Lenox, the Krofta system was contingently approved by the state for that town. Approval for

Pittsfield was widely assumed. Sure enough, the DEQE checked in with its favor in early 1984. Just to show who was boss, however, the state body required observance of a set of obsolete specifications including a special double wall needed for the previous technology but irrelevant to Krofta's Sandfloat design. The mayor stormed at the decision, but the people would pay the extra $200,-000, and no one cared at EPA.

Krofta meanwhile was busy adapting his Sandfloat device for private dwellings, and he began again by making a gift. The Mount, a grand Edwardian manor in Lenox designed by Edith Wharton and long her summer home, had become the headquarters for Shakespeare and Company, a highly successful theatrical group. The crowds at its outdoor performances, though, were over-extending the septic system, which on warm evenings lent a faint but disturbing odor to the pastoral scenes of *A Midsummer Night's Dream*. Krofta offered to install a $15,000 treatment plant, called Lakeguard, free. If it worked well he would mass-produce it and sell it to the public for $2,000 apiece. Hotels, institutions, and other private facilities promised a market for Krofta's patented devices probably exceeding even the potentially huge demands of America's small towns. In his seventies, Krofta was launching a major new business across the country.

Krofta's career displayed the process by which the externalities of capitalism become business opportunities, while the tragedy of the commons comes to afflict bureaucracy itself. The power of public taxation can create an inviting new commons, which bureaucrats themselves rush in to overgraze, while the excesses of private industry can become the target of rival entrepreneurs. Neither government nor business can alone solve the problems of pollution and other externalities. Government alone can outlaw pollution. But it cannot create the equipment required by the continuing identification of new pollutants; it cannot prevent the steady enlargement of the costs of environmental goods. Only the dynamic processes of innovation impelled by entrepreneurial capitalism can steadily diminish the pollutants of industry and the costs of a clean environment. As this process continues in the United States, industry is in fact turning to ever less obtrusive and polluting and ever more efficient and effective technologies.

Entrepreneurs, however, also cannot usually eliminate externalities alone. Caught in the logic of the commons, entrepreneurs who pay to eliminate pollution, noise, or other damage will tend to lose their markets to businessmen who impose these costs on the public. The people, in their religion and culture and finally in their politics, must define what externalities are unacceptable and determine what goods and services, what wealth and options, they are willing to forgo in quest of environmental benefits.

The expansion of Krofta's markets in both the public and private sectors could not have occurred without government action to restrict pollution, in response to a growing public demand for environmental controls. At the same time, the growing public demand for environmental goods could not be fulfilled without the entrepreneurial contributions of men like Milos Krofta. By continually lowering the cost of purification gear, he is making possible its ever wider and more effective use across the economy and around the world.

The value of a society's goods always derives from the values of its people. A democratic society that is unwilling to bar *Hustler* on public newsstands or ban billboards from beautiful views cannot justly blame capitalism for these offenses. It is up to the political, judicial, and religious institutions of the society, not other businesses, to eliminate such opportunities for ugly profit. Capitalists perform a vital role in determining what goods and services are initially offered to the public. But the people and their government determine the limits of what can be marketed. Markets provide the ultimate democracy; democracy, though, defines the marketplace.

Capitalism itself must always operate within a legal and moral order that defines its goals and limits. The tragedy of the commons bears the compelling truth that capitalism without a moral and legal context is self-destructive.

The externalities of pollution are not fundamentally different from any of the other crises overcome by entrepreneurs over the centuries. The disruption of the existing order, by whatever cause, often unleashes the entrepreneurial effort to restore it. Plagues, famines, scarcities, Malthusian pressures of population, all have fallen before the creative efforts of entrepreneurs. Ordnance for war, technologies for deterrence, electronics for space travel, all have sprung from the spirit of enterprise, fulfilling the demands of the public in an ever-changing world environment.

The challenge of pollution poses relatively simple problems in the context of a dynamic entrepreneurial economy. These externalities cause a fatal impasse only in a static system paralyzed by the coils of expertise, the claims of the past and the proven. Government can play its needed role in correcting the excesses of capitalism only if it does not pompously provide the specifics of the solution.

In this realm, the state must follow a demand-side policy. It must set general standards and goals and rely on entrepreneurs to fulfill them in ever more creative ways at ever smaller cost. When the state prescribes the particular technologies that it wants—when like the EPA it identifies in detail the "best available equipment"—it paralyzes the processes of entrepreneurial progress which are indispensable to overcome the perennial crises of human life.

The ultimate flaw in the tragic logic of the commons is its failure to recognize the redemptive logic of positive externalities. Capitalism can indeed produce negative side effects and occasion the need for government limits. But the entire history of capitalism is dominated by the positive externalities of entrepreneurship.

In producing the first workable examples of air flotation technology, Adka had no intention of eliminating carcinogens in the water of Pittsfield, Massachusetts. But Adka's innovation reached far beyond its own internal accounts and made a significant contribution far beyond its ken. In pursuing the promise of the industrial revolution, no particular entrepreneur imagined that the process would end in abolishing serious material poverty in all industrial nations and extend human longevity beyond seventy-five years. In laboriously launching their first airplane, the Wright brothers never imagined the 747, an aircraft as long and high as their first successful flight, or conceived of a trip to the moon.

The negative externalities of capitalism seem notable chiefly because they are dwarfed by the colossal benefits casually offered without charge. That is the lesson of the career of Milos Krofta and his foaming cleanser. The man who wanted to clean the water in Lenox, Massachusetts, is now showing, by his own example offered free of charge, a way to clean the waters of the world.

And in his own life, Milos Krofta's creative response to the guilts and disruptions of his early years had finally, on the other side of the globe, restored in the Berkshires the established position in a beautiful rural land that his family had held and lost in Yugoslavia. By a process of radical uprooting and innovation, he had at last succeeded in conserving the values of his youth and passing them on to future generations.

On his front lawn in Lenox, Krofta provided a sign that he saw the connection. He erected a white marble monument in memory of the family that had raised him, trained him, and made him manager of a mill, only to be abandoned in their time of greatest need. The elegant stone, however, also symbolizes—does it not?—their final triumph through a wayward son, who had worried about the water for half a century and found purity and peace, and expiation for the past, in an entrepreneurial revolution halfway around the world.

5

THE CUBAN MIRACLE

To break away from the nets and maps of the past usually requires a powerful psychic push or surrounding convulsion. As the tribulations of Simplot, Masters, and Krofta suggest, business breakthroughs spring more often from mental breakdowns than from lucky breaks, lucrative deals, or academic prizes. Entrepreneurs are more likely to find inspiration in a pink slip than in a promotion.

The entrepreneurial crisis may take many forms. But A. David Silver, perhaps the leading student of the psychology of entrepreneurs, discovered in an extensive survey of major American successes that most were driven by conscious feelings of deprivation and guilt stemming from broken families and connections. Many had lost their fathers in childhood through death or divorce; many later lost their wives. Some, like Vietnam veteran Fred Smith, the swashbuckling hero of Federal Express, underwent a wrenching trauma of combat and returned with a fierce drive to win the war at home. Entrepreneurs normally feel a deep commitment to traditional values, to family and children, but the gyrations of their careers often lead to marital strains and divorces, setbacks and betrayals. Resulting pangs of guilt and failure may unleash in certain men a tremendous personal drive to vindicate themselves and retrieve a family order.

In the modern age, however, the paramount source of entrepreneurial disruption and guilt is the turbulent politics of a tyrannous and war-torn world. In nearly every nation, many of the most notable entrepreneurs are immigrants. Immigration usually entails violation of ancestral ties and parental obligations. Dealing in their youths with convulsive change, thrown back on their own devices to create a productive existence, ripped untimely from the womb of a settled life, immigrants everywhere suffer the guilts of disconnection from their homes and families and ally easily with the forces of the future against the claims of the past. Shaped by a fractured or betrayed conservativism, however, the immigrant's most revolutionary creations usually reverberate with remembered values. In forging a new world, he continually restores the old.

In the history of the United States, each new flood of immigrants has enacted this essential drama of abandonment and rebuilding, revolution and redemption. But in recent years, no group has played out the entrepreneurial synthesis of past and future, nostalgia and restoration, with the energy and resourcefulness of the Cubans who fled Castro's Cuba in rage and fear and settled first in Miami, Florida.

The city did not seem ready for them. For the economy of central Miami, 1961 was a grim year. In the inner-city area around the Tamiami Trail, more than 1,000 homes, with FHA mortgages, had been vacated, and many were vandalized for their copper pipe and electrical fixtures. The Little League baseball field had become *el parque de la marijuana;* local shops gasped for customers and went broke; forty-year-old Burdine's, the chief downtown department store, was languishing helplessly, as its clientele moved toward the suburbs. Even Miami Beach, the supreme American resort across the Bay of Biscayne, was slipping perceptibly past its prime, as wealthy northern tourists increasingly passed it by for mellower island shores to the south.

To many observers, the arrival of the Cubans seemed a deadly blow to the city's hope for recovery. Some 200,000 had already fled Castro's burgeoning dictatorship, and more arrived daily. Castro had proclaimed a new law of *potestas patria* under which he was abolishing Catholic schools, establishing centers for communist indoctrination, incarcerating dissidents, and commandeering lawyers and other white-collar people for labor in the sugar fields. Refugees flocked the Miami airport, in painful confusion; then clustered five or more to a room in Miami bungalows and apartments, looking for jobs, nonexistent in the struggling Dade economy, and confidently awaiting deliverance—and vicarious vengeance—through a brutal charge of U.S. Marines onto the benches of Cuba, ordered by America's macho new president, John F. Kennedy.

Some 13,314 of the immigrants came as unaccompanied children, landing in Miami without kin, without English, and many with only a vague connection in the United States. They had been packed off by desperate parents and left to be processed in refugee camps and then passed on to orphanages and foster homes. Many of the immigrants of all ages were channeled first to other communities, but most of them gravitated back to southern Florida, the area closest to their prior home and most acculturated with Cubans.

All statistical projections were dismal. Experts foresaw a prolonged siege of medical crises, economic stresses, and ethnic frictions; a teeming burden of "social disorders," needs for housing, welfare, and simple hygiene, an impossible load for the already afflicted social services of the city. Here in one economically stagnant urban area, over a period of just two years, thronged some 200,000 penurious immigrants: more than the total of black unemployed youths in all America's urban areas at the time, concentrated in the hard core of one central city. It was an influx about one-fifth the size of the entire Dade County population in 1960, an inundation more rapid and overwhelming than any previous migration to one American city. Few of the arrivals spoke English, and virtually none had arranged for jobs or housing. Many had been reasonably well educated and well employed in Cuba, but their experience and credentials were often irrelevant in the United States. Doctors, architects, and lawyers escaped the sugar fields only to work as busboys, bootblacks, and parking-lot attendants. Nearly 60 percent of the exiles had been common laborers even in Cuba, and all had lost most of what they had accumulated at home. Poring through the press coverage and political comment of the day, it is difficult to find any observers who saw this human flood as anything but a tribulation for southern Florida or a problem to be solved by saviors at HEW and the Immigration and Naturalization Service (INS), or the U.S. Marines.

The Cubans' saviors, however, were already at hand. They would be saved by themselves: not chiefly by a trickle-down of grants from the government, but by the upsurge of their own productive efforts. They would be saved by people like José Pinero, penniless on Eighth Street, having invested his last dollars in some second-hand records to peddle door to door; by Armando Codina—one of the 14,000 children in Operation Pedro Pan—then a frightened gangly youth, with just two words of English, "hamburger" and "Coke," assigned to a refugee camp awaiting passage to an orphanage in New Jersey; by Felipe Valls, washing dishes in a restaurant, living in a house with his pregnant wife, two children, and twelve other Cubans; by Amaury Betancourt—with a wife, six children, a mother-in-law, money running low—an unemployed lending officer looking for months for some clerical billet in a bank; by Ramon Oyarzun, once a doctor in Cuba, now hunched over a desk, processing paper in Mercy Hospital, living in a three-bedroom bungalow in Miami Beach with fifteen other Cubans; by thousands of other men and women.

They were then unemployed, unpromising and unsettled, living in accommodations comprehensively in violation of code, but they were already at work, seething with the spirit of enterprise, figuring out how to transfigure Southwest Eighth Street into Calle Ocho, the main drag of a new Little Havana. It would soon become more effervescently thriving than its crushed prototype, soon would percolate with the forbidden commerce of the dying island to the south: the Cafe Bustano, the Refrescos Cawy, the Competidora and El Cuño cigarettes, the *guyaberas* (cotton shirts), the Latin music pulsing from the storefronts, the pyramids of mangoes and tubers, gourds and plantains, the iced coconuts served with a straw, the peeled oranges and grapefruits peddled in plastic bags to cars on the boulevard, the new theaters showing the latest anti-Castro comedies, the domino gaming plaza under the banyan trees at the center of town; the *botánicos*, vending ancient voodoo herbs and elixirs waxed into a giant candle (or a large spray can with the same potions and an implausible caveat: "This container holds no supernatural powers"); with restaurants and cafeterias galore, twenty-four hours a day of thick *cafe cubano* and the long hard loaves of Cuban bread; all comprising in a once ghostly three and a half square miles what the Latin Chamber of Commerce catalogues as 97 restaurants and cafeterias, 81 groceries and supermarkets, 49 gas stations, 48 clothing stores, 46 barber and beauty shops, 46 jewelry stores, 34 *farmacias*, 33 furniture outlets, 21 bakeries, 20 cigar factories, 20 law and real estate firms, 17 *florerias*, 17 photo studios, 13 optical shops, 13 hardware stores, 10 private clinics and hospitals, 10 bookstores, 10 tailors, 8 travel agencies, 7 funeral parlors, and 5 banks. The Chamber of Commerce counters, however, apparently overlooked several theaters, nightclubs, import/export companies, auto repair shops, discotheques, driving schools, doctors' offices, and vendors of *artículos religiosos*, not to mention the numerous *botánicos* and ten more Cuban banks, in the continuing eruptions of Cuban business in the city, reaching out to the north and south, and by 1980 comprising some 10,000 Cuban-owned companies in Dade County.

The men and women who conjured up this commercial miracle—and the immigration they led—proved to be anything but a problem for Miami; they in fact bore the antidote to Miami's decay: a comprehensive total solution, what Brookings sociologist Robert Bach called "one of the fastest and most far reaching transformations of any urban area in U.S. history." Not only did they solve the problems that their arrival precipitated; they created jobs for hundreds of thousands of other Americans. Not only did they revive Miami's stagnant inner city; they transformed the entire Miami economy, making it into a new gateway to Latin American commerce, a new financial axis between Europe, the United States, and the thirty nations and 342 million people to the south.

What was widely depicted as a burden for the existing capacity of the city's crawling economy was in fact a teeming source of new life, a winged force of international growth bursting the confines of a parochial downtown—giving forth supplies which would at once create, fulfill, and overflow their own demands. Among the dismal scientists predicting Miami's demise once again had arisen the perpetual error of demand economics: the vision of human beings essentially as mouths, but not minds—as "consumers" of goods and services, but not producers of them, as users of jobs but not as creators of new work.

José Pinero began creating new work within weeks after he began peddling the secondhand records on Eighth Street. For thirty days or so he saved up his profits from the album sales. Eventually he accumulated enough to rent and refurbish a small shop near the popular Tower Cinema for $100 per month. He named his store Ultra, after the leading department store in downtown Havana, and began selling favorite Latin imports to the movie crowds and others on the street. Also in mid-1961, Amaury Betancourt, the elegant unemployed banker with six children, had found a job as a clerk at the Coconut Grove Bank. Although it was one of the three oldest banks in Miami, he noticed it lacked an international department. Within six months he became assistant vice-president, was allowed to stop punching a time clock, and was assigned the challenge of forming an international division, in part to deal with a rising commerce with Latin America.

Meanwhile Felipe Valls's wife gave birth to a baby girl, adding to the burdens on Miami social services and lowering her family still deeper into the statistics of per capita poverty. Felipe quickly tired of his dishwasher work and found a job as a salesman in a restaurant supply company that was encountering a rise in the demand for restaurant goods in Little Havana. At the same time, still living in crowded quarters on Miami Beach, Dr. Oyarzun began studying to pass the Foreign Medical Board examinations, which would allow him to practice, in a limited way, in the United States. By early 1963, Armando Codina—"a slim 5 ft. 8 inch 13 year old," according to the records, "who likes to read adventure fiction and wants to be a mechanical engineer"—moved out of the orphanage and into a foster home with the O'Brien family, in Pompton Lakes, New Jersey. The O'Briens already had five children of their own, but they managed somehow to make space at the table for the young Cuban, who entered high school in New Jersey.

This group of immigrants was making clear progress. But with their large families and mostly nonworking wives, their halting English and questionable skills, their congested housing and low-paying jobs—and with what the press called "shockingly low benefits" and small enlistments in Florida's welfare system—they constituted a further increment to the poverty problem that was then preoccupying the bureaucracies of Washington, a clear part of the statistical ghetto of "invisible poor" to be uncovered indignantly later that year in Michael Harrington's *The Other America*. Enterprise begins with savings, with forgone consumption, which appears, from a sufficient distance and height of abstraction, identical to poverty. But welfare families with adequate income and housing can seem fine in the data though they remain, by any relevant measure of prospects, mired in real and intractable privation.

By 1964, however, some three years after their arrival, four of the immigrant families of our story were beginning to make significant contributions to the Miami economy. Ultra Records was thriving on Calle Ocho, and Pinero was planning to open another store in a new shopping center. Valls was growing restive as a salesman of restaurant equipment and was trying to persuade his boss to begin importing espresso machines from Spain, in order to accommodate the coffee thirst of the rapidly growing Cuban community. His boss, however, saw these devices as a troublesome specialty item, requiring complicated maintenance, and he refused to add them to his line of refrigerators, dishwashers, stainless-steel stoves, and other larger, simpler, and, so he believed, more profitable inventory. Valls thereupon borrowed some money from a friend ("at high interest," he says) and began importing the espresso machines himself. He knew his market. Paying $300 apiece and selling them for $1,200, he soon was able to pay back his loan, hire a mechanic named Gomez to install and service the equipment, and rent a shop on North Miami Avenue for his new International Equipment Corporation. With another loan, a second mortgage, and a low down payment, he also managed to move his family into the $17,500 house in southwest Miami that they occupied until 1982.

At the same time, Dr. Oyarzun had managed to improve his English enough to pass his medical boards, though at first he assumed he had failed and was doomed to another year of paperwork and penury as a clerk at Mercy Hospital—another period of dependency in the crowded homes of friends and relatives. Although the other students already had been informed of their test scores, the mail truck failed to stop at Oyarzun's place that morning and plunged the household into despair. When the postman returned later with the large brown envelope, he was ambushed in the driveway with hugs and kisses from Mrs. Oyarzun.

In 1965, Armando Codina returned from New Jersey to meet his mother, who had managed finally to escape Cuba and was living in Jacksonville, Florida. Codina attended his final years of high school in Jacksonville, learned several thousand more words of English, and won a scholaraship in mathematics to Jacksonville University. But his mother had never held a job in Cuba, and with Mr. Codina absent and divorced, Armando saw that "either she would have to go to work or I would." He rejected his scholarship and never attended college. Instead, at age seventeen, he took a job as a messenger, running checks at Jacksonville's American National Bank, while moonlighting as a bag boy at the neighborhood Winn Dixie. It looked very much like a setback for the young Cuban. But at American National Bank, Codina fell in love—with computers.

Back in Miami, Pinero had yet to learn English or even locate a university, but his record business was expanding rapidly, and he opened new Ultra stores in two new shopping malls and began to import records from Latin America and the Caribbean. Amaury Betancourt had risen to the position of vice-president in charge of the rapidly growing international division of Coconut Grove, and Felipe Valls, after several years of supplying restaurants, had become a contractor and consultant, designing and building them. Following a long period of work in hospitals, Dr. Oyarzun had established himself in practice and was considering the possibility of buying out his American colleague.

By 1970, the Cubans were securely established in the city. The census counted some 291,000 of them, or 23 percent of the population in Dade County. During the next decade—those stagnant years of the 1970s so pregnant with change and growth—the number would more than double, rising to 41 percent of the citizenry. Through most of this period, however, the Florida economy grew far faster than the rest of the country's, with lower unemployment and smaller welfare burdens. Every new influx of Cubans brought new fears and alarms, new demands for federal aid and management, while the Miami economy continued to expand far faster than those of the regions from which the aid was solicited. Despite the unimpeachable lessons of the long history of American immigration, the American people greeted each new siege as an economic problem rather than the economic boon it demonstrably became.

During the 1970s, each of the five immigrants in this story made important contributions to the triumph of the Cubans in Miami, one became a significant national business figure, and their children were moving rapidly into productive jobs in Dade County and across the country. Amaury Betancourt became president and chairman of one of Miami's fifteen Cuban-owned banks, Totalbank. Under the name Americas Bank, it had begun in 1974 in a mobile bank trailer at the corner of Southwest 27th Avenue and Coral Way. Located between Little Havana and Coral Gables, the new trailer was well situated to accommodate the increasing movement of Cubans into the plusher parts of Miami, then unserved by Cuban institutions. Another thriving Cuban bank, Intercontinental, advertises this concept: "The best way we can grow is to help you grow." Totalbank surged with the upsurge of its clientele. As of June 30, 1975, the deposits of Totalbank amounted to $8,485,008, and the bank's staff numbered seventeen. By 1982, when Betancourt retired, the bank's assets were some $120 million and growing at a pace of 12 percent a year, and it did business in branches throughout the city. It eschewed only the large cash deposits from "Colombia cowboys" that enriched less scrupulous local institutions and that jaded journalists identify as the source of Miami's success.

Drug money on occasion has poured into many other cities around the world, from New Orleans and Detroit to Ankara and Marseille—and poured out—without so transforming and enriching the populace. The pusher mentality of the big score is, in fact, a source of poverty and demoralization everywhere it arises. Hot money does not build capital; it debauches the human motives and values, energies and commitments which fuel real growth. The drug theory of Miami's wealth follows in a long "liberal" tradition of disparaging every new immigrant enterprise—from Chinese laundries to Italian florists—as either a "sweatshop" exploiting child labor or a cover for the transactions of crime. The real offense is a refusal to acknowledge the incredible efforts and sacrifices—and earned rewards—of the foreigners in our midst who give the lie to the myth of a closed economy.

José Pinero opened branches of Ultra Records in Central Shopping Plaza, Westchester Mall, Midway Mall, and Downtown Capital Mall to go with his original outlet on Calle Ocho. From a warehouse at 38th Place in Hialeah, moreover, Ultra imports records from throughout the Caribbean and Latin America and distributes them across the country. Dr. Oyarzun became one of the most prominent doctors in the city, the head of the League Against Cancer, and the owner of the medical building in which he first went into practice. In the early 1970s, Felipe Valls decided to plunge more deeply and directly into the restaurant and real estate fields. His restaurants were small sidewalk cafeterias, open twenty-four hours a day, serving small cups of *cafe cubano* and Cuban sandwiches. He would open one of these establishments, make it thrive, and then sell it to get a down payment on a more commodious place.

Valls's breakthrough came in 1971, when he purchased a large flower shop on Calle Ocho and turned it into Versailles, a large L-shaped gallery of mirrors and chandeliers, now the most popular Cuban restaurant in Miami. Valls estimates that the restaurant serves some 500 to 600 daily, and in a week consumes some 300 pounds of coffee, 500 pounds of rice, 400 pounds of beans, and more than half a ton of *pan cubano*.

Since 1971, Versailles has been joined in the neighborhood by four other ambitious Cuban restaurants, including La Carreta ("The Sugar Cart") across the street, an equally large and successful, though somewhat cheaper and less comely, competitor for Versailles, specializing in Creole food. Valls is indulgent toward La Carreta, flaunting its huge neon cartwheel sign across Calle Ocho. He knows that resourceful competition expands the market. And who could be a more resourceful competitor than the founder of Versailles? It is Valls himself who opened La Carreta and the other Versailles rivals nearby, and the market still grows to meet the rising supplies of good Cuban and Spanish-American food.

Valls's first five restaurants grossed some $6 million in 1981 and were increasing their take at some 10 percent a year, while he opened three new ones in 1982, including a new Carreta that seats some 340 people in a former Black Angus Steak House on Bird Road in the Westchester section of Miami. The conversion was easy, as Valls explains: "The Black Angus was already full of wagon wheels. We just kept them and called them cart wheels."

Throughout this period, like most successful businessmen operating within the U.S. tax structure, Felipe Valls has been deepening his engagement in the real estate market, presumably to shield the profits he earns elsewhere. Through his Twin Homes Development Company, he has also constructed scores of duplex condominiums at a lakeshore site in suburban Miami. According to his son, who manages one of the restaurants, the essential secret of Valls's success is a readiness to listen to anyone with an idea and a confident disposition to give credit to others. "He knows that in the long run the credit will return to him." He also takes little from his businesses for his own use. It was not until 1982, after he had built scores of houses for others, that he finally moved his family out of the small place in Hialeah that he bought for $17,500 some twenty years earlier.

Such continuing enterprise ensured that through 1982, despite the dreaded influx of 125,000 Mariel boat people (including Castro's notorious complement of criminals), and despite the arrival of some 45,000 Haitians, Florida still had one of the lowest rates of unemployment in the country; and Dade County, at 6.8 percent, had the lowest rate of unemployment in Florida. By 1980, Cuban households in Florida had higher incomes than other Floridians. In the recovery of 1983, Florida with 392,000 new jobs lagged only behind the twice as populous California (449.000 new jobs) in creation of employment and led third-place Texas by 139,000 new jobs. Not coincidentally these states were also the nation's three leading immigrant havens. By 1984, 95 percent of the Mariel group in Miami had found or created work. Among thousands of successful Cuban entrepreneurs were at least 200 millionaires. By some measures, it had been the most successful large immigration in the history of a nation of immigrants, and just as previous floods of foreigners had impelled New York into the front rank of American cities, so this latest tide is lifting Miami into a new role in the 1980s as a paramount world city, declared by Ecuador's president the very capital of Latin America.

"The best thing that's happened to Miami since air conditioning," says Chamber of Commerce leader Lester Freeman, "was when Fidel Castro read Karl Marx." Castro, in fact, by dint of totalitarian socialist planning, had managed in just two decades to lift a Cuban city to the forefront of the metropolises of the world. He erred only in supposing that this preeminent Cuban city would be in Cuba rather than in the United States.

In this sense, Castro has been the greatest benefactor of the U.S. economy since Adolf Hitler, whose horrors contributed to the United States many of its most valuable citizens, or even Czar Alexander III, whose totalitarian oppressions ultimately revived America with some 2 million Jews. Like the Cuban ruler, the Czar provoked mass flight by focusing his offenses on children, taking Jewish boys away at age twelve or earlier for six years of indoctrination in Greek Orthodox schools, followed by twenty-five years of military service, and by arousing public hostility against financiers.

The entire history of American economic and social progress is in part a chronicle of exiles and immigrations that echoes a prior chronicle of foreign tyranny and excess. A million Germans came to the United States in the tyrannous wake of the Revolution of 1848; a million Irish fled famine and British rule to reach America during those same turbulent years. Maoist oppression in China—like the Ming Dynasty before—contributed millions of overseas Chinese to Asian economies, and scores of recent thousands, pouring through Hong Kong, ultimately reached San Francisco and other American cities. The triumph of communism in Indochina is leading to corresponding triumphs of boat people in the United States. Within the entire heroic history of immigrants and exiles, sojourners and refugees on American soil, however, the saga of the Cubans in Miami in the decades after Castro remains unique. Only the Jews swarming into New York from Russia during the two decades before World War I came faster and in greater numbers. But they never exceeded one-sixth of the city's population, while Cubans ultimately constituted almost half of Miami's. No other immigrant group so inundated a city, and transformed it so quickly and successfully, while achieving such multifarious business breakthroughs as the nearly 600,000 fugitives from Castro's regime who made Miami their home after 1960.

The most important effect of government plans and controls, confiscations and harassments, predatory taxes and xenophobic laws is usually to enrich the economies of others by driving overseas a nation's most valuable resource: its most enterprising and creative citizens. Like so many socialist tyrants before him, Castro imagined that by expropriating the capitalists, he was gaining command of his nation's most important capital. In fact, he was giving it to America.

As crucial as their own knowledge and skills, however, in their legacy to America was what the Cubans imparted to their own children: attitudes, disciplines, and aspirations which ensure that, in the usual pattern of immigrant progress, many in the new generation will soon excel the achievements of their parents. The young offspring of the Betancourts, Vallses, Pineros, and Oyarzuns, for example, include several executives in their parents' firms, a bank vice-president, a general contractor, a reporter, and an oil company controller, all in their twenties and early thirties, as well as a number of younger college students learning business, engineering, and other needed skills. In fact, according to the 1980 census, the incomes of Cuban families whose household heads were under age thirty-four already exceeded the incomes of comparable non-Latin white families by nearly 20 percent.

The immigrant to Miami who was achieving the most in the 1980s, however, was thirty-four-year-old Armando Codina, who had come without any parents at all some twenty years before. By 1967, he had attracted the attention of bank executives at American National Bank in Jacksonville and received a promotion from messenger boy to teller. This gave him a chance to put his fascination with computers to practical use. In his new role, he noticed that when tellers left for lunch or other purposes, they destroyed accountability for errors and cash shortages; it was impossible at the end of the day to ascertain just who had botched the balances. This made it hard to appraise the performances of tellers and thus diminished the appeal of the job as an entry to higher levels, demoralized the tellers, and led to more errors. The teenaged Codina set to work during nights and weekends to devise a software program to computerize the teller accounting system.

In a few weeks, he succeeded and was put in charge of other computer operations at the bank. By the time he moved to Miami with his mother two years later, he was so adept at computer banking that he was named a loan officer at Miami's Republic National. The youngest bank executive in the state, he was assigned the job of making loans to businesses on the basis of accounts receivable.

It was routine work, in general, checking through the billings and other receivables of potential borrowers: the kind of work that puts some minds to sleep, allows others to wander, and provokes men like Armando Codina to look at it for opportunities. One opportunity, too eagerly grasped, came close to halting the young Cuban's upward ascent in banking; but in his struggle to retrieve his position, he created for himself a new job—and a new company.

One day he was approached by a distinguished Miami physician who was embroiled in an argument with Medicare officials and needed a loan to carry him over until the dispute was resolved. Impressed with the doctor's reputation, Codina readily granted the loan, though his department was restricted to conventional business lending. Then he went before the bank's board of directors and secured approval for the new commitment. Returning to the doctor to tell him the good news, he began to negotiate the details of the loan. Because the amount was to be based on the doctor's receivables, Codina first inquired how much he was owed.

"Ask Katy—she'll know," said the doctor. But the nurse didn't know either. Looking at the mess of the doctor's records—the endless Blue Cross, Blue Shield, and other insurance forms, Medicaid forms, Medicare forms, bills and invoices, checks and receipts, all piling up in an inscrutable scramble—Codina realized he had made a terrible mistake. The doctor's records were in no way presentable enough to justify the bank's granting him a major loan.

Unwilling to explain the situation to his superiors—or to tell the eminent doctor that he was not bankable—Codina set to work for several weeks in the doctor's office after hours to get the accounts in order. As he pored through the paperwork maze, Codina came up with the idea that was to sweep him altogether out of the banking business and into national prominence on a tide of money by the time he was thirty-two. His idea was that this doctor could not be alone in his labyrinth of insurance forms and billing documents; that if he could package a software program to deal with this problem, he could reach a market encompassing most of the nation's 300,000 physicians. While breaking the software bottleneck for an entire new industry, he could release many of the nation's independent doctors and nurses from a bondage to paperwork and allow them to concentrate their attentions on their patients.

Codina's company began slowly, against the resistance of a conservative profession. He started with a urologist named William Glantz. Every night for some ten months, Codina and three Cuban assistants would arrive at the doctor's office just as he was leaving, and much of the time they would still be there when the doctor returned the next morning. In the beginning, Codina continued his work at the bank, leaving sleep for subsequent years, but as time passed, he became ever more engrossed in his software project.

Codina had to figure out, in a way the doctor himself probably never had, the intricacies of his business life: exactly how his insurance forms and billings were filled out and computed; what the acceptable Medicare and Medicaid charges were; which costs were assigned to which accounts; what procedures were followed on which kinds of overdue receivables; how all these operations interacted with one another; and a host of further complications.

Then he had to design a program that put all this material in a simple, logical, and accessible data base, created useful report formats and display layouts, and in general performed the paperwork that was rapidly glutting and engorging doctors' offices in America in the early 1970s: paperwork that was reducing reputable physicians, with six-figure incomes, like Codina's first client, into a financial stupor—"Ask Katy—she'll know"—unbankable and scarcely insurable but perpetually liable for all the claims and disappointments of an aging, aching, and accident-prone society.

During those nights with the computer in the office of Dr. Glantz,

Codina and his company of Cuban teenagers first focused on the needs of urologists—their particular diagnoses, operations, and procedures. He designed new charts for diagnoses and billings, and a standardized form for insurance claims—from Blue Cross and private carriers to Medicaid and Medicare—and eventually he got them adopted by the state. In the end, this high school graduate from a foreign land had learned most of what there was to know about the nonmedical side of the practice of urology.

He was spending all this time and effort, however, entirely on spec, with no assurance that any doctor—even Dr. Glantz—would ever use his package, or that any funds could be raised to finance its production and marketing. He was working on through the night with no certainty that any number of the many thousands of software firms cropping up across the country would not already have under way a large number of competitive software projects, being executed by highly trained and experienced teams of experts, with access to finance and marketing skills. Codina had seen a need and had a concept for a company. He was even then creating and investing the most important capital: himself and his work. He would solve all subsequent problems as they came up.

Finally, he completed the system to the doctor's satisfaction and set forth to get a loan. With the help of Dr. Glantz and his banking contacts, he got $18,000 from the Small Business Administration. It turned out, barely, to be enough. Professional Automated Services struggled painfully into the marketplace, but almost no one noticed that it was there.

At Christmas that year, 1971, Codina's financial problems drove him into manufacturing candles to pay the rent. More promising, though, was his marriage to Margarita, then an airline stewardess, who supported them into the next year. Finally, with the help of presentations by Dr. Glantz to the local Urological Society, the program began to catch on: first with a few associates of Dr. Glantz's, then with urologists across the state of Florida, and eventually—as Codina adapted its package to other medical specialties—with some 700 doctors and clinics. Licensing its product with seven branch offices across the country, the firm grew from Codina himself and his three friends to 220 employees in Miami alone, with offices in Jacksonville, Orlando, and Tampa. It grew until, in 1978, Codina sold it for between $3 and $4 million to Itel Corporation, then flying high on Wall Street as one of the nation's fastest-growing and most opportunistic companies. When Itel crashed in 1980—amid a collapsing paper tower of kited and cantilevered leases on suddenly obsolete computers—Codina repurchased PAS and resold it the same year to NLT Corporation, an insurance services conglomerate.

Like most American entrepreneurs who make large sums of money, Armando Codina has now turned from the fields he knows best and moved into the less taxable domains of real estate. His IntrAmerican Investment Corporation is channeling funds from throughout Latin America into land speculation in downtown Miami. Like several of the city's Cubans, rich from other enterprises, who now dominate central Miami real estate, Codina's faith in Miami has never wavered, through recession, riot, and an alarming wave of crime, and his faith was being requited with handsome profits through 1982. As his land surged upward in value, he led a syndicate of local investors together with interests from Britain and Spain in the purchase of a $7.5 million development site off Biscayne Boulevard. Codina plans a major development to go with his landholdings, which are among the city's best locations.

Codina, however, is still too young to suppress his entrepreneurial drive to form new companies. Upstairs from IntrAmerican is his new project, Biotechnology, Inc., begun in 1980 to manufacture a portable exercise monitor for joggers called the Coach, which gives runners a continuous medical accounting, a recommended pace, and constant readings of speed, distance, aerobic improvement, and calories consumed. With such a multifarious gauge of motor performance, the jogger, plodding his weary way through the suburbs, will no longer have to feel epistemically inferior to drivers of sports cars roaring by.

Supply, apparently, creates its own demand in this area. The Coach sold well in test marketings at Burdine's and in Italy. Codina may possibly have discovered a new human need. No doubt there will be many more. A compulsive inventor who has patented several kinds of locks, Codina is always alert to technological opportunity. And, it is easy to forget, he is only thirty-five.

As he moved into the 1980s, however, Codina seemed to be reaching for a higher role. He was becoming another of those "upstart boosters"—prominent on the American frontier and vividly depicted in Daniel Boorstin's *The Americans*—who adopt an entire city as their sphere and spearhead of enterprise. Boorstin quotes William B. Ogden—the greatest of them all, projector and embodiment of Chicago's upsurge in the mid-nineteenth century: "I was born close by a saw mill, was early left an orphan, was cradled in a sugar-trough, christened in a mill-pond, graduated at a log school house, and at fourteen fancied I could do anything I turned my hand to, and that nothing was impossible. And ever since, Madame, I have been trying to prove it, and with some success." His rhetoric was grand, but, according to Boorstin's source, "the most striking trait of [Ogden's] character was his absolute faith in Chicago. He saw in 1836, not only the Chicago of today, but in the future, the great City of the continent." And indeed, Ogden more than any other man was crucial in launching the businesses, bridges, roads, and railways that made Chicago the fulfillment of his vision.

Now Codina and the other Cuban entrepreneurs speak of Miami with the same fervor and faith. As Codina says, "There is no place in the world like the U.S. and there is no place in the U.S. like Miami. Its structure is wide open, an environment of opportunity, devoid of an established hierarchy, like Pittsburgh or Boston or Dallas. It is a city of the future."

Codina at thirty-five is emerging as a major civic leader. He is on the board of directors of the Catholic Boystown camp that received him as an orphan twenty years ago. He is vice-president of the Miami Chamber of Commerce, and an officer of numerous other civic and philanthropic organizations. He serves on Vice-President George Bush's Task Force on Crime and has hired Bush's son Jeb to work in his office. He was instrumental in bringing the new Insurance Exchange—modeled on Lloyd's of London—to the city. "But in a hundred years I could not repay my debt to Miami."

In a speech in 1980, he declared to a Junior Achievement dinner: "You've heard about the American dream, the American pie, and whether they are still alive. Well, let me tell you, the American dream is alive and well. And if you want a part of the pie, all the ingredients are out there still. All you have to do is identify them, put them together, and work hard. . . . If you can do that you can still bake the biggest damn pie you ever saw in your life. . . . What has been accomplished in Miami serves as a showcase to *America* and to what free men and women can do when they work together in a spirit of harmony and cooperation for a common goal."

Nonetheless, the Cuban miracle was neither confined to Miami, nor dependent on the presence of a compatible Cuban culture, nor reliant on Latin American flight capital and cocaine for stimuli. The 42 percent of Cuban-Americans who live in other states earn 15 percent higher median incomes than Cubans in Florida. Many of the most successful Cubans never made it to Miami to benefit from the alleged magic of laundered money or a wide-open urban society.

Perhaps the most impressive Cuban success story outside Miami occurred in Atlanta, Georgia. In October 1960, when Castro confiscated Coca-Cola's Cuban bottling plant in Havana, he drove into exile a young chemist named Roberto Goizueta. Goizueta became an area chemist with Coca-Cola in Nassau, came to the United States, rose quickly through the ranks, and in 1981 became chief executive and chairman of the board of this $5 billion company. Castro got the bottling equipment; the United States got a major industrial leader. Goizueta later explained: "One thing I have learned is that the things you carry in your head, no one can take away from you. . . . Don't attach too much importance to material things, because, as I know so well from my own experience in Cuba, one individual can take all those material things away from you." In other words, what Goizueta and the other Cubans brought with them to America was far more important that what they left behind.

Another refugee, Juan Benitez, was to become a central figure in the new enterprise of J. R. Simplot in Boise, Idaho. When Fidel Castro in 1959 confiscated the business of Benitez's father—built up from nothing over a lifetime—the ten-year-old boy saw his family home plunged into bitterness and fear. By age thirteen, in 1962, the bright, energetic boy—short, with a warm smile and a gleam in his eye—resolved to leave for Miami. But in October the missile crisis cut off emigration and he was forced to delay his departure until early in 1965. Finally at age fifteen he made it to Mexico City.

Faced with six months of waiting for a visa to the United States, he flew to Canada instead, where the boy entered a Catholic seminary in Toronto. With the arrival of his visa in the summer of 1965, he took a train to Kansas City, where a brother had come to work for Hallmark.

Hoping to earn enough money to bring his parents to America, the sixteen-year-old Juan took no less than three jobs, all at or below the minimum wage. He worked part-time at Auto Trim, a shop repairing automobile seat covers; he inspected tortillas at a tortilla factory, reaching into the ovens barehanded to remove defective wafers; and at night he served as a custodian and toilet cleaner at the Federal Avenue Building in downtown Kansas City. By age nineteen, he also managed to finish high school, partly through correspondence at night, and following his father's rule to "save three pennies from every two you earn," he accumulated enough money to head for the Engineering School of the University of Missouri Rolla campus. With a combination of savings, work in the library, and a number of government-guaranteed loans, Juan made it through college in mechanical engineering.

After graduation in May 1972, he found work in tooling and process management at the GM auto assembly plant in St. Louis. Then, after a layoff at GM in the year of the energy crisis, he went to Hitchner Manufacturing, also in St. Louis. There he mastered a complex ceramic molding process before the firm sank in 1975.

From Hitchner, Juan went to Ethicon, a branch of Johnson & Johnson that produced the majority of the world's sutures. Moving from process engineering to facilities construction, he managed two major plant expansions for Ethicon, learned the intricacies of clean-room engineering, and attracted the attention of a headhunting firm on assignment for Mostek in Dallas, which needed dust-free facilities for semiconductor fabrication.

Mostek, by that time, though still one of the world's leading semiconductor firms, was suffering slow sclerosis under remote management from its new owners at United Technologies. Benitez began to chafe at the rigidities of a system in which he saw that "if you begin in facilities management, you die in facilities management." Juan Benitez wanted to build a new plant from scratch. Then a tiny three-line ad in the *Wall Street Journal* caught his eye: "Small start-up semiconductor company in the Pacific Northwest looking for individual to be responsible for overall construction of a Metal Oxide Semiconductor facility." He answered it.

A full three months later, Benitez received a phone call from a lady in Idaho who wanted to connect him to a Mr. Ward Parkinson. The conversation went well; he was hired. Juan Benitez soon was immersed as a central figure in one of the most momentous semiconductor construction projects—and supreme entrepreneurial endeavors—in the history of American industry.

Juan Benitez, though unusual, was not unique. Cuban immigrants can be found in high positions in many U.S. high-technology firms, from Xicor in Silicon Valley to Storage Technology in Boulder, Colorado. The faith of Benitez, Armando Codina and the other Cuban entrepreneurs is the spirit of enterprise that built America. It is a faith that now burns most intensely in the hearts of men who come here from abroad and understand the full horror of the slide into socialism.

But this is nothing new. The Cubans are just another in the long line of immigrant swarms on the ever-changing American frontier, and their upsurge differs only in speed and number from any other in the continuing saga of American revival. Vietnamese, Central Americans, Lebanese, and even the much abused Haitians are making similar breakthroughs. The triumph of socialism and tyranny usually results in the enrichment of America, as the "burdens" of immigration swiftly become the boons of entrepreneurial growth. Against the jaded expertise of bureaucracy and privilege, the dismal sciences of a secular professoriat, and the oppressive plans of Washington regulators, the faith of unlettered outsiders will prevail.

It has always been immigrants who have revitalized America's faith. As long as the United States is open to these flows from afar, it is open to its own revival: a continuing rebirth from the well-springs of its own historic mission in the world.

THE
EUTHANASIA
OF THE
ENTREPRENEUR

A SAD HEART IN
A PERSONAL JET

Wayne E. Copeland, Jr., is a born entrepreneur who has recently found what he sees as his best investment. Most of the time he is rich—wealthy enough to fly a personal jet from his home in Norman, Oklahoma, to distant airports to meet with writers on economics and tell his story. I got the treatment one night—a ride in the yellow-and-blue-striped Sabre Liner from Orlando to Clearwater, Florida; Milton Friedman was next on the schedule. Wayne Copeland was that rich; rich enough to run a yellow-and-blue taxi for Milton Friedman. But his story—being a distinctly American tale of the 1970s and early-1980s economy—is not altogether a success story, and his "best investment" was not exactly what one would expect from a thirty-nine-year-old entrepreneur with an ambition to change sharply the architectural and intellectual horizons of his city, now renowned chiefly as the home of the University of Oklahoma football team. Wayne Copeland is devoting his "best investment" to the politics of transforming the U.S. tax structure, with its nominally high rates riddled with loopholes, into a simple flat-rate system.

Like so many business venturers, he was thrust into the role as a small boy when his father—another compulsive entrepreneur—left the family in Oklahoma to seek his fortune in California; Wayne Junior found himself assuming the male role in the family. Also like many other entrepreneurs from broken homes, he was very close to his mother. She was quite something to be close to. A gorgeous brunette and former Miss Oklahoma who at age sixteen launched a chain of dancing schools in small Oklahoma towns, she managed to cope after her divorce by running an eleven-man chainsaw crew. They were clearing land for an amusement park called Frontier City. Later she became a talent scout and discovered Anita Bryant.

First, though, she discovered little Wayne. Flat-footed, he would never make it in Oklahoma football, but he showed entrepreneurial talent from the age of eight. She lent him money to buy lawn-mowers to rent to boys in the neighborhood. He made money, the boys made money, his mother was satisfied, and the lawns got mowed. It was a positive-sum lesson in capitalism, to be followed by many more. At age eleven, he sold cold drinks and hot dogs from a dirt-floored shack to golfers stranded away from the club-house after finishing nine holes on the municipal golf course: a matter of serving the needs of others, finding a market niche.

At college, in the early 1960s, Wayne began Legends, which in fast-moving Oklahoma is now the state's oldest full-service restaurant serving lunch and dinner. It started as a pizza stand, for delivery only, in a $75-per-month space behind a coin laundry in an abandoned naval base. Since no customers would bother them at this remote spot, Wayne and his colleague Orin could concentrate on making and marketing pizzas. The key to their marketing success was Orin's idea of writing a personal note on the box of every pizza sold to each of their some 4,000 customers, whose idiosyncrasies he kept on file.

One day, when Dr. J. Herbert Holloman—then president of Oklahoma University—ordered thirty pizzas for students at his home and got thirty different personal handwritten messages to boot, he decided to find the proprietor and invest in him. Holloman put in a prestigious $10,000, which, together with a similar investment from a Copeland roommate, at first nearly ruined him and Legends. The easy money lured him prematurely out of the naval base and into the treacherous arena of Norman's real estate and restaurant markets.

Wayne bought a downtown lot, constructed a new building, hired the leading French chef in Oklahoma City, and set out to take Norman by storm. But the pizza traffic got in the way of the French chef, who soon departed, and Wayne dismayed his lifelong banker, Jack Black, by remodeling the premises four times. Wayne and his new partners ended up staying open sixteen hours a day to pay the bills and dealing with gang fights in the parking lot at three in the morning. He learned a key principle of the entrepreneurial life: Don't diversify. Concentrate on what you do best. Corner the most available market, the demand for your own unique talent and experience. Invest first in your own monopoly: yourself.

His father presumably failed to apply this lesson to his personal life, diversifying into five marriages. But he too is an entrepreneur who mastered one thing, etching multilayer circuit boards and inventing several patented techniques for manufacturing them. His innovations gave him a worldwide reputation in the field and a lucrative contract for making the key mother boards for Minuteman missile guidance computers. In 1969 he sold his firm to a public company for several hundred thousand dollars. Unfortunately he was going through a divorce at the time and his wife got most of the money.

Starting anew from scratch, he began improving his process and applying it to new products. Eventually, through a serendipitous meeting in a Los Angeles bar, he stumbled into a multimillion-dollar contract etching and producing xeroradiographic cassettes as the worldwide sole source to Xerox. The cassettes were used at the time in every major hospital for the detection of breast cancer, and through a technical breakthrough, Copeland provided them very profitably at one-eighth the price of Xerox's previous supplier. But success was nearly ruining the elder Copeland.

He had taken over the company when it had $78 in the bank and $250,000 in current payables and was losing $20,000 a month, but had no line of products. He had an option to buy it for book value from its parent firm if he could pay back the debt and make the business profitable. But the Xerox profits were suddenly so big and the demands for expansion so imperious that he could no longer afford to buy the firm without giving half the equity to financial backers. Worse, he was going through yet another divorce and would have to give much of the rest of the equity to his wife.

So he called Wayne Junior, who had learned much of his father's business during summer stints in California, and asked him if he could raise the $450,000 needed to buy the company. The younger Copeland had never borrowed more than $70,000 in his life, but his restaurant and real estate were finally beginning to prosper and he was still on good terms with Jack Black. He gulped and said he would try. He would call back in a few weeks. The father said that wouldn't do; he needed the money in four days, including the weekend days ahead. Wayne gulped again and said he would try.

Jack Black, though, was out of town. Wayne had to turn instead to John H. Patten, the president and majority stockholder of Norman's largest bank, Security National, whom Wayne scarcely knew. Two days later, after sitting in the anteroom to his office for several hours, Wayne finally got in to see Patten and make the case for the loan. He was startled when Patten, on the basis of the Xerox contract alone, agreed to the deal and began the usual extended process for issuing the check. Copeland said he needed the money immediately. Patten gulped and gave it to him. Wayne was suddenly in the xeroradiographic cassette business. He renamed the firm Hipoint Research, after a street which ran by Wayne Senior's Malibu Lake home. Within less than six months, he repaid the loan from earnings and had compiled a bank balance of some $500,000. He used it to buy Norman real estate.

The reason Wayne Copeland does not regard his family story as altogether one of success, despite his own wealth, is that his father could not convert his technological genius and tenacity into an adequate pension, and his mother struggled for a lifetime with several small businesses. But Wayne Junior could parlay his unexpected skills in fund-raising, together with a bold use of leverage and ingenuity with the tax code, into a sad heart and a personal jet.

Wayne Copeland has not made much money in pizzas, or restaurants, or Dolphin Airlines in Florida, or circuit board technology, or even oil, though he has done reasonably well in all these fields at various times. But he became a multimillionaire at thirty-seven by buying real estate with borrowed money, writing off the interest payments, and rapidly depreciating the buildings for tax purposes while they soared in value, before they were sold for profits, taxed at the relatively low rate of capital gains, or refinanced to yield a tax-free flow of funds.

For the last two decades, while the government ran down the dollar, punished savers with inflation-adjusted taxes on interest of more than 100 percent, and gouged income earners at rates which rose with their productivity, many thousands of Americans became millionaires through real estate dealings while paying hardly any taxes at all. Fully half the new multimillionaires listed by *Fortune* in 1978 became so in real estate.

Wayne Copeland, Jr., is indignant at the economic waste and distortion that the tax system inflicts. He is taxed at a lower rate for putting together property deals with depreciation and refinancing finagles than his father was taxed for developing ingenious manufacturing techniques for building missile guidance computers or new ways to fight breast cancer or than his mother paid on relatively meager earnings from her dance studio in the upstairs bedroom of his grandmother's home.

He sums up the problem. Today, if he made a series of nonrecourse loans through a limited partnership to heave up another apartment building for the already glutted apartment markets in Norman, he would get so many tax credits, depreciation benefits, interest write-offs, and financing options that he would scarcely need to care if anyone rented the rooms or if the building fell down. But if he invested the same amount in a small company manufacturing a new technology, he might well lose all his money (perhaps in paying for lawyers to defend him from product liability suits or in preparing an endless series of environmental impact statements), and he would be liable for the loans. Or if he made significant profits he would face several levels of taxation on them, first through corporate income taxes, then through personal income taxes, and finally, perhaps years later, on the capital gains, even if a large portion, or all of them, merely reflected inflation. This huge disproportion between the treatment of enterprise and the prizes of shelter gets Wayne Copeland, Jr., angry, and has led to his latest investment, which he regards as his best, a contribution in politics. Here—in politics—is where the shelter economy begins.

Wayne Copeland's problem is the essential affliction of Western capitalism: the stultification and demoralization of the spirit of enterprise. Economists, however, have little idea of what is going on. To most of them, taxes and inflation may reduce the level of investment by depriving the businessman of funds and increasing his hurdle rate of return: the yield necessary to induce a capital purchase. But tax shelters, tax credits, and accelerated depreciation schedules help to restore the balance by allowing the investor to keep more of his income and profits and directing them into socially approved activities. Nothing essential is lost. Indeed, to the extent that the tax code channels funds toward high-priority fields, such as oil and gas exploration, low-cost housing, commercial real estate, coal mining, plant and equipment, research and development projects, and farm animals, the economist might imagine that shelters foster economic growth, enhance levels of capital formation, and fulfill social needs for food, energy, housing, and innovation.

In fact, real estate and oil and gas programs, accounting for some two-thirds of measured shelter activity, did substantially relieve a slump in rental housing in some areas and provided an attractive channel for financing a 60 percent increase in U.S. drilling activity after the 1979 OPEC hike in oil prices. But as Copeland points out, these tax benefits would have been entirely superfluous but for price controls on oil and gas and rent controls in many cities. In addition, high tax rates and loopholes foster a cynical and panicky financial climate that leads to bad investments. The media's focus on bizarre shelters—such as butterfly commodity straddles, boxcar leases, flower funds, weeping fig partnerships, and write-offs in porn films—may be useful in arousing public indignation at the loopholes of the rich. But the major damage to the economy comes from commoner shelters and from the high tax rates that the loopholes produce for others.

Even though the damage eludes economic measurement, it is indeed devastating and sharply retards real U.S. capital formation. The effects come not in a drop in the measurable levels of investment or in a growing gap between the rich, who use the shelters, and the poor, who don't. The problem arises in the erosion and dissolution of the invisible yield of enterprise: the knowledge, spirit, and skills of entrepreneurs, which make up the metaphysical capital of the system. Those unseen returns are more important for growth and progress than all the accumulations of buildings, plant, and equipment. To tax away these intangible resources is to demoralize and stultify the nation's wealth. That is what was happening to Wayne Copeland, Jr.

In order to comprehend the idea of a mind tax—admittedly a curious concept—one has to imagine what it is like to make money in America. Even before an entrepreneur begins receiving any funds, he undergoes the transforming experience of every suddenly successful citizen. It is a metamorphosis from a producer of goods to a manipulator of finance. Although it is bad for the economy, it begins with an offer from the government that is too good to refuse.

He is told that unless he accepts the government terms, he would have to relinquish some 60 percent of his incremental income to various tax collectors, federal, state, and local, thereby pretty much eliminating himself as a factor in American capital formation. He also would have to hire an accountant to keep track of his growing cash flow and channel appropriate amounts of it quarterly to the IRS, in accordance with complex estimates of expected income, accompanied by suitable paperwork. Meanwhile, he would watch inflation erode his purchasing power, in recent years at a pace of between 4 and 9 percent a year. If he therefore parked his wealth in a money market fund, in order to take advantage of what are widely described as soaring interest rates, he would find he had succeeded only in retarding the rate of erosion of his capital; the governments in Washington and most states would tax between 50 and 60 percent of his nominal interest: a levy of well over 100 percent of his real return after inflation. In sum, he is faced with a sudden rise in overhead costs, a quick jolt back into the middle class of income earners, and a summary end to his career as a productive entrepreneur.

Such is the fate that indeed befalls a small number of baffled winners of lottery sweepstakes, confused inheritors of modest fortunes, punch-drunk boxing champions, and one-shot windfall millionaires. But it is a fate entirely unacceptable to any red-blooded American entrepreneur who does not plan on immediate retirement from the field. For him the government has another proposition. In essence, it says that *all* his profits can be restored to him, tax-free, on one condition: that he liquidate his entire fund of metaphysical capital; that he give up the spirit of enterprise and become a certified antipreneur, an epistemic bankrupt.

Rather than using the productive knowledge that made him rich and that could contribute to the further enrichment of his country and community, he must surrender his wealth to the relatively unproductive and sterile knowledge of tax lawyers, planners, tax accountants, partnership packagers, and real estate consultants (or, as Wayne Copeland, Jr., did, become such an expert himself).

Though useless to the nation, tax sheltering will turn out to be demanding work. The entrepreneur will have to learn to discriminate among the crooks and the cranks and the practical advisers. He will have to study many proposals. On an airplane trip (in first class), he will learn of a man named Mario in Beverly Hills, favored by many movie stars and producers, who opens all the windows and turns on a loud fan when you enter the room, and who gives his advice only in a virtually inaudible whisper. His approach entails heavy use of $100 bills, withdrawn from the bank on days that your diary describes elaborate business events, such as cocktail parties and dinners in which most of the expenses—for waiters, cooks, limousine drivers, bartenders, logs for the fireplace, and food for the table—are defrayed in cash payments of under $25 apiece. To disarm natural skepticism, Mario urges that the diary also report a large number of apparently business-related activities, such as lunches with your good friend the agent, which, out of evident scruple, are not deducted. In general, however, he requires living a totally documented life, except for a few whopping fictions: large deductible business parties and a long succession of $22 drinking sessions at plush metropolitan bars with business associates. This approach, though, seems more plausible for a producer in Malibu than for your usual businessman, and it leaves our entrepreneur with the minor task of disposing of the $100 bills accumulated during a long series of such drinking bouts and business parties.

"No sweat," says another entrepreneurial friend, flaunting a large red book, from the Practicing Law Institute in New York, titled *How to Use Foreign Tax Havens*. To the afflicted taxpayer, swollen with cash, this tome offers temporary relief from the depredations of tax lawyers in the United States only to deliver him into the hands of an occult and labyrinthine circle of tax lawyers around the world: large swarthy men, according to one report, replete with 24-karat body jewelry, leather-trimmed cowboy hats, rococo boots, and arcane lore about the tax benefits of expatriated money. The crucial step, he will inform you, is establishing a corporation in a low-tax colony of a country with a double taxation treaty with the United States ("Curaçao in the Netherlands Antilles is a key to intelligent tax planning"), after forming a subsidiary in a low-tax haven such as the Cayman Islands or the New Hebrides, which in turn invests in an offshore fund situated in the Bahamas. This firm can divert your income flow via Curaçao into relatively tax-free investments in the United States, provided your lawyer has contrived an effective way to circumvent the dreaded effect of what have been described by a leading expert as "certain extremely complex provisions of Subpart F of the Internal Revenue Code." Subpart F requires investors to report, as part of taxable income, any share of profits that correspond to an ownership or beneficial position in a foreign entity, even if it generates no U.S. income. Failure to report foreign dealings in sufficient detail to permit the IRS to determine liabilities under Subpart F opens the taxpayer to criminal prosecution as a tax evader, which in turn will free him from the ministrations of the occult circle of swarthy international lawyers only to deliver him into the hands of sallower tax lawyers in the United States, which, as the reader may recall, is where he began.

In defense of foreign tax havens, however, it should be recognized that the IRS is extremely unlikely to uncover or successfully prosecute a sufficiently ingenious scheme and that most of these havens offer extraordinary opportunities for deductible investment in frosted rum daiquiris and suntan oils, plied among balmy statuesque women on some of the world's most beautiful beaches. On the other hand, anyone who invests the time and effort required to create three murky corporate entities between himself and his money could probably have achieved a similar effect more enjoyably at Aqueduct or Las Vegas, and could have escaped taxation equally well in the United States real estate market.

Before dismissing these foreign money beaches as a Byzantine minefield, however, it is only fair to mention that some 60,000 corporations, including 11,000 firms and 357 banks on Grand Cayman alone, have not. There is some $100 billion deposited in offshore banks in the Caribbean. If your sudden riches are sufficiently great, it may be worthwhile to contrive an arrangement like the one Touche Ross International, a big-eight accounting firm, nego-

tiated for an eminent bunch of British punk rockers, who had ca-
terwauled their way to a platinum single in the United States. As
described in a Touche Ross publication, the shelter entailed formation of a company (NV) in Curaçao, in the Netherlands Antilles (remember the role of Curaçao in any intelligent tax planning). To this
company was assigned the distribution rights for an album containing the hit song. This company, in turn, formed a Dutch subsidiary (BV) and licensed it to sell recordings in the United States. A
U.S. record company purchased the distribution rights from the
Dutch firm in exchange for royalties.

According to Touche Ross, "The TRI plan provided several advantages: Elimination of U.S. withholding tax (some 30 percent) on
royalty payments to BV by virtue of a U.S.A.-Netherlands treaty; a
favorable tax ruling to BV in Holland allowing deduction of 93 percent of its royalty income from the U.S., as royalty expense, to NV
in the Antilles; elimination of withholding taxes in Holland on royalty payments; and declaration of net after-tax income in Holland
as a dividend to NV free of Dutch withholding tax" and presumably subject only to the nominal taxation of the Antilles.

In general, though, the tax-haven route is suitable for larger corporations or cosmopolitan taxpayers who already have made their
pile, whether legally or not, and are willing to devote most of their
time to maintaining it. Active entrepreneurs will shelter their
money closer to home. One favored method, described by the be-
jeweled international lawyer, involves purchase of shares in a limited partnership owning rights in a domestic coalfield. Shelters in
coal were proffered entrepreneurs from many directions in 1981.

There is both good news and bad news involved in Kentucky
coal mine partnerships. The good news seems to be that with tax
exemption for interest payments, deduction of certain mine development costs, tax credits and depreciation on mining equipment,
and possible decades of percentage depletion allowances on the
coal as it is produced, you can write off between five and seven
times your initial investment. The bad news is that *you* probably
will have to mine the coal. The further good news, though, is that in
many Kentucky properties, there isn't any coal. The bad news is
that under the tax reform act of 1978 and the economic recovery act
of 1981, you will be responsible for paying off the loan anyway.
The interest costs, though, will still be deductible, and, according to
Barron's, you may have the penurious enjoyment (the best things in
life being free) of seeing some of the vendors of these coal mine
shares face criminal prosecution.

Nonetheless, as the lawyer explained, a series of investments in
valid coal mines, as in producible stands of timber, can provide

ample tax shelters for decades. Coal, moreover, may offer less risk, though also fewer deductions, than similar investments in oil and gas partnerships. Oil and gas allow all the short-term benefits of coal, plus the immediate write-offs of so-called "intangible drilling costs" (for everything from labor to chemicals and other nonsalvageable materials), and can give a larger short-term payoff if you hit oil or gas. All the energy programs, of course, but particularly coal mines, decline in attractiveness in an era of declining energy prices. Since fuel prices—barring major war, new price controls, or other relevant catastrophes—are likely to continue down in real terms for the rest of the century, the wise entrepreneur will approach these proposals with caution.

In time the seeker of shelter will return from the mines, oil rigs, and palm trees to the palpable bricks and mortar of domestic real estate to protect him from the elements, whether sleet and rain or IRS. The real estate shelters that essentially made Wayne Copeland's fortune actually were improved by the Capital Cost Recovery provisions in the 1981 tax act. In contrast to an average effective depreciation period of twenty-eight years under the old law, the 1981 bill allowed depreciation of rental structures over ten years and commercial buildings over fifteen, together with the usual 10 percent tax credit for equipment purchases, and credits of up to 25 percent for rehabilitating commercial buildings, depending on their age and historic value. Real estate shelters, moreover, are the only programs that still allow purchase with non-recourse loans. No matter what happens to the building, whether it generates income or not, the limited partner cannot be held liable for the mortgage payments.

The magic of real estate partnerships, however, still chiefly derives from the depreciation allowance for structures that typically increase in value. Unlike the depletion allowance for oil, gas, coal, and timber, which actually are depleted, and unlike the depreciation allowance for capital equipment, which in fact does wear out or become obsolete rapidly, the depreciation allowance for real estate projects does not correspond to anything real that often happens to buildings. If they are well constructed and well maintained, they will last and even appreciate indefinitely. For investors in the 50 percent bracket, therefore, the allowance constitutes a virtual tax credit spread out over ten or fifteen years, for half the cost of the building, on top of the various credits available on purchase and the deductions for interest on the mortgage, maintenance, and other expenses. Although the depreciation is theoretically recapturable when the building is sold, many investors avoid such a taxable transaction by trading the structure for another under a Section 1031 real estate swap, or by refinancing the appreciated equity with another mortgage to gain tax-free cash. But even if the depreciation is eventually taxed, it represents an extended tax-free loan to the investor. Through all these devices, real estate shelters have provided a golden road to riches for scores of thousands of Americans.

All these shelters, and many others, séduce the entrepreneur from his chosen field and into alien activity. They divert money from entrepreneurial ventures, with dynamic potentials and taxable yields, first into the huge and essentially unproductive industry of tax planning and then into a vast array of relatively artificial projects, governed by the tectonics of taxation. These projects tend to be managed from afar and mandated only to combine a balance of cash flow with a large maw of contrived tax losses. Front-loaded with fees and deductions in early years, tax shelters tend to shorten the horizons of capital. They separate the benefits of the investment from the long-lived assets themselves and attach them to their disposable packaging of financial paper. The results are shoddy buildings, shallow investments, wasteful losses, lower productivity, higher interest rates, and larger federal deficits. And because they reduce the government's revenues from the rich, retard expansion of the tax base, and diminish the quality of capital formation, the shelters tend to restrict the opportunities of the poor and middle classes while making them pay the taxes the rich avoid (as loopholes gape open, social security taxes leap ever upward). All of these qualitative and long-term changes attract little notice from economists, who focus on quantitative and essentially timeless accounts of capital formation. But the shelter system, insidiously and ubiquitously affecting all investment decisions in the economy, constitutes what is perhaps the government's most influential instrument of policy.

It always should be understood that shelters are not limited to the declared programs of tax planners and investment firms. Tax considerations bear heavily on every investment made in the economy. The shelters merely embody the most striking and conspicuous effects, not necessarily the most important.

Nonetheless, it is worth roughly measuring these distortions. Tax planning, mostly for corporations, is the fastest-growing segment of the accounting business in the big-eight international firms, amounting to 20 percent of their work; but a survey for the profession estimates that eight times as much business, mostly for individuals, is administered by small local firms of tax attorneys and accountants. Stanley Surrey has estimated that in 1972, before the massive onset of mid-1970s bracket creep, the average taxpayer in the $100,000 to $500,000 bracket gained $29,264 in tax benefits, while the average taxpayer in the $1 million bracket received no less than $725,000. These figures suggest that tax considerations dominate all other factors in shaping the finances of our most active capitalists. Even if such loophole gains were decisive in only half of the investments of the rich, shelters can be seen to play an overwhelming role in determining the shape and quality of capital.

Beyond the hundreds of billions channeled offshore, a Brookings Institution study suggests that the bias in the tax structure has increased investment in real estate in recent decades by some 50 percent, signifying further hundreds of billions of fiscally distorted architecture. Almost $30 billion in debt and equity was loosely disbursed by Real Estate Investment Trusts (REITs), a major tax shelter device for large investors during the mid-1970s. The quality of this capital formation may be judged by the loss of 80 percent of the equity value and at least partial default on more than half of the mortgages since the REITs began booming in 1969. Nor was the REIT debacle simply an effect of the 1974–75 recession. The REITs followed a well-worn path of boom and bust in tax-favored construction projects, including the similar syndicates favored by tax-shy investors during the 1950s and early 1960s.

Using Treasury analyses of the 1981 profile of income tax payments, Michael Evans has computed an estimate of some $70 billion in tax-sheltered income. But other evidence suggests that this is a substantial underestimate. The Treasury projects some 4.1 million families with adjusted gross incomes over $50,000. These families average some $81,000. If, contrary to Surrey's esimates, each manages to shelter only 20 percent of its income, the total would approximate the Evans projection. Market surveys, however, find three times as many individuals and families with incomes over $50,000, implying a much larger quantity of sheltered income. It is likely that taxes shape the disposal of some $200 billion of personal earnings, or the bulk of some $300 billion of gross personal savings. High taxes on earnings and interest income also drastically reduce the savings rate. Thus they heavily restrict both the quantity and the quality of capital formation in the United States.

The usual response to such data is to urge the closing of loopholes. But as long as the rates remain so high and progressive, such tax "reforms" are futile. In general, people do not get into the top bracket by being stupid. If they face marginal taxation at rates over

40 percent, the evidence shows that they simply halt activity generating income in taxable forms. For example, in the late 1970s, wealthy taxpayers earned virtually no taxable income at all in interest or dividends. Such economic activity would merely constitute a disguised way of retiring from enterprise.

A tax code perforated for avoidance is preferable to a system of the same rates without loopholes. Loopholes allow the economy to breathe. High progressive and unnegotiable gouges like those in Sweden and England drive people altogether out of the country into offshore tax havens, out of income-generating activities into perks and leisure pursuits, out of money and savings into collectibles and gold, and, most important, out of small business ventures into the cosseting arms of large established corporations and government bureaucracies. The result is the demoralization of entrepreneurs and the stultification of capital. The experimental knowledge that informs and refines the processes of economic growth is stifled, and the metaphysical capital in the system collapses, even while all the indices of capital formation rise.

Tax shelters are a honeyed trap for entrepreneurs. But after all is said and done, shelters do help them to keep sufficient after-tax income to continue in enterprise. Progressive rates effectively enforced without loopholes destroy entrepreneurship altogether. The tax reform movement, therefore, with its neglect of rates and focus on loopholes, would make the system worse. The only desirable reform is reduction in the tax rates.

Wayne Copeland, Jr., is a man of enterprise, with a vision and a cause, because he sees beyond the economic throes of the early 1980s to a new world beyond—to a series of technologies that can radically change all our lives, if they are allowed to prevail. "The beauty and elegance of solid-state technology can save us all from material want," he said during our jet ride together. "It can change the way we do everything, use everything, see everything, from education to resources, to energy, to food, to shelter, to capital formation. . . . The reason the integrated circuit is so powerful is that it is, in a way, an exquisite form of physical truth. Essentially weightless, it is nearly pure idea.

"If you give a man your shirt, you no longer have it. That is the world before the integrated circuit. But if you give a man an idea, you both have it. That is the magic of the solid-state world; it is essentially an ever-expanding circuitry of ideas. A truth that sets us free. . . ."

He looked out the window of the jet into the pink clouds, suffused with setting sunlight. That is why he then saw his best investment, with the most effective use of leverage, as not his real estate properties, oil and gas exploration and development packages, his father's xeroradiographic business, his intrastate airlines, or his restaurant Legends, but a regular $10,000 contribution he made to the Republican Senate Campaign Committee's Senatorial Trust. One day in 1983, it allowed him to give a silicon chip to Ronald Reagan, who was meeting with the group and who thus became the first American president to actually touch the truth of America's future. By moving toward a flat tax, Reagan also was reaching toward the key to a similarly explosive and elegant truth in fiscal policy. A flat tax or at least a less jagged and intricate one, Copeland believes, could do more to unleash the onrushing new technologies than any other policy change.

Michael Evans's careful computations of tax shelter activity and underground earnings, together with an extremely cautious estimate of dynamic effects on productivity and work effort, have convinced him that revenues can be maximized with a top rate between 25 and 30 percent. Milton Friedman and other Copeland passengers believe the optimal level is lower still. Arthur Laffer has proposed a flat tax of 11.5 percent, with deductions only for mortgage interest and charities, that would apply to all personal incomes and corporate value added. Even with static computations, this levy would bring more revenue than the current tax structure. With the dynamic benefits of such a simpler system, without shelters and finagles, the government would be flooded with revenue. Through his membership in the Senatorial Trust, Copeland hoped to make his case persuasively—and against his clear interests as a beneficiary of the current code—to all the key Republican senators. He thinks he made some headway.

But politics is as slow and frustrating as tax shelters are diversionary and demoralizing, and Wayne Copeland, Jr., understands Washington much less well than entrepreneurship. So he remained a sad heart in his sleek personal jet, with its yellow and blue vertical stripes and its tax benefits, which thrust him up, far above his Oklahoma origins, to seminars with senators and Nobel economists and to conferences with Buckminster Fuller, opening new horizons among the roseate clouds in the glory of the American skies . . . until his sudden crash in late 1982.

For there in his Sabre Liner with me early in the year were the seeds of his undoing as an antipreneur. Next to his seat was a large pile of maps and geophysical reports on the Fletcher natural gas project of the young man who was then Oklahoma's fastest-moving oil and gas entrepreneur, Bill Saxon. As chairman of and 80 percent owner of Saxon Oil Company, a firm recently taken public by

Goldman-Sachs, Saxon had a personal statement, as they say in Oklahoma, of some $340 million. In the jet, Copeland said he was skeptical of Saxon's plans. But as time passed and more and more of Oklahoma's smartest money moved into the project, Copeland became sorely tempted.

Then on January 24, 1982, he was invited to breakfast with Bill Saxon at the Oklahoma City Golf and Country Club. Saxon outlined an inspiring vision of a huge gas field that would help create in America a methane economy, emancipating the country once and for all from bondage to OPEC. According to Saxon's computations, moreover, Copeland's proposed participation of $3 million, with some limited exposure to debt, would eventually be worth at least $100 million. Saxon wrote the estimate on an Oklahoma City Golf and Country Club napkin, together with the words "It's got to be true," and his bold signature, "Bill Saxon."

Saxon's vision was indeed bold and true under the conditions of the time. Saxon himself was a self-made oilman entrepreneur with a keen sense of realities under the rig. His Fletcher field project was one of the most promising in North America. But it was "deep gas." Thus its profitability was dependent on continuation of the price-control system then in effect, which snarled oil exploration and shallower gas projects and jacked up world fuel prices, while leaving deep gas free of regulation. This system allowed prices of up to $10 per 1,000 cubic feet (MCF) for deep gas, while forcing all other gas to be sold at prices between 15 cents and $3.

With the increasing effectiveness of fuel conservation and with Reagan's decontrol of oil prices, however, the entire pricing structure began to collapse and deep gas could no longer be profitably produced. Hundreds of oil and gas tax shelter partnerships began to crumble. Local banks teetered; Penn Square fell; Seafirst and Continental Illinois watched a massacre of oil- and gas-based assets. Faced with payables of $120 million, Saxon Oil neared bankruptcy; the Fletcher properties became worthless. Wayne Copeland not only lost his $3 million but found himself exposed to several times that amount in debt suddenly due. Once rich, he was now selling assets for economic survival. He even went to the extreme of grounding his personal jet.

No longer in the air, however, he became again a real entrepreneur, at ground level, creating new value out of refuse. He returned to what he knew best, the Norman real estate market. But this time he would not fool around with apartments and tax shelter partnerships. He would bring to Norman a project so grand and beautiful, so distinguished in architecture and artificial setting, that it would make the city a cynosure of the region. Putting up most of his remaining assets, he packaged a group of loans and investments totaling $17 million to purchase some 300 acres of rolling land, with a river flowing through and clumps of trees, and armadillos in the underbrush.

It was on the "wrong" side of the thruway, I-35, and dominated at the time by a huge garbage dump. But in Copeland's vision the dump stretched out as a large curvaceous lake glimmering in the sunset below the clubhouse of a golf course designed by Robert Trent Jones, and yes, he signed up Jones for the job. Surrounding the course would be residential sites, a hotel, a market, a health club, restaurants and lakeside cafés, a garden and nursery lakewalk, an education and entertainment park, and a high-technology research and development center to bring Copeland's city his beloved semiconductor chips.

The project would be designed by William Pereira, one of the world's leading architects and land-use planners, with the Transamerica Pyramid Complex in San Francisco and Cape Canaveral among his many credits. Copeland discovered him on the cover of *Time*. Pereira, it turned out, keeps a model of an elegant Sabre Liner on his desk, and he agreed to do the project after a ride in Copeland's jet. When on October 4, 1983, the Norman City Council approved the development after a presentation by Pereira, Copeland's garbage dump investment, in trust to his son, was estimated already to be worth some $60 million.

Wayne Copeland, Jr., no longer has time for sad ruminations on politics and the elegance of integrated circuitry. He is going for his own entrepreneurial truth, as a projector of cities like William Ogden of old in Chicago and Armando Codina and the other entrepreneurs and architects transforming Miami. Copeland may not make it. He still needed some $3 billion of further investments. But his dream is already changing all the values of Norman real estate and dramatizing the metaphysical capital of ideas that is the true substance of economic growth.

It is a project of such dimensions and such risk that it overwhelms most of the narrow computations of tax shelters. Copeland's success, he is sure, will depend on the success of the U.S. economy, on the success of scores of other entrepreneurs across the country, embracing the new technologies and grand hopes of the American future, unleashing the dynamic of growth. Thus in the end, the dream in Norman will depend upon the realization, in part, of Copeland's earlier political dream high in his jet of reforming taxes and overcoming a last rival social democratic fantasy of capitalism without capitalists.

7

CAPITALISM WITHOUT CAPITALISTS

The essential problem of enterprise in the West is not so much the lingering appeal of socialism as an even more tantalizing vision in the minds of the political elite. Glimmering on the horizons of every social democratic platform, every neoliberal testament, every new mandate for reindustrialization, every learned demand for cooperation among business, labor, and government and an end to the adversarial spirit in American enterprise, every new citation of industrial strategy among the Japanese, every encouraging reference to the *dirigisme* of the French, every new disguise for the discredited ghost of the Reconstruction Finance Corporation from New Deal–depressed America, every call for a "fair distribution" of the burdens of change, an "equitable" reform of taxation, or a "reasonable" return on capital, every evangelical writ on the limits of growth, the scarcity of resources, the burden of population, the gap between the rich and the poor, every appeal for economic democracy, social control of corporations, and an end to untrammeled commercialism—suffusing all the most visionary and idealistic prose of leftist economics is the same essential dream of the same static and technocratic destiny: capitalism without capitalists. Wealth without the rich, choice without too many things to choose, political and intellectual freedom without a vulgarian welter of individual money and goods, a social revolution every week or so without all this disruptive enterprise. The progressive professors of the left would reduce human and scientific progress to "appropriate technologies" (mostly books) without this Pandora's swarm of anarchic invention. They would remake the world in the image of their own lives: a bucolic campus, with compensation in willowy co-eds, and free time, and large expanses of lawn. Enterprise without all that coarse bustle of business and trade. Prometheus burned out and bureaucratized, dimmed and insulated, presented a Freedom Medal and called to lead a new national Center on Invention and Productivity.

The dream, in its always unexpected and unwanted way, is drearily coming to pass throughout the social democratic domains of Western Europe. But even in the United States the pressure mounts to move this way. The agenda is simple: the stealthy and unannounced euthanasia of the entrepreneur. It can be accomplished easily by following two seductive themes of policy: lowering tax and interest costs for large corporations and a few other favored institutions, while shifting the burden increasingly to individuals and families. By reducing corporate taxes, subsidizing corporate loans, sponsoring a wide range of favored borrowers, institutionalizing personal savings, and discreetly allowing taxes to rise on personal income, government can painlessly extinguish the disposable wealth of entrepreneurs. It can enact a bold and comprehensive program—full of stimuli for "capital formation" and "job creation," replete with policies to favor business and rhetoric to inspire Republicans—that swiftly steals in and stifles the nation's spirit of enterprise.

The most fertile margins of the economy are always in people's minds: thoughts and plans and projects yet unborn to business. The future emerges centrifugally and at first invisibly, on the fringes of existing companies and industries. The fastest-growing new firms often arise through defections of restive managers and engineers from large corporations or through the initiatives of immigrants and outcasts beyond the established circles of commerce. All programs that favor established companies, certified borrowers, immobile forms of pay, pensions, and perquisites, institutionally managed savings and wealth, against mobile capital, personal earnings, disposable savings, and small business borrowing, tend to thwart the turbulent, creative, and unpredictable processes of innovation and growth.

Much of this program is well under way in the United States. The high interest rates that have afflicted small businesses most were not the product of some conspiracy of monetarists at the Federal Reserve, or some fit of deficit spending by prodigal Republicans. The prime source of soaring interest costs has been the increasing politicization of savings and credit, as the government created a captive capital market full of tax-exempt havens for obedient cash and capacious channels for subsidized borrowing, yet replete with traps and gouges for small businesses and small savers outside the charmed circles of the code.

The fundamental criterion, determining the reward for savings, was control. If the *saver* was willing to relinquish command of the cash and channel it to a pension or trust fund, run in accord with the rule of the "prudent man," to an IRA or Keogh plan, with their restrictive terms, to an insurance firm, with their well-managed portfolios, or to the bonds of a municipality, his interest payments could pile up untaxed at an unprecedented real rate. But if he wished to keep his money in a disposable form, he would pay taxes of nearly 100 percent on his interest, adjusted for inflation.

Similarly, if a *borrower* wished to pay tuition at school, or purchase a commercial building or a rental property, or partake of a tax shelter of any kind, or if the borrower was an established business with large profits against which to deduct interest payments, or wished to build housing for the elderly or "low-to-middle-income" earners, or lived in an area certified for disaster relief, or was borrowing funds for investment in a capital good with a predictable return and tax credits and depreciation, or if a company sought funds to merge with another firm with high profitability, under all these favored circumstances the loan would come essentially free of real interest charges.

As a result of these distortions, the interest rate after taxes and inflation was below zero for loans to profitable business corporations during thirteen of the seventeen years between 1966 and 1982; and the post-tax, post-inflation yield on Treasury bills was below zero for median-bracket savers for twelve of those seventeen years. This means that borrowing has been free (or even subsidized) for most established companies and saving has been punished heavily for the average depositor.

It often is assumed that this situation substantially changed in the early 1980s. But residual savers still faced tax rates of over 100 percent on their real interest, and profitable large corporations still could borrow at low or negative real interest costs. With 5 percent inflation and total marginal tax rate (federal and state) of over 50 percent, a 12 percent interest cost dissolves entirely, while a 10 percent interest yield is effectively confiscated.

Under these circumstances, the federally favored users of confectionary capital crowd out the entrepreneurs. Even though inflation during the 1970s and early 1980s was skewing the system toward a crash, inflicting unsustainable distortions and tumors of morbid growth—a housing market careening out of control as an inflation shelter, a hypertrophied market in gold and collectibles, a runaway underground economy, a collapse of personal savings, a depletion of productive capital—the economy was adapting itself to its diseases. Every tumor gained a constituency, every distortion found political leverage. The only unrepresented faction was the future: the companies yet to be founded or the firms yet to achieve their paths of ascent.

In the United States, though, the programs of capitalism without capitalists never fully prevailed except for a few years in the mid-1970s. The best evidence of the futility of these policies—and of the efficacy of unleashing entrepreneurs—comes in the contrast in the recent economic history of two island economies, both populated by talented and industrious people, on two sides of the globe. The two countries are Britain and Japan, and the commanding reason for the success of one and the failure of the other is tax policy.

Britain's economy has stagnated since World War I not because of foreign exchange foibles, as some suggest, or because of any inexorable trend to post–Victorian decline, but because British taxes on personal income have persistently stifled and stultified its entrepreneurs. The problem began during the 1920s, a period of stagnation in England, yet known as the Roaring Twenties in the United States. The twenties roared in America chiefly because, unlike the British authorities, U.S. presidents Harding and Coolidge rescinded the high tax rates of World War I. The United States did not restore confiscatory rates until the 1930s under Hoover and Roosevelt. Britain, by contrast, retained rates near 90 percent throughout the 1920s, and during World War II, the top rate rose to 99 percent and was little reduced in following years.

These gouges were justified in the name of equality. The paradox of progressivity, however, is that the poor suffer most when others are prevented from efficiently getting, keeping, and reinvesting wealth. For example, British enactment of the highest and most progressive rates during the 1940s ended up by increasing the tax payments of the poor by nearly four times more than the payments of the rich. But the American tax cuts of the 1920s—reducing the top rate from 73 percent to 25 percent in four years—increased the actual tax payments of the rich by nearly 200 percent and raised the share of total taxes paid at the top from 27 percent to 63 percent. The less dramatic Kennedy-Johnson tax cuts of 1964 and 1965 had similar, though smaller, effects, and the cut in the top rate from 70 percent to 50 percent in 1981 led to an increase of 11 percent in payments by the rich in fiscal 1982, giving them the highest share of total income tax payments in over a decade. This pattern continued through 1983 and into 1984. Payments by millionaires actually rose 42 percent in 1982, in the midst of the recession, and 37.4 percent as a share of all payments, amid plummeting prices for gold, collectibles, real estate, and other tax-protected investments.

Highly progressive tax rates do not redistribute incomes; they redistribute taxpayers: from taxable to untaxable activities, from domestic investment to foreign currency plays, from offices and factories to golf courses, fox hunts, and tropical beaches, from documented business to underground barter and cash exchanges, from productive professions to excess financial intermediation and finagling, from active enterprise to socially fruitless but lucrative litigation. Most of all, high taxes redistribute the British themselves, from Great Britain to Grand Cayman and to banks and beaches in Nassau, Monaco, the Isle of Man, and other sheltered climes.

The diaspora of celebrities was most conspicuous, as British Nobel Prize winners, best-selling authors, actors, actresses, rock musicians, and business tycoons scattered to the four corners of the earth. But for every media star driven abroad, there were a thousand entrepreneurs expatriated, enervated, retired, or driven underground. Some of Silicon Valley's most notable figures—from Adam Osborne and John Ellenby in personal computers to Wilf Corrigan and John Carey in semiconductors—are Britons in flight from socialism. As long as taxes remain so high, *any* supremely ambitious British citizen must abandon the country, or at least the economy. They dispatch their money overseas or preoccupy themselves with the demoralizing pettifoggery of domestic tax avoidance, leaving ordinary immobile workers behind to pay the taxes and seethe, while learned academics pore over the peculiarities of British class and culture for clues to the causes of rising bitterness and declining growth.

What the creators of the system of capitalism without capitalists fail to comprehend is that you can't have capital gains without capital, and you can't benefit from corporate subsidies without being a corporation. To start a business requires disposable personal income, and that is what high personal rates wring out of the system. British managers and executives receive pitifully low nominal incomes (why ask for more!); but they get an amazing array of relatively untaxable perks, from company cars to business suits, from vacation resorts to scholarships, from housing to entertainment. These benefits, which cannot be saved and invested in a new company, tie down British businessmen to the existing corporate structure: the very business establishment, cobwebbed with subtle strands of governmental dependency, that is a key obstacle to progress.

Even after the Thatcher tax cuts, Britain remained a hard climate for investable funds. Despite major reductions in marginal rates, income taxes in Britain remained among the world's highest, with the top rates of 60 percent on earned income and 75 percent on unearned income hitting family earnings as low as 27,000 pounds ($38,000). By contrast, even before the Reagan tax cuts, the top American rates both were lower than the new British rates and applied only to incomes over $65,000. Both the American and the British, however, specialize in punishingly progressive rates (and sluggish growth). Until Mitterand, the top French rate of 60 percent applied only to earnings nearly twice as high as comparable British rates. The top German rate of 56 percent hit earnings nearly three times as high. The Japanese rates, left over from the American occupation, are nominally huge, at between 75 and 80 percent, but they apply only to incomes above $396,924, after allowing the deduction of most personal savings. On comparable incomes, Japanese tax rates are the lowest in the capitalist world. Only Sweden has been willing to excel Britain in the contest of confiscatory levies.

Mrs. Thatcher's income tax cuts were substantial only in comparison with the utterly stifling rates she inherited, an incredible 60 percent rate on earnings of 12,501 pounds, reaching 83 percent at just 24,000 pounds (and 98 percent on "unearned" incomes). These rates she slashed by some 25 percent in one year, a politically bold and dramatic step that served to halt the long slide in income tax revenues that followed the huge Wilson-Healey tax hikes of 1975. From a level of some 14.5 billion pounds in 1975 and 1976, revenues dropped steadily (in 1975 pounds) to a level of approximately 12 billion in 1979. But despite the deep recession, the yield from the personal income tax actually rose slightly in real terms in 1980 and 1981. At a time of appalling adversity, Mrs. Thatcher's tax cuts did actually produce more revenue than the old rates. This record should be compared with the strikingly meager returns of Britain's tax *increases*. Real social security revenues actually *dropped* despite a 50 percent rate hike since 1976; and Value Added Tax (VAT) revenues rose a mere 45 percent after the near doubling of the rates.

Although designed to compensate for cuts in income tax rates, the whopping tax hikes in VAT and social security—devastating to entrepreneurs and small businesses—in fact gave Britain the worst unemployment in the West and together with the resulting welfare burden reduced available revenue. Nonetheless, Mrs. Thatcher had moved decisively in the right direction on the income tax and laid the foundation for the more entrepreneurial British economy that was emerging in the mid-1980s. Further substantial cuts in personal income tax rates, particularly in the top brackets and on investment income, could foster an exciting revival of enterprise in Britain without any cost in government revenues.

Fully demonstrating the possibilities for such a policy is the story of the greatest economic prophet of postwar Japan. In December 1954, at the takeoff phase in the ascent of the Japanese economy, there came to the leadership of the country's Ministry of International Trade and Industry (MITI) the man who shaped the policies that unleashed Japan's entrepreneurs.

This man was Tanzan Ishibashi. As minister of finance in the first Yoshida cabinet after the war, he had run into serious trouble with the Americans by attacking an austerity program designed to halt inflation. Like contemporary supply-siders, he maintained that the Japanese crisis stemmed not fundamentally from inflation or a glut of money flowing into Japanese industry, but from a dearth of production: a problem of unused labor and factories. "The only way to solve it," he said, "is to promote production." Ishibashi was fired for his pains. But his prediction of bank failures and industrial slump under the tax system created by American academics and the restrictive monetary policy imposed by Chicago banker Joseph Dodge were vindicated by events.

Nonetheless, Ishibashi may well have been too indulgent toward unchecked money creation and inflation. But he was right about the essence of the Japanese problem. As late as 1950, Japan still suffered from a tax rate of 85 percent on moderate incomes, a tax burden of 24.1 percent of GNP, and persistent inflation. A substantial tax cut in 1951, together with Korean War procurements, pulled Japan from its doldrums while increasing the government's revenues. But by the time Ishibashi resumed office at MITI toward the end of 1954, the economy was mired in a year-long recession.

As MITI chief with the Hatoyama cabinet, Ishibashi was well known for his passionate insistence on the revival of Japan's steel industry, destroyed during the war, and his militant rejection of a pastoral solution for Japan's economy, as urged by some Americans. But Ishibashi's unique and vital contribution at MITI was his outline of the broad new policies that were to launch the following two decades of economic ascent. According to MITI vice-minister and intellectual leader Tomisaburo Hirai, "Ishibashi contributed the final theoretical formulation that all other planners had been missing."

As the Ministry of *International* Trade and Industry, MITI and its predecessors always had favored export-led growth, to be fostered through MITI aid and guidance. But Ishibashi insisted that the key to export success was not government subsidies, guarantees, or other foreign promotions, but achievement of the position of low-cost producer through economies of scale and experience in the home economy. Ishibashi maintained that the key to reviving the domestic market and ending the post–Korean War recession was not a new siege of administrative guidance and fiscal austerity, but a series of whopping tax cuts.

Ishibashi's tax cuts, in true supply-side spirit, focused on personal income and savings. Corporations bore a steadily higher relative share of the tax burden through the late 1950s, though their rates also were reduced. The first Ishibashi cut came in 1955, abolishing the tax on interest, cutting the effective rate on dividends by more than one-third, from 11 percent to 7 percent, and cutting most personal rates by about 10 percent. By contrast, the corporate profits tax was dropped merely from 42 percent to 40 percent. In 1956, tax revenues rose nearly 15 percent and the savings rate surged by more than 20 percent, to a postwar high of 31.8 percent of personal income.

After minor tax cuts and reforms in 1956, Ishibashi himself became prime minister in December, promising a revolutionary fiscal package of tax cuts on personal incomes and spending hikes for roads and other needed infrastructure. In 1957, Ishibashi succeeded in delivering most of it. While launching broad new efforts in public works, he slashed marginal rates on personal income by nearly 30 percent across the board in one year. In a fortunate coup, ensuring the future of his program, he also put the Ministry of Finance in the hands of Japan's other great supply-side leader, Hayato Ikeda.

Ikeda became better known than Ishibashi as an architect of Japan's economic miracle because of one fatal Ishibashi error. In the whirlwind of activity as he assumed command, Ishibashi forgot to wear an overcoat to an outdoor reunion at Waseda University on a raw winter day in 1957. He took sick and died on February 25, giving way as prime minister to one of MITI's most interventionist leaders, Nobusuke Kishi. But Ishibashi's legacy, carried on by Ikeda (who became head of MITI in 1959 and prime minister a year later), was to be a supply-side policy and an economic boom unequaled by any other nation.

Beyond his personal income tax cuts, the crux of his achievement is probably Japan's remarkable array of incentives to save. Not only did he abolish taxation of interest and drastically reduce taxation of dividends, he also tripled tax-exempt savings with postal-system banks and doubled the deduction for life insurance premiums. Capital gains were already tax-exempt in Japan, and after his death, a substantial amount of long-term savings was made directly deductible. Because he had demonstrated beyond cavil the effectiveness and popularity of an all-out supply-side program, complete with nominally "regressive" tax cuts, subsequent Japanese leaders followed his example for the next two decades.

As under Ishibashi, savings and revenues increased with nearly every tax cut. When analysts ascribe the Japanese miracle to the works of MITI and pore over the "special measure laws," the R&D cartels, and the mazes of administrative guidance, they should always pay the highest homage to the greatest MITI leader of them all.

Ishibashi's analytical breakthrough was as striking as his political leadership. He was the first economist to illuminate the crucial connection between supply-side fiscal policy and entrepreneurial business strategy. He showed, in fact, that supply-side tax cuts are merely a special case of business price cuts, and that the two policies can reinforce each other in a spiral of growth.

Stagnant economies—and their governments—face a predicament familiar in the world of business. They resemble large companies with a serious and persistent profit problem. As Ishibashi understood, such companies nearly always want to raise their prices: a policy of demonstrable apparent benefit to cash flow and profits. In fact, in both Britain and the United States, many leading manufacturers have chosen this inviting path. In industries as diverse as steel, automobiles, and consumer electronics, large firms have persistently reacted to profit problems and cost pressures by raising prices. In almost every case their problems have grown worse. By raising prices, a troubled company usually reduces its share of the market, attracts new competition into it, and causes a decline in efficiency and morale.

As business consulting firms have discovered, it is far more promising, in general, to *lower* prices, even in the face of computer proofs from financial officers that disaster will result. The benefits of price cuts come from a complex interplay of effects that elude easy calculation, but that have been amply demonstrated, often to the surprise of management, in thousands of companies. Lower prices bring a larger share of the market, and with larger market share come increasing economies of scale, rising morale and productivity, and unexpected competitive breakthroughs, all in a growing spiral of diminishing costs and growing profits. The aggressive and apparently risky move against the numbers can lead to dynamic gains and lower costs, which in turn allow further price cuts in the future.

These concepts of business strategy—as articulated by Ishibashi and given as a rationale for his tax program—are not ordinarily applied to government policy, but they capture the essence of the political predicament of Western welfare states. These governments can be seen in the guise of a company with a dreadful profit problem, to which it responds by raising its prices year after year. The prices of government are called taxes, and tax hikes always offer the apparent promise of solving the revenue and inflation problems. But the result of tax increases—beyond a point which has already been far exceeded by most welfare states—is to reduce the government's market share and tax base.

Contrary to most conventional analysis, democratic governments live in an intensely competitive environment, and all taxes are finally voluntary. At every decisive moment of their working lives, citizens are comparing—consciously or unconsciously—the benefits of expanded participation in the regulated and taxable realm of a particular government with the benefits of withdrawing from it.

Like troubled businesses raising their prices, troubled governments that raise their taxes and their social spending beyond a certain level find that the consequences defy all predictions, in a *downward* spiral. Their calculations of income and outgo are persistently wrong, and in the wrong direction. Government borrowing lurches out of control, and rising interest rates increase the damage. Unexpected millions of workers become unemployed; surprising numbers of families go on relief; early retirements surge. The underground economy of unreported activity booms; tax shelters proliferate; so do purchases of untaxable assets, with unreported income or benefit flows, such as residential housing and leisure goods. Productive immigrants go elsewhere; ambitious citizens emigrate; parasites throng customs and then the dole. Exports suffer, and all the indices of decline reinforce each other in an insidious but always finally unmeasurable way. And the government economists and budget officers redouble their appeals for higher tax rates.

But for countries, as for companies, there is often a way out. The dynamic of decline has a precise counterpart in a dynamic of ascent. Britain, an island nation with a record of raising taxes year after year, can find its foil in Japan, an oriental island nation that lowered its taxes nearly every year. Or Britain can emulate the other Asian capitalist stars, or even Austria, which lowered its rates by one-third in the mid-1970s, and has since perplexed the world with its remarkably stable and productive economy.

Britain could still become the Japan of the late 1980s. Its leadership is committed to reversing the record of decline. The results of

changing course, however, cannot be computed on any econometric model of the existing economic structure, because the purpose is
to transform the very environment in which the change will occur.
But the study of businesses, as of nations, shows that the favorable
results can exceed all expectations, in the same way that the logic of
decline tends to overrun its apparent boundaries. Just as the relent-
less tariff wars, huge tax increases, and epidemic bank failures of
the Great Depression launched a grim dynamic of unexpected
global collapse, so the tax and tariff cuts of the postwar era unleashed a spiral of capitalist growth beyond the imagination, let
alone the computation, of any known economist.

The success of Ishibashi's strategy in Japan is incontestable. For
twenty-five years, government revenues *in absolute terms and as a
share of world taxes* grew faster in Japan than in any other major nation, while government spending *as a share of GNP* remained lowest.
The lowest tax rates brought in the highest revenues. In 1983, the
World Bank published a study, *Taxes and Growth*, by Keith Marsden, that showed this principle at work around the world during
the 1970s. Appraising the economic performance of twenty countries, grouped in pairs of similar per capita incomes in 1970, the
study found that the countries with lower effective tax burdens
grew six times faster. Thus they could raise their government
spending and revenues on an average more than three times as fast
as the countries with higher tax burdens. The difference was larger
among Third World than industrial countries. But Japan increased
public revenues during the 1970s 33 percent faster than Sweden
(paired with it in the analysis) and 44 percent faster than Britain.
The World Bank also presented evidence that the distribution of
income tends to be more "equitable," investment higher, and inflation lower in the lower-taxed countries. Although the World Bank
analysis focused on average tax burden rather than the marginal
rates on productive activity, the conclusions of the study also apply
strongly to marginal rates. The evidence massively demonstrates
that even in the reasonably short run, raising tax rates and burdens
reduces government revenues, increases deficits, fosters inflation,
and retards economic growth. Ishibashi's supply-side success was
not a special case, dependent on the culture of Japan, but a mani-
festation of the universal culture of entrepreneurship.

A government's income is dependent on its share of the market,
the portion of world enterprise that submits to its taxation. This
measure, which might be termed global tax-base share, reflects a
government's success in fostering taxable economic activity within
its jurisdiction or attracting productive businesses and individuals

into it. As in business, market share stems more from developing one's own markets than from taking others.

Every time Ishibashi reduced the real costs of government—producing a better package of services at a lower tax price—he simultaneously lowered the costs of taxable work and enterprise and raised the incentives for productive activity in Japan. Every time he reduced the government's prices, he enabled workers and businesses to lower their own prices, expand their own markets, and enlarge their own accumulated production and sales. With more experience, Japan's private companies could lower their costs still further. As Japan's private sector expanded, public-sector revenues grew and unit costs declined, allowing the government again to improve its services and lower its prices (taxes). Japanese workers and entrepreneurs, increasing their production and enlarging their world market share as their costs dropped, were the prime agents of Japan's government in enlarging its share of the global tax base.

Ishibashi understood, moreover, that some private funds, particularly savings, are so critical to economic expansion that they should not be taxed at all. The United States and Britain treated interest income as "unearned" and presumably usurious, and subjected it to special surtaxes that usually amounted to more than 100 percent of real interest income (adjusted for the inflationary decline of principal). Japan saw interest as a crucial payment for deferring consumption and financing industrial expansion. By exempting interest from taxes, Japan ensured that it would have the lowest interest rates in the industrial world and would get back in taxes on income and profits far more than was lost on interest. This policy, emerging from Ishibashi's MITI, was far more important than excise tax exemptions and special industry laws in fostering the global expansion of such key Japanese companies as Hitachi, Matsushita, Honda, and Sony. The huge Japanese savings rate and resulting low interest charges have permitted literally millions of Japanese businesses, of all sizes, to expand their investments over the last thirty years, while at the same time permitting the Japanese government, in times of recessionary stress, to run the largest deficits in the industrial world without bringing a financial crunch of "crowding out."

This policy on interest, moreover, accelerated the expansion of Japanese industry. Just as taxes are not only the price of government but also a cost of work and enterprise, interest is not only a payment for savings but also a cost of business. By promoting savings and lowering interest rates, Japan further reduced private-sector costs and enabled its businesses to lower prices and gain market share and experience. By forgoing taxes on interest, the Japanese government greatly expanded its tax base and long-term revenues.

Japanese financial policy, however, was far more harsh on some kinds of borrowing than U.S. policy. While Japanese businesses were granted long-term loans at relatively low cost, implicitly guaranteed by the Bank of Japan, Japanese homebuyers could rarely acquire mortgages of more than three years. While the U.S. government created an array of national agencies ingeniously designed to channel savings away from industry into housing, the Japanese created a similar array of national agencies to channel savings away from households into industry.

The effect in the United States was to focus capital on residential construction, a fragmented and parochial industry, slow to innovate, choked and cobwebbed by local building codes. Through the deductibility of largely spurious interest payments (actually paying back inflated principal), through the tax depreciation of actually appreciating structures, and through tax exemption of capital gains rollovers, housing became the nation's chief tax shelter. This shifted the tax burden and required higher marginal rates (and higher interest rates) on productive activity.

By contrast, Ishibashi's policies in Japan concentrated capital on the most productive and innovative forms of industry, with the highest yields in government revenue. This revenue, on the one hand, financed productive investments in infrastructure and, on the other, allowed reduction of marginal tax rates on the nation's workers and businesses. Then during the recession of the early 1980s, Japan could turn toward improvement of Japanese housing in a judicious response to real needs. Meanwhile the United States had long since become the most lavishly housed country in the world, with 60 percent of families owning their own homes, with millions of single people possessing houses as a tax shelter and inflation hedge, and with millions of elderly couples living alone in large houses or apartments.

Within Japan's supply-side matrix, its entrepreneurs carried out the most ambitious investment program in the history of enterprise, with capital outlays rising as much as 30 percent a year, spawning new companies at a rate of nearly a million a year, and expanding established ventures at an unprecedented pace. Ishibashi's regime was followed in the early 1960s by the "income-doubling campaign" of his associate Hayato Ikeda, who assumed power in 1961 and continued the supply-side thrust. The result was a steady upsurge of domestic growth, with firms and industries rapidly gaining experience in intense rivalries at home before entering the global arena as low-cost producers, and with government cutting taxes and increasing revenues and savings.

It is from this domestic crucible of intense competition with normal rates of bankruptcy far above those in the United States, with scores of rivals in every field, that the great Japanese companies have emerged. At various times during the last three decades, for example, there have been 58 integrated steel firms, 50 motorbike companies, 12 auto firms, and 42 makers of hand-held calculators. Moving into the mid-1980s, there are 65 personal computer manufacturers, 13 makers of facsimile machines, and 250 producers of robots. Overlooking this welter are always the crested bureaucrats of MITI, sometimes offering useful aid and guidance—but at the center, deciding outcomes, have always been the entrepreneurs.

The reason the system of capitalism without capitalists is failing throughout most of Europe is that it misconceives the essential nature of growth. Poring over huge aggregations of economic data, economists see the rise to wealth as a slow upward climb achieved through the marginal productivity gains of millions of workers, through the slow accumulation of plant and machinery, and through the continued improvement of "human capital" by advances in education, training, and health. But, in fact, all these sources of growth are dwarfed by the role of entrepreneurs launching new companies based on new concepts or technologies. These gains generate the wealth that finances the welfare state, that makes possible the long-term investments in human capital that are often seen as the primary source of growth.

The key to growth is quite simple: creative men with money. The cause of stagnation is similarly clear: depriving creative individuals of financial power. To revive the slumping nations of social democracy, the prime need is to reverse the policies of entrepreneurial euthanasia. Individuals must be allowed to accumulate disposable savings and wield them in the economies of the West. The crux is individual, not corporate or collective, wealth. No discipline of the money supply or reduction in government spending, however heroic, no support scheme for innovation and enterprise, no program for creating jobs, no subsidy for productive investment, however generous and ingenious, can have any significant effect without an increase in the numbers and savings of entrepreneurs. As long as, throughout most Western economies, the very particular individuals who have good entrepreneurial ideas remain incarcerated in large corporations, contemplating flight to foreign parts or retreat to rural retirement, while the nation's savings remain institutionalized in pension funds, insurance firms, and government bonds, the West

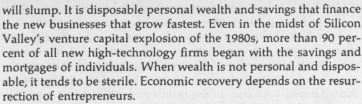

will slump. It is disposable personal wealth and savings that finance the new businesses that grow fastest. Even in the midst of Silicon Valley's venture capital explosion of the 1980s, more than 90 percent of all new high-technology firms began with the savings and mortgages of individuals. When wealth is not personal and disposable, it tends to be sterile. Economic recovery depends on the resurrection of entrepreneurs.

This resurrection cannot fully and durably occur until the ultimate arbiters of economic policy—the economists—resurrect entrepreneurship in their own influential theories. The contrary vision of capitalism without capitalists springs in part from a fundamental error of economic thought, drastically overrating the importance of physical capital formation and other quantitative measures of economic activity and drastically underestimating the decisive and controlling importance of entrepreneurial creativity.

This error affected some of the most eminent capitalist economists, beginning with Adam Smith. When Smith declared that "the extent of the division of labor"—the process of creation and specialization that propels the progress of economies—"is determined by the extent of the market," he was diametrically mistaken. Rather it is the extent of the division of labor—the reach of entrepreneurial creativity—that determines the extent of the market. It is the offering of a new good by an entrepreneur that evokes the desire of others to exchange their own property for it. Until the first good is created and offered for exchange, there is no market.

Nearly all economists from Smith to Keynes have followed Smith's error, maintaining that the market, or aggregate demand, or the money supply—in interplay with "exogenous" tastes and technologies—define the opportunities of entrepreneurs: that entrepreneurs merely scout the marketplace and mediate among existing demands, making transactions that maximize their own self-interest as expressed in power or profits. Many entrepreneurs do, indeed, play such a role, as the word "entrepreneur" implies—i.e., someone who merely interposes himself between two other actors in the marketplace. This is their function in what Thomas Kuhn calls "normal science." But the key role of entrepreneurs, like the most crucial role of scientists, is not to fill in the gaps in an existing market or theory, but to generate entirely new markets or theories. In this they are limited only by the compass of their own imaginations and powers of persuasion. They stand before a canvas as empty as any painter's; a page as blank as any poet's. Like creative artists, they bring entirely new things into the world in a process that they themselves control.

Once the products have been produced, of course, they will be exchanged in a marketplace governed by precise computations of value and scarcity that can be roughly modeled and duly celebrated by economists. The conditions of such markets for money and goods is a subject worthy of the deepest attentions of economic science. But the sources of economic growth are far outside this domain. Growth originates in the minds and wills of free men; it is determined only by their creativity and courage, persistence and faith.

The key error of economics is to subordinate in its models this higher level of creative activity to a lower level of measurement and exchange, of material products and factors of production, to assume that the market for goods somehow precedes and controls the entrepreneur who creates it. It is an error directly analogous to the error of scientists who try to subordinate the free processes of the mind to the determined processes of matter—to reduce thought to neurological chemistry. In the hierarchies of nature, the higher orders cannot be reduced to the lower ones. The long dream of physicists that by studying the structure of atoms we could comprehend all of life has proved false. Atomic structure, in fact, tells us little of value about the material objects of our lives, little about the workings of an engine, virtually nothing about our organic existences, and nothing whatever about the operations of human consciousness or human society.

Similarly, the study of markets and money yields only trivial or negative insights about economic growth and progress. Reasonably free markets and stable currencies are needed for economic growth, just as the rules and implements of chess are needed for a chess game. But they tell you little about the strategic and competitive substance of the play. Just as a poet must work within an existing vocabulary and grammar and a painter must use the instruments of his art, an entrepreneur must work within the constraints of his environment. All must observe the laws of physics and the laws of the land; the laws of money and the laws of the market. But entrepreneurship and economic growth can no more be reduced to a model of money and markets than poetry can be explained by the rules of grammar and vocabulary or art be reduced to the chemistry of paint or the dynamics of the art market.

Adam Smith's "great machine" is an absurd analogy for a system governed by unpredictable human consciousness and creativity. But even a small machine cannot be explained by the laws of physics and chemistry that govern the manufacture of its parts. A machine is a largely unintelligible mass of gears and wires until one knows its purpose. Its purpose is determined by the imagination of the engineer who creates it, the software designer who programs it, or even the businessman who uses it, not by the laws of physics and mechanics. An economy is governed by the will and imagination, creativity and persistence of its entrepreneurs. All that matters is that they be encouraged, by religion and culture, law and policy, to do their work well.

By missing this central reality, even business schools can contribute to the illusion that the system can work without free and powerful entrepreneurs. Through a stress on game theory, negotiating tactics, accounting, return on investment, and marketing analysis, most business courses present companies as sets of statistics rather than producers of goods and services, or entrepreneurial teams developing and introducing new products. The world of the business school, like the world of the economist, assumes what needs most to be explained: the existence of products and markets where there was only poverty and stagnation before.

By focusing on the tactics of negotiation and exchange—the most perfunctory and least characteristic feature of capitalism—business analysts and business school courses ignore the moral center of the system—the laborious, sacrificial, and risky creation of new value—and stress the amoral mechanisms more prominent in static or socialist systems than in a growing capitalist economy. Business schools thus tend to turn out cynical manipulators of existing values rather than entrepreneurial creators of new value. Leading professors at Harvard Business School, preoccupied by the calculable maximization of self-interest, show a pathetic incapacity to comprehend the essence of entrepreneurship.

Entrepreneurs are always the victims of the economics of aggregation that has dominated Western universities, the economics of incremental change that prevails among the theorists of growth, the economics of the mechanical fallacy propounded even by Adam Smith. For there is no place for an entrepreneur in a mechanism, or an aggregate, or a process of incremental change. The policies based on these assumptions will always leave him out.

Intellectuals and politicians seem attracted to these policies because they deny the key fact of economic life: that all of us are dependent for our livelihood and progress not on a vast and predictable machine, but on the creativity and courage of the particular men who accept the risks which generate our riches. The machine age is the paramount era not of depersonalized masses but of individual achievement on the curve of growth.

THE
GREAT
TRANSITION

8

THE CURVE OF GROWTH

The eruption of new industries is the prime mode of economic revival in all capitalist countries. In this historic process of industrial creation and transformation can be found the secret dynamics of pricing strategy, tax policy, and competitive struggle among nations and entrepreneurs.

In the late 1970s in the United States, the industry that erupted, as decisively as automobiles in the twenties, radios in the thirties, and housing and television after World War II, was computers, in all their forms and applications. The spearhead of this new growth—the product that changed the industry from a provider of esoteric capital goods into a driving force in the consumer economy—was personal computers.

In 1982, Steven Jobs of Apple made the cover of *Time*, and in 1983, the personal computer usurped the entire human race and became *Time*'s "Machine of the Year." Within sixteen months during 1981 and 1982, the number of computer retail outlets rose from several hundred to more than 35,000 and continued rising at an annual rate of about 30 percent. Radio Shack, Tandy's sometimes seedy vendor of consumer electronics, began opening more than 500 stores a year and took the lead among all mass retailers in gross margin on sales (59 percent). Commodore sold 1.2 million units of its Model 64 in 1983; in 1984 IBM began producing its various PCs at an annual rate of more than 5 million.

Creative destruction, however, plays no favorites. No sooner were computers anointed by *Time* and swamped with demand than a shakeout began. In the midst of the record year of 1983, computer companies and divisions began crashing on all sides and computer stocks teetered acrophobically and tumbled from their peaks. Texas Instruments, one of the semiconductor firms that made personal computers possible in the first place, fled from the market for cheap home computers after pretax losses of some $660 million on the product. Timex followed. In the arms of Warner Communications, Atari gasped for breath after losing some $100 million. Mattel dropped from the business after suffering a $238 million deficit in the first nine months of 1983. Victor Technologies, maker of Europe's best-selling small business machine, suddenly collapsed after a record-breaking quarter in unit sales. Adam Osborne, the man who wrote the first book on personal computers, was forced to add Chapter 11 to the saga when his meteoric Osborne Computer company stumbled into bankruptcy after a year of over $100 million sales. What had happened?

In part, the rise in bankruptcies paralleled the rise of business failures in the national economy as growth and progress accelerated. Entrepreneurs in the vanguard of the great transition were the first to hit its traps and pitfalls, its most treacherous markets and most baffling challenges. In part, the precariousness of success among computer entrepreneurs stemmed from the nature of their technology.

The personal computer industry is more a user than a creator of innovations. The theory and practice of computing, after all, was essentially set in the mid-nineteenth century during the era of Charles Babbage's analytical engine, a leviathan mechanical calculator with software concepts provided by Lady Lovelace, the daughter of Lord Byron. The computer science breakthrough that shapes the current computer revolution came more than three decades ago in the late 1940s, when John Von Neumann put the software in the computer's own changeable working memory. This innovation freed computers from a rigid internal program and allowed creation of flexible multipurpose machines such as the desktop or personal computers of today.

For decades, however, high costs restricted the Von Neumann concept to the data-processing departments of large corporations. The advances that created a mass market came in the semiconductor industry, which during the 1970s reduced the logic and memory of computers to tiny chips that could be sold for a few dollars apiece. The most important continuing innovations still come from chip firms and software creators. The computer entrepreneur still is repeatedly buffeted by innovations that originate in these outside founts of technical creativity, and are suddenly introduced by others.

More important, though, the turbulence in the industry was a product of its movement from an initial phase dominated by technical ingenuity and into a new phase dominated by product definition, strategic marketing, and manufacturing efficiency. Technical skills, though indispensable, particularly in manufacturing, could not prevail alone.

This process of transformation affects nearly all industries and observes discernible laws demonstrated over the centuries of capitalism. Though lying mostly beyond the bounds of economic science, these laws govern both micro- and macroeconomic events, the fates both of firms and of nations. The definitive story is the introduction early this century of the "personal car," which launched the auto-industrial age, transformed the map of the world, and redistributed its wealth through the suburbs of America. Although there are many profound and consequential differences between computers and cars, the entrepreneurial essences persist.

In 1900, fifty-seven surviving American automobile firms, out of hundreds of contenders, produced some 4,000 cars, three-quarters of which ran on steam or electricity. Companies famous for other products were entering the fray. Among them were the makers of the Pope Bicycle, the Pierce Birdcage, the Peerless Wringer, the Buick Bathtub, the White Sewing Machine, and the Briscoe Garbage Can. All vied for the market with stationary-engine makers, machine-tool manufacturers, and spinoffs of leading carriage firms, Durant and Studebaker. Among the less promising entrants seemed a lanky young engineer from Edison Illuminating Company named Henry Ford, whose Detroit Automobile Company produced twenty-five cars and failed in 1900.

In Europe, too, the competition was fierce, and the technology was even more advanced. In the contest between American and European automakers, the Europeans seemed decisively ahead in every regard, except the number of competing companies. Just as in recent years, competing against Japan in the computer industry, the United States led chiefly in the number of computer, software, and semiconductor firms, in the early twentieth century the United States excelled chiefly in the production of auto entrepreneurs, not of automobiles.

Americans seemed willing to try anything—by 1900, there were some 200 different types of vehicles, from motorized Quadricycles to plush horseless broughams, using perhaps one hundred different modes of propulsion. Many of the early companies even propelled themselves without capital. Like the personal computer buffs to come—and the deluded DeLorean of the early 1980s—these early venturers would get the necessary cash from their own mail-order customers and dealers, and build the product only after the payment arrived.

As in virtually every new industry, it was impossible to tell, in the early years, who would prevail. Even after the gasoline motor was established, enterprises rose and fell frenetically. In 1901, Ford began another company. But he soon left it after a conflict with the other shareholders. The companies that made five of the ten best-selling automobiles in 1903, including the leader, Colonel Pope's bicycle firm, went out of business within the decade. Ford, back again with $28,000 in capital and a new company named after himself, sold 658 cars of a two-cylinder design. He returned dolorously to the drawing board, an entrepreneurial failure for the third time. Of the ten top producers of 1924, only three had entered the industry by 1908. A survey of the early years in autos should not be reassuring to the leaders of the early 1980s in personal computers.

The technological turning point, perhaps, was a fire in 1901 in the plant of Ransom Olds that destroyed all his elaborate equipment for producing electric Oldsmobiles, but allowed recovery of one rejected gasoline prototype. It became the first mass-produced car, selling 7,000 during the next three years. More significant, though, it brought together in fruitful collaboration many of the engineers and entrepreneurs who would lead the industry in its future years. Among the key figures in Olds's smoke-smeared building were the Dodge brothers, who made the transmission; a designer named Fred, who gave Oldsmobile the first curvaceous body by Fisher; and Henry Leland, the pioneer of interchangeable parts from the New England rifle industry. Later to found both Cadillac and Lincoln, Leland built the first Olds engines.

Ransom Olds was himself only a partial success. But like William Shockley, the co-inventor of the transistor, originator of Silicon Valley, and mentor of its leading entrepreneurs, Olds played a seminal role in Michigan's auto industry. Not only did he assemble the strong men of varied disciplines needed for success, but he committed the industry to the internal combustion motor. This device, rapidly improved by engineers on both sides of the Atlantic and brought at last into mass production, played a part in the early auto business comparable to the role of the microprocessor central processing unit—the computer on a silicon chip—in the personal computer trade.

Like the creation of reliable mass-produced microprocessors, the gasoline engine emerged from a fierce twenty-five-year rivalry. It embraced hundreds of machine shops in Europe and America, from Daimler and Benz in Germany and Napier in England to Winton and Olds in the United States. Although most of them saw their product as a stationary engine for industrial use, factories mainly stuck with steam, while automobiles erupted as the key market. Much as the development of standard microprocessors released computers from the need for expensive and idiosyncratic software for each design and use, the gasoline motor freed autos from a chaos of competing fuels and engines. Finally the auto companies could offer a settled product. They could lure in the talent for mass production and marketing that was needed to bring cars from machine shops to mass consciousness . . . and incidentally, drive most of the pioneers out of the business.

Willie Durant, who knew all about production and selling from his carriage business, decided it was time to move into cars after several months of driving a prototype containing David Buick's valve-in-head engine—the most powerful in the world for its size—through rural Michigan in 1904. Within four years, Durant was to parlay his sturdy Buick vehicle into domination of the automobile industry, with a 25 percent share of the market in 1908, the year he founded General Motors.

His key move—paralleling the recession breakthroughs throughout business history, including the Japanese auto and semiconductor surges in 1975 and 1976—was to expand his productive capacity all the way through the panic and depression of 1907–08, which drove many producers out of the market. The 1908 selling season found Buick the only company with a full line of cars, from a $2,500 Model 5 touring car to a $900 "white streak." The streak doubled its sale to 8,485, gave Buick experience in "mass" production, and set the stage for one of the decisive confrontations in the history of capitalism.

Henry Ford made a portentous announcement: "I will build a motor car for the great multitude. It will be large enough for the family but small enough for the individual to run and care for. It will be constructed of the best materials by the best men to be hired, after the simplest designs that modern engineering can devise. But it will be so low in price that no man making a good salary will be unable to own one—and enjoy with his family the blessing of hours of pleasure in God's great open spaces."

Ford fulfilled his boast with the Model T. Its ruggedness and clearance was such, as Jonathan Hughes has written, that "boys in the West could drive out over the sage brush and rocks chasing jackrabbits"—or, as Jack Simplot would demonstrate, wild horses. One man drove a Model T to the bottom of the Grand Canyon and out. Thus Ford had overcome what seemed an insuperable short-term obstacle to the democratization of the car: the absence of roads.

Nonetheless, during the first year, at a selling price of $850, the Model T had lost money and market share to the dashing $900 Buick. To increase his profits the next year, Ford raised his price by a full $100 to $950 and saw his sales more than double to 12,292 in a mushrooming market. But his share of this market declined again as Buick, Oldsmobile, and other companies proceeded to under-price him.

This was the key entrepreneurial moment for Henry Ford: the moment when the central but often secret laws of enterprise came into play most decisively in the car business. Focusing on the rising profits that followed his price hike, his advisers urged him to raise prices again in 1910 to take advantage of a market exploding be-yond the ability of the firms to fulfill it. This was the course chosen by General Motors, which raised the price of Buick to $1,150, leav-ing Ford plenty of room to follow.

Indeed, in the usual accounting analysis, Ford had no plausible alternative to continuing the strategy that had worked for him in the past. Most analysts denied the existence of a large market for low-priced vehicles and dismissed the possibility of manufacturing them; costs were simply too high. Personal incomes, moreover, were too low for such a luxury product, which could be used only in the warmer months; the working class was not ready. Even Ford's manifesto had restricted his claim to men of "good salary." The automobile industry seemed to be settling down, as it discov-ered its "natural price" in the terms of modern economics.

Economists have long believed that inherent in most products is a set price, covering costs and making "reasonable" profits, which can be computed by accountants and toward which supply and de-mand will eventually settle. Willie Durant believed that autos had reached that point in 1910. There might always be some cheaper products offered by other companies to scrape the bottom of the market. But the way was now open to build a big auto conglomer-ate by combining the more successful small firms. To create such an industrial empire was Durant's objective. At that moment in 1910, he already was mobilizing the financial backing on Wall Street and building the manufacturing capability in Flint, Michigan, to achieve his goal.

Automotive history might have taken this course, at least for a while, if Ford had followed the GM example and raised his prices. But rather than raising his price as Buick did, Ford dropped it by nearly one-fifth, to $780. At this price Ford could break even only if he vastly expanded sales or lowered production costs.

This strategy of the self-fulfilling price is a classic gambit in the repertory of entrepreneurs. Contrary to the cliché, a company losing money on every unit sold can indeed make it up by volume. It is a prime law and governing experience of capitalism. In effect, Ford set his price not on the basis of his existing costs or sales but on the basis of the much lower costs and much expanded sales that might become possible at the lower price. The effect in the case of Henry Ford in 1910 was a 60 percent surge in sales that swept the Model T far ahead of Buick.

A major benefit of price cuts is their impact on the investment goals and expectations of competitors who are trying to maximize short-run profits. In this instance, Ford accomplished what panic and depression had failed to achieve: the discomfiture of Willie Durant's vast plans for expansion of General Motors. The bankers who had been lending money on the supremacy of the Buick lost faith and began to call in the loans, causing heavy layoffs at Durant's huge construction projects in Flint, and inflicting damage on the company that it took a decade to overcome.

Ford had learned his lesson. In the recession year of 1914, he cut prices twice, and sales surged up while other companies failed. By 1916, he had reduced the price of a Model T to $360 and increased his market share from 10 percent to 40 percent, while the share commanded by General Motors slipped from 23 percent to 8 percent. By 1921, after cutting prices 30 percent during the 1920 economic crisis, Ford commanded a 60 percent share of a market that had grown by a factor of twelve in a decade. By 1927, he had sold 15 million cars, with a sales volume of $7 billion, and the company's net worth, with no new infusions of capital since the original $28,000, had risen to $715 million, including some $600 million in cash. By the same strategy, Ford also dominated the tractor market.

Then tastes changed, shifting against open cars, but Ford did not. GM invaded the low-priced market with price cuts on a closed Chevrolet. Eventually Ford had to admit defeat. He retreated to retool for a year to launch the Model A. But Ford had already assumed a paramount place in the history of capitalism. By decisively demonstrating the key laws of an entrepreneurial economy, he overthrew the dismal calculus of Malthusian limits, the mathematical constraints of all conventional models of economics. He showed that markets are not static, or zero-sum, or dominated by a "natural" or "equilibrium" price or a limited or measurable demand.

Perhaps most important, he showed that high profits come from giving, through low prices and high wages, rather than from gouging for what the traffic will bear. This discovery is the moral core of capitalism. The policy of anticipatory pricing—making price cuts that will register losses without large and unpredictable gains in volume—is a mode of temporary sacrifice for later and undetermined reward. In the generous and optimistic spirit of enterprise, Ford *invested* in his price cuts.

Moreover, in his most historic single decision, in 1914, in the very midst of his price-cutting siege, he doubled wages, to the famous and unprecedented $5 a day. The *Wall Street Journal* attacked him for "putting Biblical teachings in places where they don't apply." His stockholders rebelled against his entire scheme of wage hikes and price reduction, accusing him of an indifference to profits. To such critics, Ford retorted triumphantly: "If you give all that, the money will fall into your hands, you can't get out of it." During this entire period up to 1920, though his margins remained low, Ford's profits on net worth ranged between 20 and 300 percent and were by far the highest in the industry.

The principle that Ford discovered is now known as the "experience curve" (or imprecisely, the "learning curve"). First articulated in these terms by Bruce Henderson of the Boston Consulting Group and further developed by Bill Bain and others at Bain and Company, by any name it is the curve of growth. It ordains that in any business, in any era, in any capitalist competition, unit costs tend to decline in predictable proportion to accumulated experience: the total number of units sold. Whatever the product (cars or computers, pounds of limestone, thousands of transistors, millions of pounds of nylon, or billions of phone calls) and whatever the performance of particular companies jumping on and off the curve, unit costs in the industry as a whole, adjusted for inflation, will tend to drop between 20 and 30 percent with every doubling of accumulated output.

Whether for golf balls or polished silicon wafers, consumer power tools or paper bags, one can compute the familiar chart, with the inexorable curve. Never is there a sign of long-run diminishing returns. In farm products, there is a curve for chicken broilers. In service industries, there are charts for kilowatt-hours in electrical utilities, for virtual processing units in computer time sharing, and for value of insurance policies sold. All drop in unit costs by the familiar 20 to 30 percent for each doubling of total volume.

What the experience curve shows is that whatever the market or product a particular business defines for itself, it will usually have to sell more than its rivals over the long run in order to have lower costs and thus potentially higher profits. Moreover, in a growing market it will have to grow to survive. It will have to retain or increase its *market share*, because the companies with larger shares are likely to have lower costs and will thus be able to lower prices still further in a spiral of ever-growing market control.

Ford was by no means the first to explore the curve. Indeed, his own success was dependent on previous successes by John D. Rockefeller in lowering the price of oil and Andrew Carnegie in lowering the price of steel. In a history of the experience curve their stories are at least as important as Ford's. But Ford was most direct and explicit in his strategy and did not confuse the principle with simple efforts to achieve economies of scale by cartelization.

In essence, the experience curve depends on a long series of dynamic effects of rising output. It begins with the original learning curve, which maintains that the number of labor hours required to produce a particular good declines with the total number of units produced. Workers improve their skills as their experience increases. One reason for the effectiveness of Ford's decision to enact the $5 wage was that it radically reduced the turnover of workers on his assembly lines; the average worker moved farther down his own learning curve. The result of this effect, plus improved worker morale, was a 20 percent increase in the output of Ford's equipment, virtually paying for the wage hike in itself.

Beyond the learning curve, cost reductions in experience stem from improvements in technology, materials, product design, and process design, as well as from simple economies of scale. Ford amply benefited from all these sources of advance. His secret import of vanadium steel from Scotland—a light, strong alloy with almost three times the tensile strength of the steel used in other cars—allowed him to make a car lower in weight relative to engine power. From the beginning (Ford's customers could have any color car they wanted "as long as it's black"), he set out to design his car for mass production, his production process for maximum output, and his prices for maximum sales. His company either adopted or launched every major breakthrough in manufacturing technology and concept, from interchangeable parts and moving assembly lines to an automatic camshaft fabricator which increased worker productivity tenfold.

All Ford's gains were linked to his strategy on price. In his autobiography, he explained: "Our policy is to reduce the price, extend the operations, and improve the article. You will note that the reduction of price comes first. We have never considered any costs as fixed. Therefore we first reduce the price to the point where we believe more sales will result. Then we go ahead and try to make the prices. We do not bother about the costs. The new price forces the costs down. The more usual way is to take the costs and then determine the price; and although that method may be scientific in the narrow sense, it is not scientific in the broad sense. . . . Although one may calculate what cost is, and of course all of our costs are carefully calculated, no one knows what a cost ought to be. One of the ways of discovering . . . is to name a price so low as to force everybody in the place to the highest point of efficiency. The low price makes everybody dig for profits. We make more discoveries concerning manufacturing and selling under this forced method than by any method of leisurely investigation."

Another way of ultimately reducing costs, he might have added, is to name a wage so high that it makes the workers willing to cooperate, by allowing them to share in the resulting profits. The entire company would move together down the curve of costs. Like the most successful high-technology firms of every era, Ford understood that the best way to enhance the productivity of workers is to give them a stake in the performance of the company.

Ford's top aide, Charles Sorenson, described the importance of Ford's approach. In the past, he wrote in *My Forty Years with Ford*, "American business had operated on the principle that prices should be kept at the highest point at which people would buy. That is still the operating principle of much French and British industry." But Ford oriented Americans to seek profits by producing large volumes at low prices. The result was that by 1926, 85 percent of the world's cars were American-made, including nearly half of those sold in Europe, which had led the United States by decades in internal combustion technology and maintained tariff barriers of over 100 percent.

In 1980, the dominant personal computers, together with needed software and accessories, sold for some $5,000. Although comparing prices across the century is perilous, let us speculate that this personal computer price is roughly equal to the price of autos in 1914, before Ford's rush down the curve. Let us further assume that the personal computer will eventually command a market broader than the personal car's, if only because the PC will be far cheaper and every car will contain one in some form.

This market merely begins with the 16 million small businesses in America and the larger numbers around the capitalist world. The personal computer is becoming the instrument of a new mass rite of passage, as indispensable in this era as McGuffey's reader, the TV, the Model T, and the Springfield rifle of other epochs. In its many changing guises, the computer is the instrument by which the productivity of human labor in the household will eventually ascend to ever higher levels, as the productivity of factories succumbs to job-displacing sieges of automation and robotics.

This low-priced market was by far the largest long-run opportunity for computers. Yet it was ignored by all the established computer companies. Echoing their predecessors in the auto industry, who denied the existence of a vast untapped personal market for so complex and demanding an item as the car, the makers of mainframes and their smaller kin, the minicomputer, spoke of the daunting complexity and problematical benefits of using personal computers in homes and small offices. Everyone wanted to sell computers to institutions, which made large buys through purchasing departments. As the industry awaited its Henry Ford, almost no one wanted to sell to the unfathomable mass of people.

For several years, it appeared that the Ford of personal computers would be Steven Jobs of Apple. An adopted son of Silicon Valley parents, Jobs had reached his eminence after a long period of searching in the wilderness for gurus and genetic forebears, sampling vegetarianism and primal scream therapy, and slouching through the seventies in jeans and sandals. But in the repeated pattern of entrepreneurs, the anxieties of his early years became the energies of upward mobility. All the emotional turmoil and restless energy of his youth—the rebellion, the failure, the guilt, the betrayals, the identity maw—suddenly fused into an irrepressible force of creation.

Defining the product, raising the money, scrambling for parts, organizing the manufacture, launching the firm, in a five-year siege of obsessive work, Jobs had at last assembled himself, body and soul, found his place and his cause, his identity and his redemption, in the ascent and sale of Apple Computers and the mystique of the computer world. By the end of 1981, the Apple II became the best-selling computer in America. More important, if Jobs had defined his share of the market correctly, he would have seen an opportunity to become truly the Ford of the new industry, establishing a bastion that even IBM could not overcome.

In computing, where smart buyers choose on the basis of available software, the crucial measure of market share is probably the share of total software usable on your machines. The crucial measure of experience is the accumulated experience of software writers with your computer's operating system. From this point of view, competitive machines using the same software strengthen a company's dominance. Even though these rivals may reduce hardware sales in the short run, they are unlikely to overtake the manufacturing and sales experience of the original company. But they extend the possible market for future products.

For example, the so-called plug-compatible mainframe and peripherals makers such as Amdahl and Storage Technology, though fought bitterly by Big Blue, are not fundamental competitors to IBM. They are part of the team. They challenge torpid managers, test new markets and technologies, exert pressure on noncompatible computer firms like Burroughs and DEC, and altogether protect and extend the empire of IBM, its software world, its prime arena of market growth.

For several years, it appeared that Apple might create a rival world of software in small computers. With a simple design and eight open slots for additional circuit boards, the Apple II was a seductive lure for software and accessories, less a finished product than an intriguing challenge. Invented in a garage by teenaged tinkerers, it had tantalized and finally captured the imagination of the current generation of America's most creative youth in the same way that the Model T captured the hearts and minds and mechanical genius of their forebears.

This was an epochal achievement. Dismantling and assembling, repairing and improving their Model Ts, the older generation, ready with wrenches and smeared with grease, had honed the skills that launched an earlier industrial revolution, won two wars, and shaped the postwar world economy. The new generation, poking and pushing at their Apples, whether with typing fingers or soldering irons, were learning the languages and technical ways of the computer age. As the first machine ardently embraced by these hackers and programmers—a spontaneous teenaged army of Apple obsessives—the Apple II quickly commanded more software by far than any other personal computer, some 14,000 programs by 1981.

This meant that Apple II had dominant market share by the relevant measure. It meant that Apple had the foundation for a new empire, rivaling IBM's and quite possibly excelling it. For Apple ruled not the old establishment but the new generation. But the company never fully understood the source and implications of its strength. At times, Jobs and co-founder Steve Wozniak implied they had won their position by technical prowess alone rather than by entrepreneurial insight. Apple II's engineering was elegant, particularly in Wozniak's eight-chip disk controller, performing a task requiring at least thirty chips in other designs. But the machine had serious technical limitations. Indeed, the obsolescence of the 6502 microprocessor was a major weakness of the company, and having it upgraded should have been its most urgent business.

Apple's technical conceit led the company into several crucial errors. First, it tried with some considerable success to stop other companies from imitating its equipment and even drove Franklin to try to make IBM-compatible machines. This policy reduced the total installed base using Apple software and stopped Apple from establishing the effective industry standard. Apple refused to allow the emergence of a plug-compatible world of cheaper or more specialized Apple imitations. Adam Osborne believes that but for this error Apple's software dominance would have become so overwhelming that IBM (and Osborne) in entering the industry would have been forced to make Apple-compatible equipment.

In a second and related error, Apple introduced three new technically sophisticated computers, the Apple III, the Lisa, and the Macintosh, that were incompatible with the Apple II and mostly incompatible with each other. Adopting Motorola's radically different 68000 microprocessor family, with a software base mostly in scientific and engineering workstations, Apple initiated no program with the semiconductor industry to create 16-bit and 32-bit versions of the Apple II's 6502. Third, while preventing the creation of Apple-compatible equipment, it priced its own products mostly beyond the reach of the largest potential personal computer market, persons in the home.

Thus the company arrogantly threw aside its real asset in software share and began competing from scratch in hardware with IBM and other firms that possessed at least equal technical ability and a larger base in software for the new level of 16-bit machines. During the crucial year of 1981, while Jobs prepared to pose for *Time* and made plans for a new Apple Campus headquarters of green glass, Apple was still blithely, blindly at work on the technically obsolescent and incompatible 8-bit Model III. It was fiercely protecting in the courts the technically obsolete Apple II from imitation or improvement by others. And it developed no 16-bit models to use Apple II software.

The company thus frittered away its chance to become the dominant force in the industry. While vaunting itself as the chief alternative to Big Brother IBM, Apple had in fact opened the way wide for IBM's far from inevitable ascendancy in personal computers. To win the 16-bit market, IBM had merely to copy—with certain improvements—the strategy Apple had employed in the 8-bit market and then abandoned to IBM for future products.

It was not until 1984 that Apple showed signs of understanding the nature of the business by making the Lisa II compatible with the Macintosh and pricing the Apple II near the home market range. After an outside firm spontaneously created a prototype 16-bit 6502, Apple even began aggressively to plan upgrades for the microprocessor that still drove 95 percent of its installed base of some 1.5 million machines. But however successful the Macintosh family, it came too late to make Apple number one. Although Apple might stay number two in personal computing, Jobs had failed to win the mantle of Henry Ford, who ruled his industry for nearly twenty years.

With the indecision of Jobs, the personal computer industry remained paralyzed on the threshold of the new era, still looking for a Henry Ford to lead it into the huge consumer market. Several entrepreneurs, however, took the lead on a bolder course, exploiting the experience curve in uncharted territory. Among them were Fred Bucy and Mark Shepherd of TI, Jack Tramiel of Commodore, Adam Osborne of Osborne, and Philip Hwang of Televideo. Their several stories—their considerable achievements and crushing setbacks alike—illustrate many of the principles and perplexities of industrial creation on the curve of growth.

In its modern guise, the experience curve was born at Texas Instruments, where Patrick Haggerty articulated its principles and his successors gave it a name and a controversial history. In the early 1970s, the company worked first with the Boston Consulting Group to refine the concept, and then with Bill Bain and several other founders of Bain and Company as they applied it to their move into consumer electronics, climaxed with the home computer.

Many companies in Silicon Valley had noticed the radical drop in costs that attends increased volume in chips, but they imagined that it was a peculiarity of their own industry. Often the learning curve was confused with the wafer yield curve (the increase in the proportion of working chips as volumes rise) or with the density curve in integrated circuits, as in (Gordon) Moore's law, which predicts a doubling of memory capacities every two years. TI together with Henderson and Bain subsumed all these phenomena into the more powerful general theory of an experience curve in all industries.

In its 1973 report to the stockholders, the company identified the keys to international competitiveness as "market share" and "market growth." In a statement worthy of Henry Ford, the company declared it was challenging the Japanese in consumer electronics through a strategy of "aggressive pricing," continuing cost reduction, expansion of capacity "ahead of demand," and exploitation of "shared experience." The pursuit of shared experience meant that TI would produce products using technology in which TI already was far down the experience curve, namely semiconductors.

It was obviously a high-risk strategy. But to entrepreneurs like Shepherd and Bucy, proud and nationalistic Texans, it seemed a necessary decision. As Bucy said: "TI is competing head on with the Japanese . . . in semiconductors, calculators, and watches. What is to stop them from taking over these businesses as they have done in radios, stereos, TV sets, motorbikes, and steel?"

Bucy had the answer: "I think the big difference is that TI is the first major non-Japanese company they have run into that understands and uses the learning curve. . . . TI has used this concept formally and informally for many years. . . . It is absolutely mandatory to compete successfully with the Japanese."

TI was faithful to its word. Not only did it use the strategy to retain the world lead in most semiconductor markets against the Japanese. It also blasted into calculators in the early 1970s and took a leading 27 percent market share by 1973. Even though TI's clear advantage in experience applied only to integrated circuits—which in turn represented a steadily diminishing portion of the cost—TI maintained dominance in the growing calculator trade until the early 1980s. TI even made a big splash on the experience curve in digital watches, driving the price down to $9.95 before giving way to the more fashionable Swiss and Japanese. Then in 1980 the firm entered the fray in personal computers.

With Bucy and Shepherd, there had been no paralysis on the threshold of the huge home market. Watching the hundreds of companies focusing on the American office and businessman, TI did not say, "We understand businessmen better than Apple does, computers better than Tandy, and we're bigger than both of them together plus any fifty of the other firms in Silicon Valley." To the amazement of industry observers, TI said, "Forget it," and put its professional "Pegasus" project on a shelf for later. There are 16 million businesses, TI reckoned, and 160 makers of business computers. There were 80 million homes and perhaps three serious makers of home computers: Commodore, Atari, and Tandy. Of those three, only Atari focused on the home, but its software was mostly games. TI went for the crowd, rather than with it.

TI conceived a machine that both could play the games and educational software that were crucial to the home and could potentially handle the most popular tasks of successful personal computers, such as word processing, spreadsheet finance, and data-base management. For a microprocessor central processing unit (CPU), TI chose its own powerful 16-bit 9900 and resolved to have appropriate software provided, preferably in the plug-in solid-state software modules (read-only memories or ROMs) pioneered in TI's programmable calculators. With its 16-bit processor, TI's home computer would offer a CPU more powerful than any other personal or small business machine on the market at the time, whatever the price.

In May 1980, the machine arrived in the stores, chiefly J. C. Penney's, where there was no one who knew how to sell it, and the few computer shops of the day, where no one wanted to sell it. The problem in the computer stores was too low a price to justify the sales effort required. The problem at J. C. Penney's was too high a price (nearly $1,000) and unfamiliarity with the product. With a dearth of software, everyone agreed the machine was a "dog."

TI, though, is not a company that is daunted by difficulties. It went to work on the software and pricing problems, hiring programmers and making a study of consumer businesses to determine the appropriate price. The study concluded that the 35mm camera was the most comparable product and that the home computer price therefore should be $199.

This price was about one-third the Atari and Commodore prices at the time. It was considered impossible to sell a computer profitably for anywhere near this amount. But this was the kind of problem that TI—with its long experience in semiconductors—fully understood and even relished. Such a price, it knew, would radically transform and expand the market. In itself, the new price would drastically raise volumes and reduce costs.

Meanwhile, TI ramped up software production from ten packages to 130, eighty of them in solid-state plug-in ROMs that obviated the snags and uncertainties of mechanical disk drives. Outsiders provided some 2,000 additional programs, including several appealing games. By Christmas 1980 the price was dropped to under $500 and the machine began to eke out of the stores. The "dog" at last, ever so slowly, was beginning to wag its tail.

By the third quarter of 1981, TI dropped the price to below $400, and fourth-quarter volume rose to a respectable 20,000, enough to please TI with the sign of potential, but not enough seriously to alarm Atari and Commodore. In 1982, TI cut the price to $299, well below the level of profitable production, but sales began to surge at last. By May the company had sold 90,000, three times the total in 1981, and forced drastic reduction to a similar price by its competitors.

The market began to explode, with analysts predicting total sales close to $1 billion, compared to $120 million in 1981. Most observers, though, still saw TI as a distant third in the competition, with Commodore and Atari, with their more extensive software and greater marketing savvy, as the likely leaders. When Atari, Tandy, and Commodore moved to make further price cuts, TI spokesmen feigned distress, ascribed the move to "weakness," and implied that the Texas company would not contemplate anything so silly and self-destructive.

TI, however, was in fact planning a radical drop in price. It would not be achieved, however, through a simple price reduction. The home computer executives instead proposed to Bucy a $100 rebate, more than one-third of the price. It would be the largest in business history for such a low-priced item, thus gaining publicity. It would bring the product to the targeted price of $199. It would gain TI a large list of names, all potential customers for the accessories and software modules on which it hoped to make a profit. And it would be revealed to the distributors at the last minute before they printed their Christmas catalogs, thus preventing an easy response.

Bucy was thrilled. "This is what we needed," he told his team. "Let's suck it up and go for it." The timing seemed perfect. TI got into the two major Christmas catalogs with the rebate featured, while Atari and Commodore were left with their previous prices well over $200 for much less powerful machines. Although the conventional wisdom still saw Atari and Commodore as likely winners in the Christmas period, visitors to TI reported elation in the consumer products division.

Nonetheless, as usual, the price cut was more effective than anticipated even by TI. For all its experience on the learning curve, the company, according to Bucy, "grossly underestimated the demand generated by the rebate" and failed to put enough capacity in line to fulfill it. Still, at the beginning of 1983, *Business Week* could report, in an article entitled "Texas Instruments Comes Roaring Back," that the company "has grabbed a leading 35 percent share of the market for microcomputers selling for less than $1,000, finishing 1982 with 700,000 of its units in use."

The Texans had moved fastest down the curve. But they were not the only entrepreneurs ready radically to transform the computer market in 1981. One of the others, moreover, was a conscious and declared aspirant to the mantle of Henry Ford, with an explicit strategy directly addressed toward creating a true mass market in personal computers. That man was Adam Osborne, a British immigrant with no formal training in electronics, computer science, or business, who had written and published the best-selling manuals on microprocessors. He planned to exploit an intersecting series of experience curves in the computer components industry to put together a cheap, portable machine that could use the CP/M operating system, then dominant in small business software.

He announced: "We are not planning to go and compete with larger micro and mini computers. We will be emphasizing high volume, low cost, high performance products...." And he would never raise the price of the Osborne I. "We could even drop the price significantly." As for other personal computer firms, "they can either adopt the same policies—or they can go into some other line of business. I am today," he declared, "where Henry Ford was in the auto industry in 1910. Like Ford we are going to amass a billion dollars."

By its second year, 1982, the new computer vindicated the Osborne strategy by selling more than 125,000 and bringing in revenues of some $125 million. This performance gave Osborne the dominant share both of the market he pioneered for transportable computers and of the market for computers selling for between $1,000 and $2,000. He prepared for an even more devastating 1983. . . .

Both Osborne and TI had used the price-cutting strategies of the experience curve to dominate their targeted markets; 1983 would see still more dramatic price reductions. These, though, would be the unplanned price cuts of desperation rather than the gambits of a brilliant strategy. Somehow these once unique and splendid products had abruptly entered the annals of famous business fiascos. Their purchasers, once proud of their fashionable acquisitions, now mumbled the names and wondered where they could find replacement parts or service. Business critics, once agog at the productive brilliance of TI and the prophetic luminosity of Osborne, wrote mordant epitaphs for the companies and their computers. Business magazines intensified their ongoing critiques of the experience curve, as if it were an optional facet of business life rather than the essence of it.

No company working in the shadows of Japanese productivity, however, can escape the constraints of the curve. The company that beat TI in home computers in 1983 was Commodore, which Jack Tramiel, its five-foot-four-inch Auschwitz-survivor president, had thrust three years before into the low-cost market. In a tumultuous meeting with his board, he pounded the table and persuaded them to endorse his program to create a serious computer to sell under $300. If Commodore didn't do it, he said, the Japanese would. Like TI, he was right. Unlike TI, he effectively executed his plan.

A veteran of the calculator wars, Tramiel had suffered one of the repeated traumas of his career when TI's tough pricing had nearly banished him into bankruptcy in the early 1970s. While selling calculator chip sets to Commodore for $19, the Texans began marketing an entire machine for $19, all on one chip.

Tramiel saved his business only by bringing in Irving Gould, an outside investor, and by indulging in a fast financial shuffle that left several creditors empty-handed and angry. The episode left a stain on the astonishing story—and perhaps a scar on the calloused conscience—of this immigrant shopkeeper who rose in twenty-five years from Auschwitz to the commanding heights of the world economy. A "graduate survivor," as he called himself, he hunkered down for two years and turned the company around. Vowing never again to be ambushed by the rapid changes in the world of chips, he purchased two small semiconductor firms, MOS Technology and Frontier. When Tramiel faced TI once again, this time in home computers, he was ready to fight on the frontiers of technology.

With its 16-bit microprocessor and its production skills, TI seemed to have the clear advantage in this fight on the curve. Aggressive pricing is effective, however, only if it is combined with aggressive cost reduction and appropriate product definition. Even though TI designed a splendid small computer, it made several serious errors of positioning. The $199 device was heavily advertised for capabilities that required expensive additional memory. Indeed, a key advantage of a 16-bit processor is that it can command at least four times the memory of an 8-bit device. But Commodore, despite its much less powerful processor, began selling its new model 64 with four times more memory than TI's. Commodore's new computer could perform most of the feats advertised for TI's, such as word processing and advanced games, without additional costs; and by 1983 was selling widely for about the same price. While TI offered much more possible computing power—if the customer had the money and patience to pursue it—Commodore was providing much more immediate capability. The mass market purchasers of low-priced computers preferred Commodore's onboard capability to TI's high-tech specs. (Or else they bought the still cheaper Commodore VIC-20, much less powerful but loaded with software.)

Commodore could provide a better real package to the consumer because Tramiel, loser to TI in calculators in 1975, grimly and personally remembered the lesson of the earlier contest, while TI's corporate winners blithely forgot it. Though a novice in semiconductors, Tramiel vividly recalled the pace of change in chips and what it could do to manufacturing costs. Spread through the divisions of a $4 billion firm, TI's superior expertise never focused clearly on this one product. Just as important, Tramiel was an entrepreneur fully in control of the home computer and dependent on it for the life of his company. Responsible for thousands of products, TI's executives never concentrated with Tramiel's ferocity on that one key market.

In any event, TI essentially froze its home computer technology in 1981 and went for volume. By the time Commodore in late 1982 and 1983 came close to TI's prices, the Commodore machines were using some one-third fewer chips. Where TI was still wiring together large numbers of devices, Commodore was using advanced integrated circuits that combined all the functions on one chip without wiring, as TI had shown them six years before. Where TI was still using 16K DRAMs (memory chips containing 16,000 bits of information), Commodore in its home computer turned rapidly to 64K DRAMs. Experience-curve pricing depends on being the low-cost producer. TI dropped the price on schedule, but it failed to drop its costs as fast as Commodore or define its product as well. In the end, TI beat everyone in home computers but Jack Tramiel.

Osborne suffered a similar fate. An unabashed proponent of both experience-curve pricing and software share, he was defeated by companies that maintained equal or lower costs on products that could use IBM's vast repertory of programs. Although he opposed the decision, his company even overpriced its new product, the Executive. Citing the costs of the first month of production, the new president, a man from Consolidated Foods, pointed out with a laugh that at $1,995 "the company would be losing money on every unit sold but trying to make it up on volume." He was absolutely right, of course. But a man so innocent of the fierce constraints of the curve could not save a computer firm in 1983.

More successful was a Korean immigrant named Philip Hwang, who began his career waiting on tables at a Lake Tahoe hotel and managed to work his way down the learning curve by manufacturing video display and networking terminals. Then in 1983 and 1984, his rapidly growing company, Televideo, launched an array of IBM-compatible machines, including a portable. His sales in 1983 totaled $168 million, and his gross profit margins of nearly 50 percent, largely achieved through manufacturing efficiencies in Korean plants, were larger than IBM's. Because he could win no venture capital in the early years of his company, he retained most of the shares and was worth some $600 million after his public offering.

Even Apple was learning at last. By reducing by two-thirds the number of chips in the at last expanded Apple II line of computers and by huge investments in automation, Apple at last became a significant force in the low-cost sweepstakes. Its impressive, though mouse-infested, Macintosh was designed above all for simple mass production in one of the world's most labor-free plants. Jobs declared, "We have to be the lowest-cost producer in the world by the time the Japanese figure out how to build a good computer." Apple was clearly improving its strategy in 1984. Still more dramatic, however, was the rising entrepreneurial resourcefulness of IBM.

Contrary to widespread opinion, IBM's dominance of personal

computers was by no means predictable. IBM's history, from its "Stretch" system fiasco of 1955 (a $77 million loss in 1983 dollars), to its supercomputer bust of 1965 (worth $408 million), to its equally costly and humbling retreat from superfast Josephson Junctions in 1983, is as full of missed opportunities and bungled ventures as of brilliant coups like its System/360 in 1964. This system at once introduced semiconductor circuitry and broad software compatibility to the IBM product line and garnered over $1 billion in orders in its first month. But outside this mainframe world, the botched 5100 desktop computer of 1973 is more typical of IBM than its brilliant entry into PCs in 1981.

Steve Jobs was essentially on target at Apple's 1984 annual meeting when he regaled his audience with a short series of vignettes of his great competitor:

"It is 1958," he began. "IBM passes up the chance to buy a small company that has perfected a new method called Xerography, discounting the technology as 'unimportant.'

"Now it is 1968," he continued. "IBM dismisses Digital Equipment's minicomputer as competition, saying its computers are too small to do real computing.

"Now it is 1978," Jobs intoned, working toward a crescendo. "Apple Computer releases the personal computer as we know it today. IBM dismisses it as too small to do real computing.

"In 1981, IBM came out with its own personal computer." Jobs then boomed out to an uproarious crowd: "Now it is nineteen eighty-four . . . and IBM announces that it wants it all!" IBM's new claims ring with some disturbing plausibility only because its entry into personal computers was executed with an entrepreneurial defiance of many of the principles that governed its past performance.

While TI, Commodore, and Apple still imitated IBM's old strategy of tying its customers to unique software and systems, IBM itself at last set them loose and accepted the principle of software share. In a remarkable act of corporate abnegation, it manufactured virtually no components itself, licensed for its operating system the freely available MS-DOS, and chose for its central processing unit perhaps the world's most accessible microprocessor: Intel's 8088, which accepts both 8-bit and 16-bit oriented software. Thus, unlike Apple, it assured and invited the widespread production of emulative machines. By disclosing all the details of the "open architecture" of its PC long before its release, IBM assured a massive effort by the software industry to supply it with programs. Long the lofty and inscrutable master of the "gotcha"—by which it induces customers for its mainframe to buy all IBM software and peripherals—IBM adopted for this market a policy of permissiveness more characteristic of an Osborne who had no choice.

At the same time it adopted with fierce resolve the mandate of the experience curve. The change began in 1977 when IBM cut prices by one-third on two obsolescent models in the 370 series. As usual in the long history of industrial price cuts, sales soared far "beyond expectations." This experience prompted a new strategy of aggressive price cuts and massive investments in manufacturing technology. While IBM eschewed technical advances in designing its personal computer, the PC assembly plant in Boca Raton is one of the most fully automated major factories in the industry. While Wall Street worried about the company's shrinking profit margins and IBM's annual outlays for plant and equipment more than doubled in real terms between 1977 and 1983, profits surged, and return on equity rose to over 22 percent, highest among major industrial companies. IBM is not effectively stopping the output of imitations, but it is making sure that it will be the lowest-cost producer, with the highest share of the market that its permissiveness is fostering. As long as it follows this open policy, IBM is likely to remain dominant in the mass markets for computers.

The winners in the computer marketplace, like successful automobile companies since the time of Henry Ford, will be the companies that comprehend the most fundamental of all learning curves: the growing experience of potential customers as they learn more about the product and how to acquire its best features—whether standard software, more responsive service, or more portable hardware—at the lowest possible cost.

This consumers' curve, however, is usually treated by strategic analysts only as a problem for a growing company. Michael Porter of Harvard Business School maintains in his book *Competitive Strategy* that as consumers become more sophisticated, they achieve more bargaining power and buying expertise and become an increasingly difficult market. They begin demanding lower prices or more options and service, and in general put pressure on the profit margins of inadequately experienced companies. In Porter's view, a smart company tries to focus its sales on dumb buyers, "inexperienced with the product, particularly those whose purchasing characteristics tend to make them learn slowly." Porter points out that "products have a tendency to become *more like commodities* [his italics] over time as buyers become more sophisticated and purchasing tends to be based on better information."

To avoid this low-margin trap implicit in the experience curve, Porter recommends alternative strategies of "differentiation" and "focus," generic approaches that allow companies to exploit the most lucrative niches of consumer ignorance or bargaining weakness. But Porter's alternative strategies, in fact, merely expound the techniques for creating new experience curves. By focusing on a particular geographical market, groups of potential buyers, or part of a larger product line—or in differentiating a product by service, image, or special features—a company will create or discover a new experience curve applicable to the new market chosen.

By a strategy of "focus" on wealthy customers and "differentiation" by quality, for example, Mercedes and Grid Systems compete in luxury markets, one in cars and the other in lap-sized portable computers. But they still face an experience curve in these products. As their once exclusive features are continuously adopted by mass-market rivals, the elite producers must continuously create new challenges of quality. Mercedes must continuously meet competition from other luxury cars, or from cars produced by firms such as Chrysler and Honda that imitate Mercedes style and features and offer them at lower prices. Similarly, the once rare virtues of the Grid Compass, with its electroluminescent screen, sleek styling, bubble memory, and briefcase portability, appear increasingly in products from companies such as Radio Shack and Hewlett-Packard.

What Porter is, in fact, describing in his discourse on the learning of buyers is the process by which the experience curve exerts its sway over companies that think they escape it by pursuing specialized niches. One critic complains that believers in the learning curve assume "about 80 percent of all products are commodities. Well, they aren't." He is right. But even Porter shows that all products in time have a tendency to become commodities. The customers insist on it as they move down their own curve in buying and using the product.

Indeed, the transforming of special items into commodities is the prime function of entrepreneurship. By educating customers, lowering prices, expanding sales, and multiplying uses, entrepreneurs enlarge the total experience of buyers at the same time that their own productive experience soars. By adjusting their product for the largest possible markets and advertising its advantages, suppliers create their own demands and lend capitalism its democratic thrust. Previously narrow selling channels—whether for marvelous automobiles once available only to the rich or for fabulous computer power once available only to great institutions—broaden into mass markets. Once-elite luxuries become popular "commodities." When the price of a good is dropping, people invent more applications for it; thus its value increases even more rapidly than its sales in a continuing spiral of capitalist progress.

Economics is never static; entrepreneurs can never rest. In the long run, there are no generic niches or modes of focus and differentiation which seal a company from the continuing process of improvement and discovery, learning and illumination by producers and consumers, in a world of flux and challenge. Scarce resources of mind and matter always can be used in better and more efficient ways, and new products are continually launched by creative men. The knowledge—of inventors, entrepreneurs, producers and consumers—which accumulates through the ongoing waves of human experience is the most crucial curve and capital of industrial progress. By going for the smart buyers, rather than avoiding them, the entrepreneur gets to ride this rising tide of knowledge rather than be swept away by it.

The fundamental misconception that misleads the economic profession, dominates the media, and twists American public opinion is the idea that learning can stop in a free economy—that economic change and transformation can be halted by protections and subsidies. But every investment, business, or business project serves as a test of an entrepreneurial idea, with results not only financial but also epistemological. Knowledge grows even when profits fall; and when profits rise, the learning process accelerates as entrepreneurs buy new experience by further investment and experiment. Economic progress can be driven abroad, to other countries that embrace it, but as long as capitalism survives in the world, the growth of experience is inexorable.

When Tanzan Ishibashi launched his program of tax cuts in Japan, he was allowing the Japanese economy to race down the learning curve, accumulating the entrepreneurial knowledge that is the most explosive capital of the system. As the Japanese companies gained experience, lowered prices, and expanded market share, the Japanese government also enlarged its take—its share of the world tax base. The fact was, though, Japan had no other choice except slow stagnation. As taxpayers move down their own experience curve, they learn how to avoid any existing structure of excessive rates. High taxes will eventually cripple any capitalist economy. Tax cuts, like price cuts, are indispensable to keeping the system on the curve of growth.

9

JAPAN'S ENTREPRENEURS

In 1950, the leading Western expert on Japan, Edwin O. Reischauer of Harvard, declared the country a nearly hopeless case: "The economic situation in Japan may be fundamentally so unsound that no policies, no matter how wise, can save her from slow economic starvation." Instead of starving, however, Japan's economy, growing at a real average rate of nearly 10 percent annually for the last thirty years—with national income increasing by a factor of nine since 1950—has outperformed any other in the history of the human race.

Japan offers a challenge to much of the conventional wisdom of the world's intelligentsia, both right and left, about how economies grow. It will not do, for example, for conservatives to present Japan simply as an example of laissez-faire. No theory of invisible hands and free markets alone can explain the pattern of Japanese growth, as it was mustered and massaged by a many-handed state, led by Japan's intelligent and resourceful Ministry of International Trade and Industry (MITI). MITI from time to time controlled and subsidized credit, excluded imports, financed exports, guaranteed risks, organized cartels and group R&D, named and anointed "sunrise" technologies, protected "infant" industries on into burly adulthood, nursed out gently its declining companies, and in general planned and postured, nudged and signaled, pushed and regulated widely, as it waved wands and batons of "administrative guidance" over the nation's businesses.

Yet the voices of the left will have equal trouble in claiming for their side an economy that boasts the lowest taxes, welfare benefits, and share of government spending in the industrialized world, as well as some of the weakest unions, most rigid sex roles, and most repressive social disciplines of any modern society. The planning powers of MITI also seem doubtful as an explanation of Japan's success. In appraising the importance of a bureaucracy like MITI, however brilliantly it sometimes prophesies technological trends, it is always wise to avoid the chanticleer fallacy: the idea, for example, that "sunrise" industries rise up on the horizon chiefly because the Ministry of International Trade and Industry—or some other preening bureaucracy of planners—chimes cock-a-doodle-doo.

Nor will it do to avoid the question of Japan's miracle altogether by referring to vague racial characteristics or inimitable cultural traits or historic fortuities. Japanese racial and cultural characteristics previously produced a unique history of civil violence and disharmony, economic chaos and political upheaval, resolved only in catastrophic militarism and war. Something entirely new happened amid the ruins of postwar Japan. In learning from this amazing history, it is well to begin with the lesson we so laboriously taught the Japanese: humility.

At the outset, few Japanese institutions had survived. Civilian bureaucracies reemerged forcefully under the Allied government. Otherwise all was chaos. Many companies that escaped Allied bombs were leveled later by Allied bans against all militarily useful enterprise. The leading cartels were dissolved and all wartime activists and officials were removed from power. Even the gods were banished, forbidden to smile on the emperor or, even under the guise of moral teaching, to contaminate the schools. What were left were men and memories. It is from them that the new Japan was largely created.

For clues to the miracle, let us look, therefore, at some of the godforsaken men among the ruins. There is a former businessman, age fifty-one (four years to go before the conventional Japanese year of retirement). The son of a peasant farmer, before the war he ran a large company manufacturing electric motors and other electrical devices; now he is making plans to produce radios and other audio equipment. His name is Konosuke Matsushita (Mat*soosh*ta), and his prospects do not seem panasonic.

Then there are two young dabblers in electronics recently discharged from a research project for the Japanese navy, with little in the way of capital beyond a dilapidated Datsun truck. They are struggling to produce automatic rice cookers in a small corner room on the third floor of the war-ravaged Shirokiya department store in downtown Tokyo. Masaru Ibuka and Akio Morita are their names; they will build a hundred rice cookers, but the cookers too often burn the rice. They will sell none. To avoid bankruptcy, they need funds and are summoning courage to get them from the older Mr. Morita, Akio's sake-magnate father. Soon they will found Sony.

There is "Mr. Thunder" himself, a rakish lad who dropped out of school to race automobiles (he nearly died in a racing crash). He is Soichiro Honda, running a motor repair shop in Hamamatsu, dousing impertinent tax men with a fire hose, and driving a car full of geishas off a bridge (all survived).

There is Genichi Kawakami, returning from a trip to the United States with the bright idea that what the defeated rabble of his country would need is fun and games; he resolved to revive his company, Yamaha, hitherto focused on wooden furniture and pianos, and transform it into a developer of leisure industries.

Such diverse entrepreneurs and their companies cover a gamut of Japanese business in many of the fields—from consumer electronics and automobiles to musical instruments and semiconductor devices—in which Japan has broken most massively into the U.S. market. Low interest rates, rapid depreciation, or grand strategic designs never sold a rice cooker, built a marketable radio, debugged a computer microcode, constructed, at low cost, a resonant piano, or fashioned a workable power turbine. "Administrative guidance" never cast a satisfactory piston ring, or wrought a reliable semiconductor from scratch, as Sony did in its tiny factory. At the root and origin of all great empires of industry can usually be found a perspiring entrepreneur, often frustrated and fatigued, struggling over a machine that won't quite work.

Honda, for example, was to become the world's single most brilliant and successful entrepreneur of mechanical engineering since Henry Ford. But only the perspiration of genius was in sight during that period before the war when he embarked on a siege of day-and-night study and experiment in the techniques of casting, in his attempt to make a piston ring. He lived at the factory, turning from a gay blade into a hirsute and harried hermit, stinking of grease and sweat, while his savings ran out, his friends fretted, his parents reminded him of promising opportunities in auto repair, and he pawned his wife's jewelry for funds. Finally, the unschooled youth added to his nearly sleepless schedule a series of classes in industrial engineering at the Hamamatsu School of Technology, under a professor who had laughed at young Honda's excuse for a piston ring.

Within the year of 1938, Honda succeeded in manufacturing identifiably round and functional devices. But out of a 50,000-unit order, Toyota, which had just sold most of its loom business and was starting to build trucks for the military, sampled fifty rings and rejected marriage. Honda was forced to take his product to less stringent markets, until two years later in 1940 he could meet the

Toyota quality requirements. But he could not fulfill the orders because the government, planning for war, refused him rights to purchase cement for a needed new plant. Undaunted, he and his men set out to learn how to make their own cement. Finally, during the war, he began to receive financial support from Toyota and was capitalized at more than 1 million yen ($260,000 at the prewar exchange rate). He invented new machinery for automatic piston ring manufacture and automatic planing for aircraft propellers, allowing relatively untrained women to produce these goods as the men went off to meet the marines. He lost two factories to fire-bombings, but rushed out after each attack to pick up the extra gasoline tanks U.S. fighters shucked as they flew by. "Truman's gifts," he called the cans. They were made of nonferrous metals needed for his specialized manufacturing processes, and sometimes even retained a little gasoline at the bottom. In 1945, an earthquake—of all redundant concussions—devastated the Hamamatsu area as well as most of Honda's plant and equipment, while Allied planes were wreaking havoc still worse elsewhere in Japan.

After the surrender, Honda, who did not fancy himself as an auto company subsidiary, decided to break away from Toyota. Selling the remains of his piston ring business for $125,000, he set out to create a fast rotary weaving machine to replace the slow horizontal shuttles then used in Japan. But he ran out of funds before reaching the manufacturing stage. It was early 1947 and once again he was back at scratch, along with most of the Japanese economy.

 The most striking and paradoxical fact about the careers of successful entrepreneurs is their continual failure and frustration. As Soichiro Honda later told a graduating class at Michigan Technological University: "Many people dream of success. To me success can be achieved only through repeated failure and introspection. In fact, success represents 1 percent of your work which results only from the 99 percent that is called failure."

Chance and failure also attended, and made possible, the founding of Sony. Masaru Ibuka was available to start the corporation—and provide it with a stream of ingenious inventions—only because he failed the entry exam for lifetime employment at Tokyo-Shibaura Electric Company. Better known as Toshiba, this was Japan's oldest electrical goods firm and the biggest one as well until Hitachi overtook it in the early 1960s (Sony swept by it in net income during the late 1970s). While making a living in radio repair and selling short-wave converters to Japanese radio owners hungry for foreign news, Ibuka and Morita followed their rice cooker fiasco with a resolve to incorporate. On May 7, 1946, they formed Sony (then TTK Co., Ltd.) with a paid-in capital of 198,000 yen (worth between $500 and $600), the limit allowed under Allied command regulations for incorporation without complex paperwork.

The company's prospectus, written by Ibuka, expresses some of the visionary qualities of this extraordinary man, as he launched his tiny company: "At this time of inception of the New Japan," he wrote, "we will try to create conditions where persons could come together in a spirit of teamwork, and exercise to their hearts' desire their technological capacity . . . such an organization could bring untold pleasure and untold benefits. . . ." In addition, the management of this $600 company bravely committed itself to "eliminate any untoward profit-seeking" and to eschew "expansion of size for the sake of size."

"Rather," wrote Ibuka, "we shall emphasize activities . . . that large enterprises, because of their size, cannot enter. . . . Utilizing to the utmost the unique features of our firm, welcoming technological difficulties . . . focusing on highly sophisticated technical products of great usefulness in society . . . we shall open up through mutual cooperation channels of production and sales . . . equal to those of large business organizations."

In the meantime, to meet a cash flow problem, the company decided on divestiture of its old Datsun truck. It also began devoting days and nights and weekends to producing voltmeters, an electrical gauge designed by Ibuka. Morita estimated that they could meet their payroll by selling ten a month. Soon they were producing thirty or forty and preparing to launch, through many trials and errors, what for Japan was a truly original consumer product: the tape recorder. The tape, though, was to be made of paper.

Honda, meanwhile, his own car immobilized by the fuel shortage, was having trouble getting food for his family. He decided to solve this problem by the novel device of attaching a motor to a bicycle. His neighbors were impressed enough to ask Honda to make more. Using a small gasoline engine used for electrical generators during the war, he contrived a makeshift motorbike and sold scores from his little repair shop until the surplus motors ran out. Then he decided to build motors himself.

Faced with government controls on gasoline and restrictions on the manufacture of gasoline-using machines, Honda built a motor that ran on *pine resin*, which he recalled had been used as a substitute for aircraft fuel toward the end of the war. "We squeezed the resin from the pine root," Honda says, "then mixed it with gasoline bought on the black market. The mixture gave off such a stench of turpentine that I could insist that we were violating no gasoline controls by operating the motorbikes."

With the income from his ramshackle but popular contraptions,

Honda then set out to design and manufacture a real motorcycle—Mr. Thunder's "dream of speed"—as a means of locomotion for Japan as it overcame its postwar shortages and began again to think of moving fast and free. There was not yet a market for such a machine. But as Honda said later, in words echoed by many Japanese entrepreneurs from Morita to the Kashio brothers, "We do not make something because the demand, the market is there. With our technology, we can create demand, we can create the market." *Supply creates its own demand.*

Ibuka, too, began with an idea and an intuition rather than a manufacturing schematic. Beyond the successful voltmeter, the Sony founder, like Soichiro Honda, ended with more than a hundred patents to his credit. But in 1948, Ibuka possessed only the tantalizing image of a military tape recorder he had seen one day in Occupation Headquarters. He was convinced that such a machine could be Sony's first consumer product. But he had no patents, no recorder, and no tape. There was not even any plastic in Japan from which to manufacture tape; nor would MITI permit Sony to import it.

In retrospect, it is clear that the difficulties of creating a recorder using paper tape forced Sony to acquire the technological skills that made possible all the company's future achievements. In order to use paper, Sony would need not only to develop an entire new technology for magnetized tape, but also to produce radical improvements in tape recording hardware. By no financial calculus could these efforts be proved remotely worthwhile, when they could all be nullified by a change of opinion at MITI allowing import or licensure of the 3M plastic tape with its estimated ten-times-superior capability. Nonetheless, it was this apparently foolhardy effort that created the assets that became Sony. These assets were not measurable; they consisted of the rising metaphysical capital of knowledge, skills, technological confidence, organizational management, and marketing ability, which differentiate an enduring company from an *ad hoc* financial and production project. "Sony" was moving rapidly down a curve of accumulated experience without any unit sales at all.

Indeed, once they had manufactured the tape machine, they encountered a further problem: No one wanted the thing. Morita and Ibuka had accepted from the beginning the better-mousetrap fallacy—the mistaken idea that a new, useful product will bring the world unprompted to your door. Even after they built a demonstrably better way of catching sound, the world adamantly refused to troop to the doors of Sony. The essential problem was that the product was an innovation; therefore, no one "needed" it. No one knew what it was, how to use it, or what it was good for. Morita finally took the problem in hand. Having become a manufacturer, he would have to learn marketing.

Bemused by the mousetrap fallacy, many of the world's greatest technical companies—from Ford Motor Company in the mid-1920s to Texas Instruments in the postwar era—have failed to learn the lesson of sensibility to consumers and thus have fallen far short of their promise. Dominated by their engineers, these firms have failed to develop the altruistic dimension—the sensitivity to the responses of others—that is indispensable to all business success. The "inner-directed" creator, so celebrated in the annals of industry, is impotent without an "other-directed" sympathy and curiosity, whether he has it himself or finds it in a colleague.

Although Soichiro Honda seems supremely other-directed, his genius flourished in the "skunkworks," with a wrench in his hand, amid the smell of grease and gasoline. Honda solved the marketing problem by bringing in a full partner, Takeo Fujisawa, and giving him complete authority in finance, sales, and strategic marketing. Marketing is also key to the success of Matsushita, which uses the trade name Panasonic in the United States. An older company less bold and innovative than either Sony or Honda, it has outearned both of them, and scores of American competitors, largely through its genius in imitating and adapting better to the customers' needs products invented and launched by others, notably including Sony.

Sony's answer to the problem of marketing was to unleash Morita to become one of the world's paramount salesmen. In the end, it was salesmanship, sensitivity to consumer needs and responses, rather than technology that allowed Sony to outdo such technically superior companies as Texas Instruments in selling transistor radios and other electronic consumer goods. But in 1950, while its financial officer predicted bankruptcy, Sony and its agents remained unable to sell a single tape machine to the public. Morita began an indefatigable campaign—from cocktail parties to elementary schools—to inform the world of his marvel. The first important purchase came from a Justice Department branch in Nagoya, which used it to record proceedings in the courtroom. Morita immediately saw this sale as a crucial breakthrough, signifying a large-scale use for the machine. They rushed to the headquarters of the Ministry of Justice and managed to sell sixty more.

The sale came easily because Sony was not selling a mere machine; it was selling a use, a solution to a problem. New uses were found in schools, and several further sales led Morita to see the future of the tape recorder as an educational aid. Buoyed by this success, Masaru Kurahashi, working for Sony's retailing agent, appealed to his boss to let him take over all national distribution of the device. The boss refused, and Morita promptly hired Kurahashi and made him head of a subsidiary, soon to become Sony Sales.

The company made a key error, however. Because Yamaha was thriving through its sales of pianos to schools, Morita assumed that the company could sell tape recorders too. He was wrong. In order to sell something, you have to understand it. Yamaha did not then understand electronics. It could not explain the machine or repair it. Despite access to Yamaha's large sales network with its ties to hundreds of schools, Sony sales began to languish. Morita resolved to establish a distribution and sales network of his own, bringing Sony massively and expensively into the realm of marketing. Ibuka and his engineers, after some demurrers, finally agreed, and Sony Sales was born.

Honda, meanwhile, had succeeded in creating his "dream" machine, a sleek and powerful motorcycle with a four-cycle engine. On its test drive in July 1951, Honda remembers following behind in a car, as a young assistant, Kiyoshi Kawashima, a veteran of the pine-resin years, drove the new machine along the famed Tokaido road from Tokyo up through the treacherous Hakone Pass. As the car struggled to keep up, Honda knew he had a technical winner, like Sony's first tape machine. "We managed to catch up with Kawashima-san after a while as he was taking a rest on the mountaintop, at a point which commands a glorious view of Lake Ashinoko on the slopes of Mount Fuji. A torrential rain was coming down, matched by the tears of joy in our eyes, as we stood around the motorcycle."

Now Fujisawa, without the romance of mountaintop rains, would have to sell the machine. He began with a coup: writing letters to all the 18,000 bicycle shops in Japan. As Fujisawa recalls, a typical letter ran as follows:

"Less than one hundred years ago, your father saw the first bicycle brought in from the Western world. He knew little about it, nor how to ride it, how to make it, how to deal with the simplest problem—even how to repair a puncture. But he learned to do all those things and he learned to do them well. Because of that spirit of Japanese resourcefulness, he was able to make a comfortable living and left you with a bicycle shop and a way to earn your living. Now we are launching a new product. It will be a motor-driven bicycle. You have hardly seen one, and you do not know how to sell it or how to repair it. But we intend to help you learn to do both."

Five thousand dealers, who came to make up one of Japan's first and largest national distribution networks, responded to Fujisawa's letter. But Honda's "Dream," so it turned out, was then shared only by connoisseurs of speed and power, the limited market of motor-cyclists dominated in the United States by Harley-Davidson. Honda came to understand that a commercial breakthrough would come not to the company with roaring machines which could captivate the swashbuckling spirit of youths who wished to overtake cars through the Hakone Pass, but to the company which could lure millions of ordinary Japanese off their bicycles.

In 1952, within a year after the launch of the Dream, Honda became that company, by creating a small, cheap, and efficient "Cub" engine that either ran on Honda's red-and-white frame or clipped conveniently onto a bicycle. It was this relatively quiet machine, contrary to his own rambunctious inclinations, which brought Honda the roaring success he sought. It sold massively through Fujisawa's network of bicycle shops, and Honda was awarded an emperor's blue ribbon in 1952 for his contributions to Japanese industry.

Nonetheless, Honda's relations with the Japanese establishment of Todo University graduates and former zaibatsu (conglomerates) were always strained. He spurned the nation's powerful business lobbies and associations—led by the Keidanren and Nikkeiren—with their demands for government aid and protection; and only with great difficulty could he be lured into a white tie and cutaway to receive the emperor's medal.

In an exchange with the emperor's younger brother after the ceremony, though, Honda offered a vivid image of his work and its motives. To the prince's remark that "it must be an exacting task to invent or contrive something new," Honda replied, "I don't really find it very exacting because I am doing what I like to do. As the proverb goes, 'Love shortens distances.' " Honda's trek to the summit of Japanese industry, through war, frustration, and treacherous mountain passes, had indeed been shortened by his love for machines.

Fujisawa's key contribution, during this early period shortly after Honda's award, came not in sales but in finance. Although Fujisawa had no training in financial matters, he was well prepared for the precarious finagling of Japanese entrepreneurship by his childhood in the household of a frequently failing small businessman. Facing down angry creditors, bluffing bankers, juggling books, kiting paper on a breath of hope, buying time with smiles, Fujisawa's father had given him a superb education in crisis management that would well serve Honda through its many hard times.

They began in 1953 after Honda, capitalized at $165,000, decided to meet the threat of foreign competition so feared among his business colleagues by purchasing $1 million worth of advanced machine tools from Europe and America. He paid with a series of short-term notes and proceeded to set up a modern factory to produce what would be Honda's new breakthrough, perhaps the Super-Cub that orbited the company in the mid-1950s. Honda and Fujisawa had made a crucial miscalculation, however. They counted on continued boom in the Japanese economy to sustain sales of their existing machines while the debt was paid off. But the early-1950s boom in Japan was in part a product of special procurements for the Korean War. As the war wound down in the mid-1950s, so did the Japanese economy. Unable to pay off the debt, Honda confronted the fate he had most feared since his early postwar escape from the maw of Toyota. He was on the verge of slipping into the net of the Mitsubishi *keiretsu*, the conglomerate of industrial dependencies of the giant Mitsubishi bank, which for several years had been trying to merge Honda with Mitsubishi Heavy Industries.

Fujisawa, however, had several years earlier befriended a high-level Mitsubishi official and had induced the bank to accept Honda's deposits, with the implication of future acceptance of loans. Mitsubishi had made the loans. In 1955, the official interceded for Honda and persuaded the bank to extend the loans. With the help of Fujisawa's maneuvers with other creditors and his workers' willingness to give up their bonuses, Honda pulled through as an independent company, with the capacity two years later to launch the Super-Cub.

The Super-Cub turned out to be one of those breakthrough products that transform and consolidate an industry. Before the Super-Cub there were fifty motorcycle companies in Japan purveying a variety of equipment, ranging from new versions of Italian scooters to huge swashbuckling Harleys. The motorcycle field appeared to be a hopelessly fragmented and thoroughly mature market, full of special niches, to be served by small companies with possibly high margins, but without much promise for long-term growth. Motorbikes seemed to be an "inferior" good, like potatoes, on which people tend to spend less as they grow richer—precisely the kind of product that MITI wished to discourage in Japanese industry. The motorcycle market, in fact, appeared to be the perfect arena for use of the kind of "generic strategies" of differentiation and focus that Michael Porter offered as a refuge from the exigencies of the experience curve.

The Super-Cub changed all that. Honda produced a step-through bike that combined the power and excitement of big machines with the convenience and efficiency of scooters, built it in his modern integrated factory, advertised it to a mass market ("You meet the nicest people on a Honda"), priced it well below the competition, and roared down the curve like Kawashima through Hakone Pass. By the time the dust had settled ten years later, the fifty Japanese motorcycle companies had dwindled to four and Honda dominated the world market for motorbikes.

During the same period in the early 1950s that Honda was conceiving his Super-Cub, Masaru Ibuka of Sony visited the United States to inquire into American uses of the tape recorder and stumbled instead onto the magical threshold of semiconductor technology. It was a world already teeming with activity in the United States, but still a matter of glints and rumors in Japan.

At first, Ibuka saw transistor technology as a way to solve a nagging problem of his company: what to do with the array of advanced metallurgists, mechanical engineers, physicists, and other miscellaneous miracle workers he had hired to overcome the challenges of recording faithfully on paper tape. Sony was by then manufacturing fine recorders with magnetic plastic tape, and after selling them to most of the schools in Japan, had broken through to a mass market of radio stations, banks, police, and many thousands of private purchasers. The company was working on an array of other audio and video projects. But Ibuka realized that his company's greatest asset was not its impending products but its technical manpower. He worried that these products would not suffice to hold their interest. Perhaps the transistor would do it.

The initial price, $25,000 down to license the technology from Bell, seemed steep for the still-small company. It would need approval from MITI, which then controlled all imports of foreign equipment and access to foreign exchange and had previously denied Sony the right to import plastic tape. On the grinding two-day airplane trip back to Tokyo, however, Ibuka was pierced by one of those fixating ideas that give him the same indomitable drive that he discerned as "unique" in Soichiro Honda and Edwin Land. He decided to use the transistor to make radios: "Radios," as he said on his return, "small enough so each individual will be able to carry them around for his own use, with power that will enable civilization to reach even those areas with no electric power."

Ibuka's enthusiasm carried the day with Morita and the other leaders at Sony. But MITI thought the idea preposterous. If the potential was so great, why had not Hitachi, Matsushita, or one of the other great Japanese electrical companies applied for the patent? And MITI asked, according to Nick Lyons in his history of Sony, "If the big companies are not interested, why should MITI give the allocation of foreign exchange, plus all the implicit rights for associated technological imports, to a small manufacturer of tape recorders?" MITI balked for nearly a year, while Ibuka audaciously proceeded to assign his top young technicians to the project, assemble a complete library on transistor technology, and sign a conditional agreement with Western Electric. MITI angrily protested Ibuka's presumption, but Ibuka responded with yet more passionate and well-documented arguments for his case. In early 1954, MITI gave in and Sony was on its way, undaunted by warnings from Western Electric that the device was too crude in the higher registers to use for radios.

In committing Sony to semiconductor technology, Ibuka had engaged his company, late in the game, in the fastest-moving technology in the history of science. Yet, somehow, perhaps because he could not hope to dominate semiconductor technology itself, he made his company a world leader in commercially applying it.

The entire original technology had come, piece by piece, from the United States. Ibuka and his transistor expert, Kazuo Iwama, a young geophysicist, had spent the first three months of 1954 in America. They traveled the gamut of laboratories, universities, factories, and industries involved in the several advanced technologies, from microelectronics to photographic etching and advanced crystallography, that were converging in the manufacture of transistors. They went from Bell Laboratories to Western Electric, from Raytheon to Union Carbide. Most important were several conferences held by Bell specifically to explain and popularize the technology. Nearly every night Iwama would dispatch back to a team of technicians in Tokyo a long detailed letter, of as much as seven or eight pages, of diagrams and technical English interspersed with Japanese characters, Roman numerals, and American place names, filled with instructions for imports and purchases. Occasionally Ibuka would send a telegram: NEED HEAVY DUTY DIFFUSION FURNACE STOP; then in the light of a new discovery, he would rescind it: WAIT ON BUYING ALL EQUIPMENT UNTIL FURTHER NOTICE STOP. DETAILS IN A LETTER.

The long-distance technique worked. By April, Ibuka and Iwama returned to Japan, and by late 1954, they had produced their first, and somewhat faulty, transistor, and received a shock from Texas. A Texas Instruments subsidiary named Regency had launched the world's first transistor radio. The news of its production first jolted, then filled with joy and confidence, the team working on the project at Sony.

It is the unseen wall or uncharted chasm—the kind of expected but absolute obstacle that blighted the lives of hundreds of technicians working on power storage for electric cars—that creates the anguish in innovation. The TI breakthrough vindicated Ibuka and pushed him to still more heroic effort. All major breakthroughs in transistor radios, from pocket-size to FM, and on to the first transistor TV—and most of the commercial successes—would henceforth come from Ibuka's Japanese firm, soon to emerge as Sony. Sony's success would leave Hitachi and Matsushita some three years behind and provoke them to desperate and only partly successful efforts to catch up. It would make Sony a profitable company, grossing $2.5 million in 1955 and tripling its employees to 1,200 by 1957. It would project Japan, as early as the mid-1950s, into the vanguard of progress in consumer electronics, as Sony became known around the world as the manufacturer of the miniature "radio that works."

But did someone hear a cock-a-doodle-doo? Well, in 1956 the Ministry of Finance fluttered hurriedly to its fencepost to hail the sunrise in tape recorders and transistor radios, cutting the excise taxes on them for two years; and in June 1957, in the wake of Sony's success, MITI sponsored an "Electronics Industry Promotion Special Measures Law," permitting rapid depreciation, easy imports of technology, and other favors. Who knows, it might have helped Hitachi. But it is doubtful that any of the targeted aid was needed, or made up for the delay and obstruction of Sony two years before. The story of Honda, the other leading postwar startup, is even less favorable to the grander claims of MITI's enthusiasts.

In 1957, Soichiro Honda visited one of America's leading experts in motorcycle sales to persuade him to market the latest version of the Super-Cub in the United States. They had a warm conversation, reaching easy agreement that the agent would sell 7,500 motorcycles per period. The negotiations suddenly broke down, though, when the American indicated that "there will be no trouble selling that many motorcycles. That's a very appropriate figure" for annual sales. Honda had thought he was agreeing to 7,500 sales a month. "Seventy-five hundred a month?" the agent replied. "That's out of the question. Preposterous." By the mid-1960s Honda would sell some 20,000 per month in the United States. Such anecdotes, always presented in a spirit of wonder and excitement, are in fact ubiquitous in entrepreneurial history. Like all entrepreneurs with major projects, Soichiro Honda was defying the expert opinion. It was because the experts still believed the project "preposterous" that the opportunity survived for Honda to exploit it.

Soichiro Honda's role as one of the world's greatest entrepreneurs since Henry Ford is firmly founded on his success in achieving the impossible twice. First was his feat of transforming the apparently obsolescent motorcycle into one of the great glamorous growth products of the late twentieth century. But his second breakthrough—entering the auto industry at the top and producing one of the dominant world cars of the mid-1980s—was still more amazing. To any expert in the field, automobiles in 1966 seemed among the least accessible of world industries. The last U.S. entrant was the ill-fated Kaiser-Frazer of 1946. The dominant companies were simply too far down the experience curve to be overtaken by a newcomer.

Such a pessimistic view certainly prevailed at Japan's Ministry of International Trade and Industry. In the 1960s, as Japan began opening its economy tentatively to the world, MITI worried that its frail industries would be swamped by huge American cartels. MITI officials returned from Europe with terrifying tales of the "American Challenge" as limned in Gothic strokes by Jean-Jacques Servan-Schreiber. In particular, so they feared, Japan's imitative and fragmented auto industry—long protected from foreign competition by MITI's own policies—would tumble helplessly before the juggernaut of General Motors, Ford, and Chrysler. MITI proposed that Japan's ten auto firms be combined into two, namely Nissan and Toyota, and that new firms be prohibited from producing four-wheeled vehicles.

Although MITI's legislation for this purpose was stalled in the chaos following the student riots of 1960, the agency persuaded Nissan to absorb Prince, once a major Japanese company, and persistently nudged Mitsubishi Heavy Industries, a huge shipbuilding firm not then in the auto industry, toward merger with Isuzu. Some MITI leaders, who had opposed auto investment in the 1950s because it implied massive imports of iron and oil, Japan's scarcest resources, renewed their appeals for disinvestment in the 1960s. Although their earlier objections had failed (in part because of Korean War demand for military vehicles), they returned to the fray in the 1960s with the kind of eco-aesthetic and strategic case that Emma Rothschild later popularized in the United States in her book *The Decline of the Auto Industrial Age.* Not only were cars wasteful and polluting, but they represented a mature "sunset" industry inevitably to be dominated by established foreign companies.

Japan's entrepreneurs, however, refused to see it that way. The creation of new auto companies actually picked up as MITI's protections and subsidies were removed. By the mid-1960s, Suzuki, a Honda rival in motorcycles, already had entered with a minicar, and Toyo Kogyo, a machine-tool firm, was contemplating introduction of a Mazda with a Wankel rotary engine. Then in May 1969, Mitsubishi Heavy Industries, the spearhead of the giant Mitsubishi *keiretsu* (which had been attempting to absorb Honda), finally demolished once and for all the MITI plan. In an act that the MITI Heavy Industries chief described as hitting him like a pail of water poured into his ear while he was sleeping, Mitsubishi announced an agreement not with Isuzu or Honda, but with Chrysler, a dread foreign leviathan, to form an entirely new auto company in Japan. By the end of the year, the "Colt Gallant Hardtop," soon to become the "Dodge Colt" in the United States, began streaming off Mitsubishi's assembly lines, and a year later the firm had leapt into third place in Japan's auto industry. Shortly thereafter, General Motors bought 34 percent of Isuzu and Ford invested in Toyo Kogyo. Meanwhile, European governments began nationalizing— or otherwise reinforcing through their national treasuries—a further array of automobile behemoths, including France's Renault, British Leyland, Germany's Volkswagen (40 percent owned by a provincial government), Sweden's Volvo and Italy's massive Fiat. Such was the phalanx of Honda's worldwide competition by the early 1970s.

But Soichiro Honda had a plan. Although his competition was little aware of it, the plan had begun several years before. It involved none of the approaches followed by his rivals. It entailed no mergers, no government finance, no huge bond issues or even large borrowings from banks. Rather, he announced his entry in auto racing. He would build a racing car that would win at Le Mans. To fulfill this goal, he set up a separate research and development company at Honda, free of all the distractions of short-term projects, free, as Honda himself would stress, to set improbable goals and to fail.

His essential strategy was to make a series of technological breakthroughs, and he knew he needed help from the best engineering talent in Japan. He believed that the way to attract the highest-quality engineers was not by announcing plans for a commercial automobile but by declaring a resolve to develop the world's fastest racing car.

Once he had assembled his team he freed it from all the constraints of existing auto technologies and commercial ambitions.

Rather than allying itself with some great firms of the past or some great fount of finance, Honda thrust itself onto the frontiers of technology. For Soichiro, this meant thrusting himself into the middle of the skunkworks. In the context of the modern auto industry, Honda, in fact, represented a profoundly reactionary impulse. It was a movement of back to the basics, back to the skunkworks, back to the inspiration of Henry Ford, another grease monkey with no college degree, who dominated the industry largely by his obsession with machines.

The strategy was a success. Although Honda pulled his engineers off the racing car project before it achieved a victory at Le Mans, their Formula One entry won the Mexican and Italian Grand Prix, and Formula Two racers prevailed in eleven consecutive races for smaller cars in 1966. The sports car he developed from his Formula Two racer, moreover, dazzled the automotive world. As the British *Sunday Times* auto critic wrote: "The precision of the Honda's engineering, almost like a jewelled watch, has astonished every engineer I spoke to." Although a correctible flaw in the motor prevented Honda from winning at Le Mans in 1967, automotive experts agreed that he would dominate the field in future years.

By 1967, however, Honda felt he had exhausted the technical benefits of racing and abruptly withdrew from competition. In a prophetic move that put him years ahead of all other automobile companies—and ahead even of the environmental movements in the United States and Japan—he led his team of engineers into a yet more problematic and rewarding challenge: the creation of a nonpolluting car. This effort would not only reach most of its goals, embarrassing some of the world's largest corporations in the process, but it would also, as Ibuka observed, help Honda in its increasing accumulation of "a tremendous amount of unique engine technology that it alone has." Ibuka well understood the process, for the route to success was similar for him and Morita at Sony, with the paper-tape recorder and transistor projects imparting the necessary spur to technological mastery. In neither firm, it is safe to say, was the spur of MITI as important to success, though MITI's resistance may well have provided a stimulating challenge to both companies.

Both companies followed the classic course of swivel-hipped entrepreneurs, "going where they ain't," "running for daylight." As Morita says, "Sony does what others don't; we lead, others follow." At the same time these two firms offer both caution and confirmation for hard-charging champions of experience-curve pricing and market share *über alles*.

Sony's chief competitor in transistor radios was Texas Instruments. For all of Sony's inventive genius in the creation and marketing of consumer electronics over the decades, its record in pure innovation stands well below TI's catalog of semiconductor breakthroughs. Yet this superb company, with its unexcelled technical skills and its dynamic sense of strategy and pricing, lost abjectly to Sony in transistor radios, the product that made Sony a master company in consumer electronics. With all the advantages of a home market, shared experience with other semiconductor products, and prowess in manufacturing, TI could not meet the challenge of a smaller Japanese firm competing in a strange land and doing most of its marketing itself.

On the surface, TI, at the very moment of defeat, possessed a clear edge in costs and prices. Sony charged nearly $40 for its model, while TI and other American companies that followed were charging $12 or $13. But the crux of any market share strategy is not mere price per physical unit sold, but price per unit of consumer service or satisfaction. The question, in Kenichi Ohmae's terms, is how well the product fulfills the customers "objective function." In this case, the relevant curve of experience was not, as TI apparently assumed, the production and sale of transistor radios at the lowest price, but hours of satisfactory performance per dollar. By this measure Sony's product—"the radio that works"—was cheaper at $40 than its rivals at $12.95, and Sony was producing more units of consumer satisfaction, more sales with market traction, and moving farther down the curve than TI.

Sony's advantage probably stemmed in part from its inferiority to companies like TI in the advanced refinements of semiconductors. This led it to focus on the transistor radio as its main product and satisfying consumers as its primary aim. By contrast, in these early years of dizzying discovery, the American semiconductor industry fixed its market focus somewhere between Armonk and the moon. As a result the *Eagle* landed and the American computer industry leads the world. But Sony, Matsushita, and other Japanese companies dominated the field in applying this fabulous technology to the mundane and humbling task of making people happy— linking the laboratory with the sales display, connecting a miraculous but superficially baffling technology to the longings of human hearts and minds.

Because Sony's prime item was radios, it moved onto the next stage more rapidly than any other company. Ibuka immediately saw that to exploit the full potential of the transistor—to make a pocket radio—required miniaturization of all the other radio parts.

Yet most of the component manufacturers rejected the possibility of making speakers, capacitors, inductors, transformers, and batteries on that tiny scale. But Ibuka would not give up, and in the end, he personally, Sony's CEO, going from lab to factory, haggling with technicians, finance officers, and engineers, managed to persuade them one by one to attempt what they had believed was impossible in reducing the scale of their products. They were the experts in component production; they were masters of the limits of their trade. But Ibuka is a classic entrepreneur, making businesses out of impossibilities.

In the end, it happened that the subcontractors were partly right, as experts often are. It turned out to be impossible, in the time prescribed, to make the radio small enough to fit into a shirt pocket. Sony transformed this setback into a new business, making big-pocketed shirts.

The result of Ibuka's stubbornness was that by the time Sony launched its pocket radio in international markets, the company and its subcontractors, pushed and harried by Ibuka, had taken the world lead in electronic miniaturization—a lead that Sony and the other Japanese firms, from Matsushita to Casio, would never relinquish. Sony was no longer following the technology. Although it never became a leader in the broad range of semiconductor products (like other Japanese firms, Sony launched its personal computer in 1982 using Zilog and Intel microprocessors), Sony achieved dominance with its own defined specialties.

After the pocket radio, Sony pioneered a long series of consumer products, mostly derived from its mastery of transistors and miniaturization, from the first transistor TV in 1960 to the unique Trinitron one-gun, one-lens color TV (Sony's single most successful product) in 1968 and the Betamax VCR in 1975. Perhaps most impressive among its products for the 1980s are a series of new digital recording and playback devices, including the Mavica digital disk still camera and the Digital Audio Disk (DAD) system.

A list of such marvels, many of them now commonplace, conveys some of the technological resourcefulness of Sony. But many of the items have been imitated and even excelled by other companies. Matsushita (Panasonic)—the company that does what others do, *following* in the once-typical Japanese way—repeats many of the Sony products and outsells them. Not Sony but Matsushita, because of its superb skills in design and manufacturing and its global marketing prowess, with five times as many outlets as Sony and twenty-seven more years of experience, is the world's leading vendor of consumer electronics. Sony produced the Betamax, the first popular videotape recorder, but Matsushita learned that customers really wanted an eight-hour rather than a three-hour machine, and shortly dominated the market. Sony made the Walkman, but Akai imitated and improved on it, and sold the improved item for 40 percent less. The importance of Sony is not registered in its size or technological skills, as impressive as they are, but in its pioneering entrepreneurship, which transformed the image of Japan in world markets. Sony, more than MITI or Nippon Steel, epitomizes the spirit of enterprise that infused and informed the miracle of Japanese growth.

Nick Lyons sums up this Sony vision in his book by that name. He tells a favorite Morita story: "Two shoe salesmen . . . find themselves in a rustic, backward part of Africa. The first salesman wires back to his head office: 'There is no prospect of sales. Natives do not wear shoes.' The other salesman wires: 'No one wears shoes here. We can dominate the market. Send all possible stock.' " As Sony's top American salesman describes it, the key difference between Sony and other electronic firms is that the others "see a market and come up with a product to fill it. Sony's philosophy is to develop a product when there is *no* market—and then create one."

This approach, not Matsushita's, was crucial to the success and popularity of Japanese exports. If Japan had continued only to mass-produce at lower price products designed elsewhere—from automobiles and TVs to steel ingots and silicon chips, exports partly dependent on an undervalued yen, vagaries of the money markets, and government subsidies—public resentment would have flared up fiercely. American protectionists would have acquired even more strength than they have shown already, as specific jobs, income, industries, and regions seemed to be jeopardized by imports from Japan. But when Sony and other inventive Japanese firms like Casio and Yamaha brought forth their skein of sparkling surprises, they threatened nearly no one; most Americans were dazzled and grateful. A pocket radio, a tummy TV, a hand calculator that both computes your taxes and simulates flute and guitar music, a digital camera, a Walkman, a small copier which makes miniatures and enlargements, a radio which records and tells the time, a Betamax—such products did not exist; they created new markets, new wealth, new excitement. Their offerings come virtually as gifts, revealing unexpected sympathies, giving rewards well beyond their cost, surprising the purchaser with the fulfillment of unconscious wishes.

Fully in the spirit of Sony's achievement, doing what others don't, making markets out of human needs, finding opportunity in the expert's despair, was Honda's entry into the auto industry. The first results were less than auspicious: a sports car that wowed the connoisseurs of engines, but failed in the market; a minicar that seated just two Japanese-sized passengers and was tipsy at its top speed of fifty miles per hour. Even when the research and development team actually produced a motor, the CVCC (compound vortex controlled combustion engine), which eliminated most pollutants by burning or suppressing them in the combustion chamber, it was unclear that Honda could design a marketable chassis for it or that Honda's motorcycle salesmanship could suffice in the auto market. Nonetheless, while the research project was still under way, Honda had boldly constructed a huge new factory to manufacture its expected new cars. Moreover, there was good news from the United States. The Environmental Protection Agency approved the CVCC prototype as meeting all pollution requirements without the use of a catalytic converter or unleaded gasoline.

Although Detroit experts dismissed the feat, saying it was applicable only to minicars, Honda's engineers then set out to adapt first a Chevy Vega and then two Chevy Impalas to the CVCC formula. These modified cars were brought to the United States in the fall of 1973 and again, much to the embarrassment of Detroit, passed the EPA tests, with only modest reconstruction of the engines and an actual improvement in fuel economy. Honda had demonstrated its possession of a truly unique technology. At the same time, it was beginning to show some success in selling its new Civic in Japan with ordinary motors. Ford applied to sell it in the United States with the CVCC engine.

At that point, in 1974, however, Honda incurred what appeared to be two terminal setbacks, one self-inflicted, one partly imposed by OPEC. In a move exactly paralleling an earlier decision by Sony to sell all its products under its own name in the United States, Honda rejected the Ford offer. That decision, though appealing to company vanity and long-term goals, drastically reduced and delayed foreseeable sales in the United States. The second catastrophe was the worst recession in the postwar history of Japan, causing auto purchases to plummet about a third in the first quarter of 1974, while consumer prices lurched up some 2 percent a month. That seemed to portend a drastic reduction of potential sales and profits in Japan.

Honda, however, like Willie Durant in 1908 and Henry Ford in 1910, turned dire recession into a radical break in the history of the auto business. Partly because of still-rising demand and partly because of the expense of antipollution devices and the pressure of inflation, Japanese automakers had hiked their prices some 8 percent in the fall of 1973 and then by nearly 50 percent in January 1974. Because the hikes merely reflected inflation—with wholesale prices up 57 percent and manufacturing wages up 74 percent between 1972 and 1975—all Japanese auto firms were expected to go along, particularly smaller firms like Honda with shorter production runs and higher unit costs. In the event, all Japanese auto firms did go along, except Honda. By its refusal, Honda in real and competitive terms was radically lowering its prices and assuring huge losses and possible bankruptcy if sales did not massively rise. It was a classic moment of decision in business history, a bold gambit of pricing ahead of the curve. In fact, Honda's price cut was more than twice as large proportionately as the cut by which Henry Ford broke away from the field in 1910.

According to the Galbraithian school of economic analysis, the automotive industry has fundamentally changed since that era. The large companies are now in control, administering prices at will and controlling consumer responses with their huge advertising and marketing campaigns. Honda, new to the industry, commanded no such market power. In essence, it was betting the company that Galbraith was wrong about the very industry on which he focused his argument, even in Japan, a country widely alleged to be a cartelized economy. As Sol Sanders wrote in his excellent company history, the entire automobile industry held its breath to see what would happen.

Within months the outcome was settled. As usual, price elasticities of demand proved unexpectedly high. While Nissan (Datsun) and Toyota saw their sales drop by 40 percent, Honda's sales rose by 76 percent over the previous year in an upward surge which continues still nearly a decade later. Honda's pricing policies, combined with the best technology in the industry—the lowest pollution and highest fuel economy—had created a new automotive titan, the first plausible claimant to the mantle of Henry Ford.

In this case, however, Honda's own presence was primarily in spirit. Although he was reported to have strongly approved, it was his new president and protégé, Kiyoshi Kawashima, who made the decision—the same "Kawashima-san" with whom twenty-three years before Honda had celebrated his "Dream" in a rainstorm at the summit of Hakone Pass with the snowclad peak of Mount Fuji glittering, mysteriously vivid and compellingly near, in the clouds on the distant horizon.

By 1983, Honda was by far the fastest-growing auto company in the world, leaping up the list of the world's largest non-American industrial corporations (it jumped from sixty-eighth to forty-eighth in 1981), passing all Japanese automakers except Nissan and Toyota. More important, it had introduced a new model, the Honda City, which would allow it rapidly to close in on the leaders. A relatively commodious minicar, roomier than the Civic, it goes 68 miles to the gallon (45 mpg in Japanese city driving), surges through a quarter mile in 18.6 seconds, reaching 70 miles per hour, exceeds 90 miles per hour in fourth gear, and costs $3,299 in Japan ($3,631 with a briefcase portable motorbike in the trunk for use in emergencies or for transport from remote parking areas, a common problem in Japanese urban areas). The critic for *Car and Driver* magazine hails the City as "precisely the inexpensive, unpretentious, efficient and fun-to-drive car that we need to put America on wheels again." Another product of one of the company's callow research teams (average age twenty-seven), the new Honda prompted *Car and Driver* to a momentous comparison: "Just as the Model T was the right car for the first 20 years of this century, the Honda City could well be the right car for the last 20 years."

Nonetheless, this car was unavailable in America during the early 1980s. Because of the "voluntary" quotas on Japanese automobiles (termed "voluntary" because they are negotiated by the executive branch rather than enacted as law by Congress), Honda's imports have been severely limited. Like nearly all trade restrictions, the quotas brought results both perverse and ironic. The chief initial beneficiaries may well have been Nissan and Toyota, whose established market shares were protected against Honda. The chief business victims of the agreement may well turn out to have been General Motors, Ford, and Chrysler, which were faced with Honda's response: a new stress on its fancier up-market entries, the Accord and sporty new Prelude. Honda also opened a new production facility for these models in Ohio, which is projected to increase Honda's U.S. sales by 40 percent.

Inevitably hurt the most, however, were America's consumers and the businesses that serve them. By reducing as much as 50 percent the costs of automobile transportation for its purchasers, the City could have conferred a substantial stimulus to the American economy, releasing funds for growing businesses of all kinds, while in all likelihood encroaching little on Detroit's most profitable lines. In this age of economic self-abuse, though, "voluntary" trade restraints are very popular. They offer the throngs of Washington masochists as much pain and as small benefit as tax hikes and price controls without requiring the embarrassment of public enactments.

Honda is likely to surmount such obstacles of the U.S. government as easily as it overcame the obstruction of MITI. Like Sony, it is one of those great entrepreneurial companies that seem to feed on resistance and grow stronger. The question is whether these companies are in any way characteristically Japanese. Both have avoided heavy dependence on Japanese banks, both have pioneered in American equity markets, both have led their industries in building American facilities for both manufacture and marketing. Both, in the midst of meritocratic Japan, disparage the importance of academic credentials: Honda boasts only eight years of education; the well-schooled Morita even wrote a Japanese bestseller in the mid-1960s that scandalized many with its title, *Don't Mind School Records.* Some observers feel that the two companies are extraordinary anomalies in Japan—rare products of unique personalities during a period of postwar opportunity and turmoil—and that their like will not be seen soon again. As Japan faces increasing problems of pollution, overpopulation, and resource scarcity, so the argument goes, the government role in the economy will necessarily become increasingly powerful and inescapable and innovation will require ever larger business and bureaucratic structures, leaving little or no room for entrepreneurs like Honda and Ibuka.

This argument has been familiar to the United States for several decades now, and its proven fatuity here should give pause to its proponents with regard to a country that proportionately generates twice as many business starts as the United States, boasts seven times as many small manufacturing companies, and maintains reserves of savings, available to business, at least twice as large as comparable American funds. In addition, a quick perusal of the Japanese scene will reveal scores of entrepreneurs who have accomplished as much as Honda and Ibuka did at comparable ages, and with no more government aid.

Consider, for example, Kazuo Inamori, president of Kyocera, formerly Kyoto Ceramic. Though the company's name may suggest plates and pottery, ceramics in Japan represent the next step in the continuing alchemy of modern science, epitomized by the transformation of the silicon in beach sand into mind and memory. Japanese ceramic firms, led by Kyoto, are transforming the metal oxides that constitute 90 percent of the earth's crust into an array of products, new and old, from ceramic auto engines to synthetic but real rubies and emeralds. The jewels are now being mounted for Kyoto by top designers and retailed by Inamori in Beverly Hills. "Inamori's folly," say some, but Inamori offers the usual refrain: "It's the same with any new technology. You create the market."

Inamori's chief product, however, the one that projected Kyocera into the spotlight of the Japanese press as the country's best-managed and most impressively performing company in 1979, is electronic insulators. Joining the two prime feats of modern alchemy—the metamorphosis of both sand and dirt into industrial resources—Inamori commands 80 percent of the market for ceramic packages for the most dense and stress resistant semiconductor chips. From this foundation of a near-billion-dollar company, Inamori in the early 1980s entered the already overcrowded fray in personal computers, apparently another of Inamori's follies.

His eye for technical opportunity, however, made Kyocera the only Japanese company to break massively into the American market. His vehicles were the Tandy 100 and NEC portable computers. *Infoworld*'s product of the year in 1983, the Tandy was the first adequate low-priced lap-sized portable, a 3½-pound machine with an eight-line liquid crystal display and an onboard modem for telephone transmission or reception of data. Popular among writers and newspaper reporters, this device became the first successful truly portable, as opposed to luggable, computer. The NEC machine was similar to the Tandy, but with more memory and without the modem. Together these Kyocera products defined the direction for 1980s developments in personal computing.

Or take the four Kashio brothers—Tadao, Toshio, Kazuo, and Yukio—the founders of Casio, who have pioneered a novel form of specialization: novelty itself in high-quality electronics. Casio produces electronic watches and calculators in such kaleidoscopic profusion and with such rapid price curves that even Matsushita has been confounded. Hardly had Casio's wafer-thin two-inch calculator caught fire in the stores, at a high price, than Casio put the same power on a watch, brought out a model that plays music as well, and radically dropped the price of the now obsolescent original. The Kashios combine the swiftly improving technologies of product creation, such as computer-aided design and manufacturing (CAD-CAM), with a hair-trigger sensitivity to market shifts and customer velleities. Casio thus drastically accelerates the life cycles of its goods and inhibits the exploitation of its ideas by imitators.

Perhaps the most important industrial breakthrough to take place recently in Japan, however, occurred not in such capricious consumer markets but in the more deliberative domain of capital equipment. By 1984, Japan held a large world lead in the crucial area of advanced industrial robotics, with over 100,000 robots in place, nearly 70 percent of the world total and six times more than the United States had. A field that combines several advanced technologies, including computers, semiconductors, lasers, and fiber optics, it is an obvious arena for the huge companies and government-guided cartels for which Japan is sourly celebrated.

Feared for their alleged threat to employment, in fact, robots chiefly eliminate repetitious or dangerous jobs, intricate assembly work, and work near furnaces and radioactive areas that are unfit for humans. By improving the quality of products and lowering their prices, robots generate wealth, and hence new and better jobs, creating in Japan, with perhaps the world's most highly skilled work force, a shortage of skilled manpower and one of the world's lowest levels of unemployment. Because robots can be instructed to perform a variety of tasks in different ways and sequences, moreover, they allow creation of flexible manufacturing systems that can vary the output of a particular manufacturing process in response to changing inventory needs or market demands. In the long run, by reducing the need for expensive retooling of fixed automation facilities, robots can enhance productivity, flexibility, and quality of manufacturing processes while economizing on both labor and capital.

That this vital technology was a clear national imperative for Japan—a country dependent on manufacturing prowess to pay for its lifesaving imports of food and fuel—did not escape the notice of the Ministry of International Trade and Industry. But the total of public money channeled into the field during its formative years did not exceed $50 million, a small fraction of the amount invested in robotics research and development alone under U.S. space and defense programs.

To ascribe Japanese success in robots chiefly to this paltry government aid requires an almost mystical belief that MITI combines an invisible hand with a Midas touch. No doubt Japan's government helped, by taking a positive and encouraging stance. In 1980, the depreciation of robots was reduced to six years and a supplementary 13 percent allowance was created. The Japanese Development Bank and other agencies created a national robot-leasing company. There were no suits by government lawyers, as in the United States, opposing robotics research on the grounds that it causes unemployment. But by 1978, when MITI's interest in the subject began to take tangible forms, Japan already had achieved a large lead in robot production over the United States. By 1979 there were already no fewer than 133 Japanese robot producers (about five times the U.S. total), including seventy firms devoted to advanced programmable robots. The reasons for Japan's triumph in this field, as in so many others, are the amplitude of available capital and the vision of private entrepreneurs.

Like most of the technologies spurring Japan's new enterprises, robotics began in the United States, and in many facets of the business the United States still has the technical lead. The United States is losing not in science and research, but in business and production. Kawasaki Heavy Industries ($3 billion sales), for example, licensed the technology from Unimation, the technically advanced but operationally backward U.S. company that introduced the devices in 1962. Still using Unimation technology, Kawasaki has remained the Japanese leader in robot production, providing 1,500 of the machines which gave Japan the world lead in automobile productivity. In 1982, Kawasaki contracted to sell its more reliable version of the Unimate Puma robot to General Motors, the prime U.S. customer for the devices. Unimation had not even automated—or robotized—its own operations and could not seem to compete with its Japanese licensee. In 1982 Joe Engleberger, Unimation's chairman and hero of American robotics, was complaining about too many U.S. entries in the field—some thirty-five—while the number of Japanese companies rose past 200. He spoke whimsically of making a robot for the home. "It might replace the maid," he said.

Robot makers span all of Japanese industry. A quarter of them have fewer than fifty employees; a fifth have capitalization of under $500,000; but nearly all of them have access to loans and a keen sense of the nature of the marketplace and what is at stake in the world's economy. Far from a special hothouse product of government planning, the nation's robotics industry is a mostly spontaneous expression of the intense competitiveness of Japanese capitalism. Companies from all industries—from steel and screws to pens and semiconductors, from mighty Hitachi to tiny Ant—have played a part, beginning in the welter of their home market and overflowing into the world economy.

As Japanese robots now enter the United States, they manifest once again the complementary nature of these two leading economies. Hitachi, for example, normally has followed a strategy of testing and perfecting its process technologies first on its own formidable line of some 40,000 products, from TVs to nuclear power plants, before making sales to its outside customers in Japan or moving abroad. In 1981, however, it licensed most of its robotic equipment to two American firms, one large, one small, and Hitachi's technology now plays a significant role in what has been dubiously termed the reindustrialization of America. Hitachi's robots are crucial to the ambitious plans of General Electric, America's Hitachi, to transform U.S. factories by combining the dominantly American technologies of computer-aided design and manufacture, automated warehouse management, and office electronics with heavily Japanese robotics. General Motors, moreover, has joined with Fujitsu-Fanuc to form a jointly owned robotics firm in America to provide devices for GM and other American firms.

Big companies alone, however, never saved an industrial economy. Hitachi is also granting its robotic technology to one of the most promising of all America's young technology firms, Automatix of Burlington, Massachusetts. Started by Philippe Villiers, cofounder of Computervision, a world CAD-CAM leader, Automatix has assembled some of the country's top robotics experts to provide complete turnkey programs for automating industrial plants. Villiers and his associates chose Hitachi robots for one of their packages.

So Japanese firms are slated for a significant role in reviving U.S. industrial productivity, just as Japan's competition and capitalist success have galvanized the American business, labor, and political leadership to a new recognition of their common interest in economic revival and freedom. Nonetheless, as the 1980s progressed, leadership in applying most of the new technologies of the age remained in the United States and most of the flow in technology licenses still went from U.S. firms to Japanese. And the source of the American edge remained its entrepreneurs, led by the resourceful fanatics of Silicon Valley.

10

AMERICA AS NUMBER ONE

In 1957, about a decade after the invention of the transistor, Western Electric's semiconductor manufacturing plant in Allentown, Pennsylvania, employed 4,000 workers. They produced an unprofitable five transistors a day per worker. In 1983, Western Electric's Allentown plant still employed about 4,000 workers. They were still manufacturing transistors. But they produced some 6.4 trillion of them, or 5.3 million transistors per worker per day: a productivity increase of a factor of 1.06 million. Each of the some 10 million transistors sold from Allentown in 1957 cost about $2.50; in 1983 they sold for thousandths of a penny apiece.

This increase in productivity and decline in price was accompanied by a radical rise in quality. Each of the transistors made in 1983 was far cheaper to operate, far more reliable, and incomparably more useful than the earlier devices. In the late 1950s the transistor was a relatively rare and expensive component, used in pocket radios, hearing aids, and a few other specialized products. By 1983, connected by the scores of thousands in integrated circuits less than a quarter-inch square, transistors had heralded the finally triumphant computer revolution.

In 1957, Western Electric was one of eight American companies manufacturing transistors. By 1983, hundreds of companies commanded some semiconductor manufacturing capability, and some ninety firms were significant producers. But Western Electric was the only one of the original eight to remain a major force in the industry. In large degree, entrepreneurial companies springing up in the late 1960s and early 1970s—and then again in the late 1970s and early 1980s—had come to dominate semiconductor production and innovation.

After thirty-five years of producing chips for use by the telephone company, Western in 1983 was preparing to sell the devices on the open market for the first time. But the industry had developed to the point where the entry of this telephone leviathan was greeted in Silicon Valley less with fear than with indifference, accompanied with doubts that the unionized giant could compete in this cost-driven business.

Strangely, this saga of soaring productivity growth and plummeting prices has had little impact on the statistics of GNP, inflation, and productivity compiled in Washington. The bulk of chips go into computers and related instruments. Yet the Bureau of Economic Statistics can discover no evidence of their presence. In fact, the BES explicitly assumes that computers have been rising in price at a rate of 1 percent a year. Because the price of chips and of the computers they drive has been dropping at an exponential pace, the number crunchers in the government—who weigh the productivity of American labor by the inflation-adjusted market value of their product—almost entirely miss the heroics of the Allentown 4,000 and the rest of the workers in the semiconductor industry. The real yield of the semiconductor advances has been passed on, mostly free of charge and devoid of notice, to the world's consumers.

Joel Popkin, a former assistant commissioner for prices at the Bureau of Labor Statistics, estimates that the assumption of constant computer prices over the last twenty years has led to a cumulative 5 percent underestimate of the real level of GNP. That would mean, very roughly, a $150 billion mistake. The error arises when the statisticians adjust nominal GNP for the level of inflation. By failing to recognize the plummeting real price of computers, springing from their rising quality and expanding functions, the government assumes a higher rate of inflation and a lower rate of production and productivity than is actually occurring. Further evidence of the problem comes in the Standard Industrial Classification Manual, used to catalogue the economy for all detailed data collection. Among the eighty-four "major industry groups" recognized in its pages are tobacco and leather goods, but computers are lost in the field of "electrical machinery."

Even Popkin's estimate of a cumulative 5 percent error in GNP understates the significance of the government's computer oversight. Computers are not just another product, accounting for some 2 percent of national output. In the form of microprocessors and other semiconductor chips embodying software and functional intelligence, they lend marginal features and utility, reliability and appeal to most of the fastest-growing consumer products. In the form of computer-aided design, manufacturing, and engineering ar, they create the flexible and adaptive systems that are raising competitiveness of U.S. companies at ever lower capital costs. In the form of fuel use regulators and emission controllers, they allow heavy industry to restrict energy usage and pollution.

In most of these applications, computers are enhancing not the mechanical power, unit volume, resource usage, or other quantitative dimensions of a product, but its quality, features, value added, and dependability. The computerized "cabbage patch" blooms with a different doll for every child; one automobile assembly line can efficiently produce cars of every model and color, with an ever-expanding array of special features. The solid-state TV set can be made small and portable, or expanded into an entertainment medium tapping scores of channels, using video tapes and disks, and serving as a monitor for games and computing. Its microchip controls mean it virtually never breaks down. It is a product incomparably more useful than the TVs of the past to which it is compared, with relatively small adjustment in the data for quality changes. Microchips, produced by the billions by U.S. semiconductor firms, add similarly expanded powers in smaller packages to home appliances, mechanized tools, telephones, security systems, cameras, watches, sewing machines, and typewriters, among other homely products lazily tabulated by the BES.

Just as important are the scores of entrepreneurial companies providing the new producer durables that led the 1983 recovery. According to an MIT study, the new electronic capital gear yields twice the productivity increase per dollar of investment as conventional machinery. Leading the world in adoption of these devices, the United States has achieved major breakthroughs in capital efficiency virtually absent in the data. With its increasing focus on high technology, a dollar of investment in the United States supports a substantially greater expansion of real though largely unmeasured GNP and productivity than a quantitatively equal addition to the capital stock of Europe or even Japan.

The United States is purchasing no more capital equipment and few more televisions than in the past. But the equipment yields greater returns, more flexibility, and higher quality, while the TVs incorporate in their increasingly digital systems far more potent features. As Paul Hawken has put it in his book *The Next Economy*, the dominant trend in the U.S. system since the energy crisis of the early 1970s is a continuing change in the ratio of *mass*—energy and material—to information—utility, functionality, software, intelligence, craft, durability—in the goods and services produced. The colossal blunder in measuring computer prices thus reveals and symbolizes a fundamental incapacity to measure economic growth, capital accumulation, productivity, or inflation in an entrepreneurial economy undergoing a technological revolution and entering what is sometimes termed the age of knowledge or information industries.

This failure of economic understanding has led to a widespread blindness to a major American triumph in the real economy. For this new age is dominantly an American age, and the revolution is mainly an American revolution. Not only did most of the central technologies originate in the United States, but the U.S. lead in using them is still growing. To make a computer requires chips, but to apply it to useful work requires software. A computer without software is like a record player without records or a television set without programs. As a result of a frenzied rise in software entrepreneurship, encompassing thousands of new firms, the United States in 1984 commanded some four times more software and eight times more software engineers and perhaps twenty times more software entrepreneurs than Japan, its closest rival in the field.

As a result of this lead in software, the United States has opened a decisive lead in the application of the new computer technologies. Between 1981 and mid-1983, for example, U.S. purchases of information tools, mostly computers, rose by 33 percent, compared to rises of some 22 percent from a far lower base in Japan and Europe. With the recovery of 1983 and 1984, sales of producer durables—which sparked the economic revival by rising at four times the average first-year pace of previous recoveries—continued to surge, spearheaded by high-technology gear, which rose at an annual rate of 18.7 percent in real terms.

Less than 20 percent of capital equipment as recently as 1977, computers and associated products rose to more than one-third of all producer durables. High-technology capital stock per worker in the information industries, which had risen 28 percent since 1978 and more than doubled in computers, leaped forward through 1983 and into 1984. As information workers rose from 42 percent to 56 percent of the work force in fifteen years, investment per information worker surged from one-third the level per manufacturing worker to just 7 percent less. Ironically, this U.S. lead in applying high technology produced an increase of high-technology imports—mostly components and peripherals based on U.S. designs—that many observers mistook as a sign of a U.S. technical lag.

Even in the manufacture of hardware—computers and the chips

that make them possible—the United States has lost little ground. Although the Japanese lead the world in efficient electronic manufacturing, the United States in 1983 retained some 75 percent of the world market in computers. Even in integrated circuits (the most complex chips), where the Japanese have performed most brilliantly, U.S. market share in 1983 remained over 68 percent, down from 72 percent six years ago. During this period Japan's share rose only from 19 percent to 24 percent, while the European share dropped from 9 percent to 7 percent.

The U.S. semiconductor industry rivals the overall growth of the Japanese economy as the greatest success story of the postwar economic era. In fact, the breakthroughs in chips are turning out to be more important. Although economists tend to judge eras by movements in GNP and other aggregates, history is more inclined to denominate periods—from the age of steam to the atomic era—by their dominant products and technologies. By that measure this is the age of the microchip. Since semiconductors are crucial to nearly all other new technologies, from medical instruments and industrial robotics to bioengineering and space travel, the U.S. lead in this field—together with its edge in software—should give this country a central position in the world economy for years to come.

Nonetheless, some leading industry executives fear for the future. They have been building their infinitesimal castles of silicon for a decade—each one with broader portals and flights of stairs, more manifold gates, more corridors and chambers, more capacious storerooms and intricate mazes than the one before. They were still on the beach, excited and proud to be, in their usual understatement, "sucking in sand and spitting out chips." But despite record sales, the mood of invincibility had been subtly leaking away for several years and they were looking anxiously out toward storms at sea. A few of the leaders were actively seeking government protection from the great "sunami" wave gathering in the East. Protectionism is ordinarily the refuge of a business on the way down. Could it be that industrial cycles had accelerated to the point that these once-triumphant companies, little more than a decade old, were already feeling pangs of mortality?

Taking their cue from the most worried executives, U.S. politicians, journalists, and academic analysts, long indifferent to the technology, have suddenly focused on the semiconductor industry as an American asset in peril. They point to Japanese dominance in the market for what are called commodity memories: mass-produced chips that are used in virtually all computers for storage of data and programs. The industry's best-seller of 1984 was a commodity chip for the immediate retention of short-term data (working storage) called the 64K dynamic random access memory, or DRAM. It stores 64,000 basic units of information (bits) in a pronged plastic package an inch long previously holding 16,000 bits. Thus it quadruples the capacity of every computer memory socket, or with related advances in miniaturizing other components, reduces by 75 percent the size of every computer. Critics of the U.S. industry point to signs that Japan is not only prevailing in 64K DRAMs but also is dominating the next generation of commodity memories, the 256K DRAM, and shows a lead in published designs and prototypes for the megabit (1-million-bit) DRAM as well.

In addition, alarmists bewail the two-thirds rise in Japanese semiconductor exports to the United States in 1983, their apparently large edge in capital expenditures, and their lead in producing chips of gallium arsenide, a chemical hybrid, very difficult to manufacture, that allows faster memory operation. They also stress the Japanese lead to CMOS technology (complementary metal oxide semiconductors). A system of silicon chip design that results in very low power consumption and heat generation, CMOS is needed both for the densest chips (to prevent overheating and static) and for the lightweight, portable, and battery-powered equipment that is now taking over much of the personal computer market.

Such fears of Japan are joined with the observation that commodity chips require ever more expensive capital equipment, purchasable only by the largest semiconductor firms. Since the Japanese semiconductor firms are part of large electronic conglomerates, they are better able to meet the financial demands of the industry than the smaller U.S. merchant companies such as Intel and National Semiconductor that have led U.S. progress in the past. In addition, the Japanese firms, as well as several European producers, are said to benefit from larger governmental research programs and more cheaply available debt than the U.S. companies.

Alarm about the current state of the U.S. semiconductor industry reflects a deeper concern about the sources of technological progress in the contemporary era. Although admitting that entrepreneurs played a significant role in the rise of the U.S. industry, many analysts conclude that government intervention was critical to semiconductor development in both Japan and the United States and will be still more critical in the future. The age of the entrepreneurial start-up is believed to be over in major semiconductor products. The breakthroughs of the future will come to those countries that best manage a collaborative effort between government bodies and giant corporations such as IBM, Hitachi, and Siemens of Germany.

In such a contest, Japan, so the theory goes, has the crucial advantage of long experience in semiconductor industrial policy on the part of its governmental Ministry of International Trade and Industry. MITI since the early 1970s has officially targeted semiconductors as a growth industry, and in 1977 it launched a $250 million research and development cartel combining Japan's five largest electronic companies in an effort to accelerate the nation's move into very-large-scale integrated (VLSI) circuits. By 1979 the project had apparently borne fruit: Japanese firms captured 40 percent of the world market for 16K DRAMs, the memory generation that preceded the 64K device. And by 1981 Japan had taken more than 70 percent of the world market for the 64K memory.

According to the theory, Japan had targeted the U.S. chip industry just as it had targeted U.S. steel and auto companies. Soon, it was said, semiconductors might go the way of those previous American bastions of industrial strength. Semiconductor industry executives would soon be vying with textile men and beet sugar lobbyists for the parking slots of the handicapped outside the Capitol. But this time, national security as well as the future of the U.S. economy would be at stake, since these high-technology products are central to the fastest-growing and most militarily sensitive industries.

Along with the belief that MITI was chiefly responsible for Japan's success came a theory that U.S. semiconductor triumphs were largely a product of the inadvertent industrial policies of the Pentagon and the National Aeronautics and Space Administration. This notion benefits from circumstantial evidence. The military was the first and largest customer for the silicon transistor, and the Minuteman missile and the space programs were the leading early users of the integrated circuit. In addition, computers constituted a large share of the early civilian market for chips, and the chief early purchaser of computers was Washington. Pointing to this evidence—the smoking gun or missile site—the academic detectives declare that they have solved the mystery of Silicon Valley: how a relatively small group of individual engineers and entrepreneurs could have created the world's most important industry. Obviously, say the investigating professors, the government did it. In Japan it was MITI; in the United States it was NASA and DARPA (the Defense Advanced Research and Projects Administration).

Since the Japanese and European governments have the most comprehensive plans for electronic technology, the analysts believe that the future will be in Japan and Europe. American policy intellectuals yearn for charismatic concepts, futuristic projects, and visionary verbiage, particularly when combined with the magic of governmental money managed by men with advanced degrees. The theorists, therefore, bow before MITI plans and subsidies for the age of information.

All the theories, however, collide with the details of real technological progress and with the small matters of sequence and cause and effect. A detective might ask, for example, how MITI could have launched the Japanese miracle in semiconductors when the MITI program followed the industrial breakthroughs it is alleged to have caused. Similarly, it makes far more sense to maintain that the U.S. semiconductor industry made possible the Minuteman missile and the man on the moon than to argue that the military and space programs created the semiconductor industry.

The three most critical technologies in the early stages of the semiconductor industry all emerged without Pentagon or NASA aid. In 1948, when William Shockley, John Bardeen, and William Brattain of Bell Laboratories invented the transistor, Bell had yet to receive its first postwar military contract. Wartime research in atomic explosives and radar had diverted Shockley and his team from solid-state projects and delayed the development of the new device. Bell initially feared the Pentagon would further impede progress in the field by classifying the transistor, which was smaller, lighter, cooler, and more durable than the unwieldy vacuum tube that at the time accounted for fully half of all malfunctions in military gear. It was not until three years later, however, that defense officials showed major interest in the new technology.

The next breakthrough was the invention of transistors made of silicon, which could endure more heat and were therefore more valuable for military and other harsh environments than the original semiconductors made of germanium. This seminal development occurred at a small company called Texas Instruments, whose capital outlays for semiconductor research in 1953 and 1954 exceeded its entire gross earnings. TI certainly hoped to gain military contracts through its silicon research, but it was also seeking a way to create more hardy and portable seismic gear for its oil exploration arm. TI received no subsidies from the industrial policy of the time—the $50 million Production Engineering Measures (PEM) program administered by the Air Force between 1952 and 1964 to build up semiconductor manufacturing capabilities in private industry.

Similarly, the integrated circuit was invented first at TI and then at Fairchild with no direct government aid and in the face of government assistance for alternative forms of miniaturization. The PEM grants concentrated on such technologies as micromodules—small building blocks, each containing a transistor—that could be easily linked to form large electronic circuits. Fairchild initially forswore government contracts and developed the planar production process, which eventually enabled hundreds of thousands of transistors to be integrated on a single chip.

Afterward government demand gave this technology a major boost. Although Fairchild intended to pursue industrial and consumer markets, such as television electronics, the space program suddenly created a high-priced market for every integrated circuit the company could produce. An Air Force captain named Richard Alberts pushed TI into deep participation in the Minuteman program. But the invention itself was neither anticipated nor subsidized by Washington.

Washington's direct assistance, moreover, contributed little to later commercial success. Some 80 percent of the PEM grants went to Western Electric (to which they were small change) and to the vacuum-tube leviathans General Electric, Raytheon, Sylvania, RCA, Philco-Ford, and Westinghouse. Throughout the period of these subsidies, their recipients lost market share to essentially unsupported rivals, and all but Western Electric eventually left the semiconductor business altogether. (They have been struggling ever since to buy their way back in, without marked success.)

The problem was partly that the PEM monies often were attached to technologies that proved fruitless, and partly that the recipients were unwilling to exploit useful research that threatened their still-growing markets for vacuum tubes. In the end, this first venture in industrial policy was of little help to most of the key firms in the industry and was of scant importance even to the wealthy labs of Western Electric, the major early producer of semiconductor patents, and far ahead of the military in understanding the technology.

The decade between 1963 and 1973 provided a further test of the relative contributions of government policy and private creativity in fostering the semiconductor revolution. As the military and space markets for integrated circuits rapidly declined in proportion to industrial and consumer markets, the industry took off. Some fifty-five companies sprang up from the Fairchild family tree alone. The dynamic RAM, the erasable programmable memory (EPROM), the handheld calculator, the digital watch, and the microprocessor were launched. The invention of metal oxide semiconductors (MOS) and silicon gate technologies galvanized the industry.

Overall, during this period of governmental neglect, semiconductors became the driving force of growth and progress on the frontiers of the world economy and the indispensable fuel of the computer revolution. Meanwhile, TI, which continued heavy reliance on defense contracts, saw its market share in integrated circuits decline almost by half between 1964 and 1967 alone—from an industry-leading 32 percent to 17 percent of a market that had nearly doubled.

In Japan, too, both technological creativity and commercial success have sprung more from private initiative than government policy. In 1977, when MITI launched its VLSI effort, Japanese electronics conglomerates were already making rapid gains against IBM in their domestic computer market and had achieved remarkable momentum in semiconductors. By 1979, Nippon Electric (NEC), Hitachi, and Fujitsu had captured 40 percent of the U.S. market in 16K DRAMs and more than 50 percent of the Japanese market in large, mainframe computers. But the joint research and subsidies that began in 1977 could not have produced this result in items already designed and in mass production in 1977.

Oki and Matsushita, not long ago laggards in semiconductors, were excluded from the 64K VLSI subsidies, but both managed to enter the race anyway in 1982, and two consumer electronics firms, Sanyo and Sharp, entered in 1983. Oki became the world's fastest-growing major semiconductor firm and offered 256K samples before any of the participant companies. Contrary to U.S. reports, Oki developed its own memory technology from its previous efforts in watches and calculators and received no help from the government labs (now privatized) of Nippon Telephone & Telegraph (NTT), the leading customer for Oki's many telecommunications products.

The Japanese research subsidies that cause so much alarm in the United States are relatively small. Consider, for example, MITI's heralded project to develop a computer with artificial intelligence, which can understand the spoken word, recognize objects, and perform more sophisticated reasoning than conventional mainframes. The Japanese government has committed $500 million over ten years to this fifth-generation computer. But Hitachi had a research budget of $600 million in 1981 alone. And Bell Labs' annual research budget is $2 billion. MITI subsidies also pale by comparison with the French government's $4 billion Plan Calcul, a colossal monument to the folly of believing that government funds alone can achieve marketplace success. With a series of allegedly brilliant thirty-five-year-old planners from the Sorbonne pulling and pushing French engineers from one project to another and alternately luring in and kicking out American collaborators, the French have fallen steadily behind small American start-ups in key semiconductor technologies.

In 1984, although the Japanese hold a significant edge in manufacturing efficiency and are rapidly making gains in the laboratory, Americans still lead in the frontier products of semiconductors. In microprocessors, for example—the famous computer on a chip and the central processing unit of all small computers and industrial devices—American companies—chiefly Intel, Motorola, and Zilog—command a monopoly of all the dominant microprocessor designs. Every major personal computer in Japan, as well as most Japanese robots, uses American-designed microprocessors.

Despite a growing Japanese effort, all the most commercially promising devices in the new generation of advanced microprocessors also come from the United States. Because successful new microprocessors, such as devices that handle 32 bits at a time, are most useful if compatible with the software created for earlier machines, a major new entry will be difficult. Although several Japanese and U.S. companies are trying to get a piece of this market, there are no signs of any Japanese advantage. The most impressive new 32-bit microprocessors, in fact, came from National Semiconductor, Hewlett-Packard, and Western Electric. With their software-intensive nature, microprocessors play to the major American strengths in the industry—innovation and software, as opposed to commodity manufacturing. The judicial reinforcement in 1984 of copyright protection for software will help protect the U.S. position.

Beyond microprocessors, Intel has given the United States a significant lead in producing memories that, unlike dynamic RAMs, retain their contents without electric power. Among these nonvolatile memory devices are the so-called magnetic bubble, which provides a solid-state alternative to cumbersome and unreliable disk systems that is much more dependable and easy to use. In 1984 Intel introduced a 4-megabit bubble memory that put the company a whole generation ahead of Japanese competitors then releasing 1-megabit devices. Intel also began mass production of the world's smallest 256K EPROMs, a memory device more complex than a DRAM, and released prototype CMOS DRAMs comparable to Japanese offerings. In 1984, Advanced Micro Devices (AMD)—long an imitator of Intel—leapfrogged the older firm to provide a 512K EPROM.

Far from depressing the United States industry, the Japanese challenge has galvanized American companies to more efficient and resourceful performance. When Hewlett-Packard announced two years ago that Japanese RAMs showed fewer defects than American parts, U.S. firms responded with a quality campaign that readily closed the gap. When the Japanese moved impressively into CMOS, a technology invented and then largely forgotten by the Americans, U.S. companies launched a drive to excel in that crucial technology and were little behind by the middle of 1983. When the Japanese targeted the U.S. industry with collaborative projects, the Americans initiated an array of cooperative research and development projects of their own, some of them part of the Pentagon's VHSIC (very-high-speed integrated circuits) program.

Nonetheless, the long-term American prospect in semiconductors would remain as gloomy as the pundits claim if the U.S. had to depend on its established companies alone for its future. The leading Japanese firms have been increasing their capital spending and research at an annual pace nearly twice as fast and have been playing a steadily more dominant role at international technical conferences on the technology. The Japanese are graduating some twice as many electronic engineers annually as the United States, and the mathematical skills of Japan's average high school graduate excel the performance of America's top 10 percent. Japanese engineers seem to remain with their companies—and stick with particular projects—more tenaciously than their American counterparts.

The key reason the U.S. is keeping pace with this juggernaut and will probably retain its lead in the future is not the contribution, however impressive, of IBM, Bell Labs, research collaboration, or VHSIC. The key to the future of the U.S. industry is that like the U.S. auto industry competing with the technically superior Europeans early in the century, the U.S. semiconductor industry is dramatically ahead in entrepreneurs. In every field, from CMOS to gallium arsenide and semiconductor CAD-CAM, the United States is spawning start-ups. Like the now large firms of the new-company surge of the 1960s, these firms are full of fighters and fanatics: men with a lust for contest, a gleam of creation, and a drive to justify their break from the mother company; immigrants fighting for vindication and place, seeking to justify their break from the mother country; engineers with an equity stake and a vision of perfection.

Perhaps the most promising development in memory technology, for example, is the E-square PROM (electrically erasable programmable read-only memory). It represents a significant step toward the technical ideal of a cheap nonvolatile device that keeps its contents when the power goes off but is readily accessible for reading and writing like a RAM. Such a device allows the continual adaptation of software to new conditions (for example, in automobile engines as the weather shifts or in point-of-sale terminals as prices change). It allows the repair and revision of video games or the updating of credit cards over the telephone. A further development of Intel's splendid EPROMs, this technology was technically defined and dominated in 1984 by a five-year-old spinoff from Intel called Xicor, led by an Israeli immigrant named Raphael Klein. A three-year-old spinoff called SEEQ was only slightly behind, and several other start-ups were rushing up in their wake. In CMOS, newcomers have begun at least ten significant firms driving to overtake the Japanese, and one of them, Integrated Device Technology led by British and Taiwanese immigrants, was already producing the world's fastest CMOS RAMs. Close behind was a firm begun by a brilliant young Stanford graduate named T. J. Rodgers, who invented a briefly fashionable process called VMOS while he was still in school.

Outside the realm of major commodity products, entrepreneurs are exploiting the U.S. software advantage to create literally hundreds of companies for the production of custom and semicustom chips. Expected to command some 40 percent of the world semiconductor market by the end of the decade, these items are made for a particular use and customer and depend on the development of ever more sophisticated computer-aided design and manufacturing (CAD-CAM) software. In essence, the knowledge of America's some 3,000 chip design engineers is reduced to software packages that can be used by America's some 300,000 computer and systems engineers for rapid creation of special-purpose chips. With CAD-CAM, manufacturers of computer systems can order chips with unique functional specifications and get them back from the semiconductor foundry in a matter of weeks rather than years. The custom market is the fastest-growing area of the industry. Since it requires enormous creativity in software and intimate responsiveness to the customer, the United States should be able to overcome the Japanese challenge in this field.

For all the attainments and potentials of U.S. semiconductor firms, the Japanese remain extraordinarily potent competitors who will probably continue to gain share in the exploding chip markets of the coming decade. But their ascendancy, largely in manufacturing chips from American design, poses little threat to the U.S. industry. In fact, the Japanese challenge has probably been beneficial to the U.S. semiconductor industry as well as to U.S. systems houses making computers and other chip-based gear. Any further effort to exclude Japanese chips from American markets will likely hurt the U.S. economy more than the Japanese.

In 1982 the Americans enhanced their reputation as inscrutable occidentals by launching suits at once charging the Japanese with dumping and with price-fixing 64K DRAMs. But stopping 64K DRAM shipments from Japan would have provided little help for American companies. Never capable of fulfilling alone the surging demand from the makers of personal computers, by mid-1983 they had allowed their lead times to stretch beyond five months.

The chief victims of protection would have been American makers of personal computers, which could not have filled their DRAM sockets without help from Japan. The chief beneficiaries would have been Japanese personal computer makers, among them, ironically enough, Hitachi, Nippon Electric, and Fujitsu, the three leading Japanese semiconductor firms.

Still the Japanese mastery in the manufacture of DRAMs was portentous for American companies. Because DRAMs are a commodity used in virtually all electronic gear, their potential market looms in the billions of units. Companies that can master this manufacturing challenge gain experience that can be applied to all other chips. Thus DRAMs were the item that most of the major electronics firms of the world and many of their governments targeted for priority development. DRAMs were the device that would ultimately generate the largest long-term profits by giving successful producers the lowest costs for all chips. And DRAMs were the product that led many leaders of major companies to despair of the future of the U.S. industry and to predict the demise of American companies in major commodity markets.

In particular the challenge of the 64K DRAM frustrated Texas Instruments for several years, forced National Semiconductor to turn to Oki for a workable design, drove Advanced Micro Devices to withdraw from the field, balked Intel until early in 1983, left Motorola with an unworkable chip vulnerable to alpha rays, found IBM with a device too slow for many uses, and altogether confounded ITT, Siemens, Phillips, and several government-subsidized leviathans in France. Most of the world's leading electronics firms struggled and failed after expenditures approaching $100 million. By the end of 1982, with Texas Instruments facing a recall crisis and even Intel failing to produce its chip in volume, it appeared as if the 16K story would be repeated, but with higher stakes, as the Japanese charged in to exploit the disarray and disability of American memory producers. Scarcely an expert remained who did not grant to the Japanese firms a dramatic victory in the battle of the 64K DRAM. Gloom befell the U.S. industry, as its followers balefully contemplated the possible consequences of Japanese dominance on the frontiers of this technology—the driving force behind the most rapidly growing industries of the era.

At that point, however, in the first week of 1983, an American company made an astonishing announcement. In a declaration as amazing in its way as tiny TI's announcement of the silicon transistor and the integrated circuit early in the history of the industry—and three-year-old Intel's proclamation of the microprocessor in 1971—this American firm took the world lead in DRAM technology.

The company that restored to the United States the technical lead in 64K DRAMs was not Western Electric or IBM or Mostek or any of the established firms of the industry, though all would revive impressively in 1983 and 1984. Contrary to all the resolute assertions by every expert in the field—from Intel founder Robert Noyce to TI chairman Mark Shepherd—that it is "impossible" to launch a successful start-up in the commodity semiconductor business, the new cost and technology leader was an almost totally unknown firm that had shipped its first semiconductor product in October 1981, little more than a year before.

Called Micron Technology, the new company was a Boise, Idaho, consulting firm that decided in 1979 to enter the manufacturing fray in 64K DRAMs without so much as a finished design, a financing plan, or a fabrication facility of any kind. Yet scarcely more than two years later its president, Joseph Parkinson, made a revolutionary announcement of a new 64K DRAM and he revealed his company's shipments of more than a million units of its original chip in 1982, probably exceeding all American producers except TI and Motorola. And he intimated "a major breakthrough" in the design of the 256K DRAM.

It was one of the great feats in business history. Industry experts previously had estimated that to create the cheapest possible facility for production of advanced semiconductor devices would cost some $37 million in the first year: $19 million on plant and equipment and $18.5 million on personnel. But the established firms had spent an average of well over $100 million apiece to launch their own 64K devices. The Japanese had poured some $250 million into a collaborative research project between government and private industry largely devoted to developing the product. The British government had lavished nearly $200 million on Inmos, a company that was also mandated to enter the industry in 64K DRAMs, but by 1982 was producing less than one-tenth as many units as Micron. Indeed, the apparent failure of Inmos, despite its access to the British treasury and command of some of the top talent in memories, seemed to prove the futility of Micron's attempt to start at the top in this most sophisticated and demanding of all industries.

Yet Micron did it. The way it did it shows once again that the crucial capital of industry is not money or machinery, but mind and spirit, and that America—in these crucial domains of enterprise—remains number one.

11

THE RISE OF MICRON

The building stands a few miles east of Boise, off Interstate 84 and the old Federal Highway, the Oregon Trail to the Pacific Northwest. It is a desert land, fraught with dire history, strewn with gold glints from the eyes of prospectors and with the parched bones of coyotes and wild horses, and of men who never made it through the mountains to the coast.

It is also a land of business legends, of men who abandoned visions of gold and got rich on potatoes; where the father of Micron's building contractor finally gave up the ghost of his Model A and his dreams of Alaskan wealth, settling instead for life in Idaho, building heavy machinery. It is the home of J. R. Simplot and the saga of his patch of Idaho sand. It is the land to which inventor Allen Noble fled his Montana home, at age fourteen, and began milking cows and growing potatoes. It is the home of the Parkinson twins—Ward and Joe—and now it is the home of Juan Benitez.

It is the land where Farris Lind built up the state's largest oil company out of his sense of humor while sealed in an iron lung. Micron workers daily pass one of Lind's famous billboards on their way to work. "Just 84 miles to Bliss, Idaho. Stop at the Stinky," it proclaims. It is signed by a cute skunk, the trademark Lind adopted after the name he once was called by a rival resentful of Lind's low prices and rising market share. But it also bespeaks Lind's indomitability: stricken by polio from the neck down, unable to speak except on the inhale of his breath, he nonetheless led his chain of gas stations to preeminence on the highways of the state. He died in 1979, the year Micron was born.

The low-slung 50,000-square-foot structure stood without a name for several months. It was thought to be a new outpost of Hewlett-Packard, the largest electronics employer in the state. To the embarrassment of the owners, some of the workers dubbed it "the Manhattan Project," a bad joke on the company's secrecy and its goal of excelling the Japanese chip makers. More to the point, sitting in its bleak eminence four miles from the mountains and surrounded by striped asphalt, it looked like any typical transplant from any corner of Silicon Valley. But with the encroaching sagebrush and Grant's Truck and Car Stop down around the corner, not to mention the KOA Trailer Park and Idaho Used Car Auction Company, it seemed a transplant that probably would not take— that would be rejected by the surrounding tissue of economic scrap and salvage, and be pushed into Isaac's Canyon down the road.

Yet despite all appearances the Micron building differed critically from similar structures in Santa Clara County. There was a hard core of Idaho austerity behind all the architectural longing for the shade of palm trees. The parking lot was filled with old pickups and Chevys, with no flash of a California Porsche or Ferrari. There were goats and turkeys and guinea hens cleaning up around the two pools of green waste water on the edge of the grounds, bespeaking Micron's farming roots and its need to dispose of all its own refuse. Most important, the facility took half as long to build as similar plants in California, and cost one-quarter as much.

In charge of the construction was Juan Benitez, who as manager of facilities for two years at Mostek had never been allowed to build a new plant. After Mostek had been taken over by United Technologies, Benitez explained, it lost its managerial flexibility: "It was a place where if you begin in facilities management you die in facilities management." In frustration he had sold his house in Dallas and with his wife and child had left for Micron in October 1980, a month after the groundbreaking. He had understood over the phone, and had told his wife, that it was a ninety-man company. He was surprised to discover that the correct number was nine. He also found that the building design, done by outside consultants, was inadequate. The company, moreover, turned out to be even more flexible than he had bargained for. Even though Micron had no building fund, facilities designer, or working chip, the Idahoans had rushed to install the foundation and erect a shell before the early winter snows. It was all unexpected. But Benitez had left Cuba at age fifteen, headed for America, with no assurance of anything. He had arrived in Mexico City and gone to Canada before finally making it to Kansas City. Faced with the unexpected in Boise, Benitez was serene.

It was not to be an ordinary semiconductor construction job. The Micron facility would have to meet the most exacting challenge of manufacturing in the history of the industry: It would have to produce millions of 64K DRAMs each month, each chip with ten layers of differently treated silicon, containing more than 100,000 transistors, with millions of details of less than 3-micron dimensions inscribed on each layer by a photolithographic process that could admit virtually no particle of dust or hint of vibration. There was one further detail Benitez learned: the facility would have to be cheaper than any other such plant in the industry.

Although Benitez had never run a construction project before, he had seen many from the inside in his role managing maintenance at Mostek. Ignoring problems of funds, he went to work. To save money, the Micron building was largely constructed not of steel but of laminar wood. The building contractor, Ron Yanke, a major figure in the history of Micron, executed the bricks and mortar essentially at cost. Purchasing only the most indispensable equipment and eschewing all redundancy, Benitez resolved on an open-ended scheme that would allow them to add gear as the money came in. In a key decision, Benitez and Parkinson also decided to eschew the hundreds of one-horsepower fans conventionally installed in the ceilings for atmospheric management, in favor of five huge fans in an outside facility that impelled all the air through some four miles of air ducts.

Although the building process seemed fraught with confusion and crisis at the time, it ended by exceeding industry standards for dust-free clean rooms and meeting all deadlines. The ultimate test came in early 1983 when central Idaho was jolted by an earthquake that caused havoc in many parts of the state and terrified Ward Parkinson in his house on a hill overlooking Boise. Benitez in the fabrication area ("fab"), though, never knew the quake had occurred.

By May 1981, the company was moving in, and by August the momentous matter of wafer fabrication began. Micron was well on its way to one of the most extraordinary feats in the history of American enterprise. Emerging from the life and character of particular men, it was the expression of a deeply American art of creation.

* * *

Born and brought up in Blackfoot, Idaho, Joe and Ward Parkinson were sons of a local insurance agent and his schoolteacher wife. Though identical twins, one of them—probably Ward—is said to have slipped out of the sac. In any case, Joe always has been the more sleek and confident of the two brothers. Both are tall and handsome black-haired young men. But Ward shows signs of the absentminded intellectual, speaking in abrupt bursts sometimes hard to follow, while Joe commands the silken rhetoric of a born attorney.

In high school the twins led Blackfoot to the state debating championship. But Joe did most of the improvisatory speeches, leaving Ward to make the prepared statement. Even so, Joe on occasion virtually had to push his brother onto the stage, and at the state finals in Kellogg in remote northern Idaho, he nearly had to carry him there. The night before, already high from the travel and the tensions of the earlier round of debates, Ward on a bet had nearly finished a bottle of vodka in one draft.

Having apparently figured out a sure way to duck the next morning's ordeal, Ward now had to figure out a way to survive. He went into near shock and suffered six hours of retching and pain. But after a bottle of Pepto-Bismol, he announced the next morning with bleary-eyed bravado that he was ready for the showdown debate.

About halfway through his speech, however, he blanched horribly, said he didn't "feel good," and lurched from the stage in a fit of dry heaves. He headed for the door, followed by a gaggle of horrified lady schoolteachers who plied him with tea and sympathy. Somehow he recovered, while Joe managed to defend the UN with sufficient skill to win the day. The pattern of Joe's bailing out his sometimes erratic brother would recur throughout their very different but always strangely intertwined careers.

Both boys worked hard throughout their school years, often in the potato fields that supplied the Simplot empire. From time to time they shoveled manure and did other chores for farmers before school and sold groceries and hardware in local shops afterward. Eventually Ward got a job in a local mental hospital, while Joe rose from grease monkey to a salesman in the parts department of Blackfoot's Chevrolet-Cadillac dealer.

Star students in high school—and "diamonds in the rough" from the point of view of an eastern college's geographic distribution quotas—the twins were approached by Columbia University's local alumni representative, who had been alerted by their friend Terry Bowman, already a student at the college. Bowman persuaded them of the delights of the Ivy League, and they were admitted to the freshman class in September 1965.

On Morningside Heights, pursuing the two safe professions that assured lives of freedom from cowbarns and potato fields back in Idaho, Ward followed a premed curriculum and Joe decided to prepare for the law. But to earn extra money they began working after hours and soon showed signs that they were not destined to return to Blackfoot for routine careers providing legal and medical counsel to the local potato growers. As a "lark" they started a charter airline travel service to Europe, which prospered enough to pay a lot of their bills.

Nonetheless, although Joe thrived at Columbia, Ward found it a strain. When he discovered that medicine entailed endless and depressing study of human diseases, he dropped out and decided to move to more uplifting fields of learning in surroundings more inspiring than upper Manhattan. He entered a program in electrical engineering at Utah State in Logan, high in the mountains, and began to market the travel service to students in the West, while Joe managed the eastern front.

Both brothers graduated in 1969. Joe entered law school at Tulane, where he often led his class, at the same time teaching basketball at a high school in the bayous of Donaldson, Louisiana. Ward, who still seemed distinctly the less promising of the twins, rejected further academic pursuits in favor of work in the research labs at Fairchild Semiconductor in Silicon Valley.

Having suffered a hemorrhage of executives and middle management, Fairchild in 1969 was on the verge of its famous tumble from the summits of the industry. But Ward, immersed in the world of semiconductor electronics, remained oblivious to the tensions and disappointments around him. Within two years, staffing at the lab plummeted from 450 to fifteen, through layoffs and defections. But Ward had joined one of their few successful programs—creation of a new family of logic chips for a new Burroughs mainframe—and he so impressed his bosses that he was dispatched to Stanford for a year of company-financed studies leading to a master's degree in electrical engineering.

When Parkinson finished at Stanford, he rejoined his previous boss at a new start-up called Reticon, where for two years he designed development systems for the company's image sensors—essentially electronic eyes for robots and controllers. (Micron later would introduce a similar product.) But he longed to return to work in semiconductor components: chips. In 1974, he took a chance to go to Motorola in Phoenix, where he drifted toward a fateful and compelling focus on the design of semiconductor memories.

It did not take any special genius on Parkinson's part in 1976 to reach the conclusion that the future of the product lay in metal oxide semiconductors (MOS), a simpler mode of design that would soon dominate the industry. In order to learn MOS memory technology, he knew he would have to move on again to a company and a technical group that could teach it to him. The company he chose was Mostek, the fractious splitoff from Texas Instruments headed by former TI engineer L. J. Sevin (now a leading venture capitalist with semiconductor industry guru Ben Rosen).

Mostek had launched a series of MOS memory innovations. It had invented the standard 16-pin package and was sweeping the field with a brilliant new 4K DRAM introduced in February 1976.

One of Mostek's prime attractions for Parkinson, and a principal source of its design innovations, was Paul Schroeder, a quiet engineer with an MIT doctorate, who headed Mostek's development group and who would have a deep influence on Parkinson's career. But as he continued his work at the company, Parkinson came to understand that a further secret of its success was a homesick young genius from Idaho Falls named Douglas Pitman. In his mid-twenties and the son of a carpenter, Pitman was a thin dark-haired young man with a wife and three children, no checking account, and keen nostalgia for the mountains and sagebrush of Idaho.

Frustrated by the demands of abstract mathematics, Pitman had dropped out of college after just two years at Idaho State in Pocatello. Then he had contracted the silicon fevers during a course on circuit design, sponsored by American Microsystems (AMI). A Santa Clara firm with a plant in Idaho, AMI was looking for local talent. But faced with this youthful embodiment—in admittedly unpolished form—of one of the supreme talents in the industry, AMI let him slip away to Texas. He reluctantly ended up in Dallas, where he performed a key role in the detailed design of many of the memories on which Mostek based its formidable repute and profits.

Ward Parkinson, though, also made key contributions. Working with Schroeder, the sophisticated engineer from MIT, and with Pitman, the untutored prodigy of Pocatello, he designed a series of fast static RAMs which remained profitable for Mostek well into the 1980s. Fast RAMs were useful as a buffer or intermediate memory in computers, speeding them up to rates faster than their dynamic RAMs would allow. Parkinson, foreshadowing insights which would be important at Micron, chose to orient the memory toward the rapidly growing world of 8-bit microprocessors and the emerging market of personal computers. He urged that the memory use the novel scheme of 1K by eight, operating in bits of eight—a byte at a time—which would make it a perfect one-chip buffer in microprocessor applications. It was a correct decision, and it impressed Pitman with Parkinson's acute sense of the marketplace, which was manifested many times at both Motorola and Mostek.

During those years at Mostek, Parkinson felt in his element. He warmly admired Schroeder and had come to respect Pitman deeply. Parkinson's career, designing semiconductor memories, was on track at last. Then in April of 1978, the situation at Mostek changed abruptly for the worse.

The agent of the change was Richard Petritz, a smart and professorial former research director at TI who had founded Mostek with L. J. Sevin in 1969, and who split with him in 1972. Petritz persuaded Parkinson's mentor Schroeder to join him in a new venture. The new firm was to be called Inmos and would create a new generation of futuristic memories directly in competition with his former colleagues. Schroeder promised to contact Parkinson as soon as they found the necessary financing.

The trouble was that in 1978 the American venture capital industry was in a shambles. From a high of over $1 billion raised in the late 1960s, these entrepreneurial funds had plummeted some 90 percent by the mid-1970s as a result of high taxes and inflation. In particular a so-called tax reform of 1969 had doubled the capital gains tax to nearly 50 percent. Start-up firms that normally compensated with stock options for their inability to pay high salaries lost not only their chief source of finance, but also their main means of attracting talent.

Silicon Valley entrepreneurs reacted with a spirit of desperate ingenuity. The designer of IBM's breakthrough 360 series, Gene Amdahl—the world's leading computer architect—could find little money anywhere in the United States and turned in desperation to Fujitsu in Japan to finance his new start-up. Militant Americafirster Jerry Sanders of AMD (Advanced Micro Devices) sold 20 percent of his company to Siemens of West Germany. Federico Faggin, one of Intel's inventors of the microprocessor, started Zilog on a crest of Exxon's "windfall profits." Roy Stata of Analog Devices turned to Standard Oil of Indiana. Fairchild gave up its ghost to the multinational oil services giant Schlumberger. Several companies sold out to Japanese competitors, giving Toshiba, NEC, Toyo, and Seiko new windows into the Valley.

The venture capital solution found by Richard Petritz and Paul Schroeder, though unusual, thus can be understood as a sign of the times. The two American entrepreneurs made an alliance with English Labour MP Tony Benn and his National Enterprise Board and contracted to become nothing less than a prize showcase for British socialism, which had destroyed its own high-tech industry by taxes and red tape. Petritz would get a chance to show his stuff against his old colleague L. J. Sevin, Schroeder would get an opportunity to manage the design of the memories of his dream, and the British taxpayers would get the chance to pay for it all.

The ironies and complexities of the formation and financing of Inmos have confounded endless commissions of British experts from both Labour and Conservative administrations and still defy easy comprehension. It is thus understandable that Ward Parkinson and Douglas Pitman did not quite know what they were doing in July 1978 when they agreed to leave Mostek and join their former boss, Paul Schroeder, in this new venture in semiconductors and socialist politics.

On the part of one principal, however, there was no confusion or uncertainty whatsoever. L. J. Sevin reacted as though he had been raided by redcoats—and turncoats. He dashed for a plane to London, waving legal memoranda, and threatened to sue. His outrage, though, had the unexpected result of dispelling all lingering doubts of some British about the value of their investment. They gave Sevin a bureaucratic shuffle and continued with their plan. Sevin returned to Dallas and filed suit against the Inmos principals, including Parkinson and Pitman, claiming the theft of trade secrets and charging Inmos with an attempt to monopolize the key talent in memories. This antitrust claim assured triple damages if Inmos lost the suit. In addition, Mostek sought an injunction against the practice of engineering by Parkinson and Pitman. The two Idahoans had cut themselves loose from comfortable employment in one of the world's top semiconductor firms in order to become pawns in an international power struggle that could severely damage their careers. Ward did the obvious thing. He called his brother Joe.

While Ward was working himself into this legal pickle in Dallas, Joe had been continuing his ascendancy in the law with a focus on the southern circuit. From the top of his class at Tulane Law School, he went to New York University to edit the *Tax Law Review* and get his master's. In 1973, he returned to New Orleans to clerk for a judge in the Fifth Circuit Court of Appeals, and in 1974 he taught taxes at Tulane while consulting for oil and gas companies. As the energy crisis erupted he was summoned back to NYU to teach oil and gas tax law and work for Baker McKenzie, the prominent New York firm at the Seagram Building on Park Avenue.

The higher he rose and the more money he earned, though, the more dissatisfied he became with the plush carpets and voluminous paper of corporate legal practice. His wife was a lively blonde named Barbara from the mountains of Montana (Ward had followed his brother's example and married her sister Sue). When Barbara announced she was pregnant and "would not raise a baby amid the dog doo of Washington Square," Joe left New York to return to a large firm in Boise. There, his New York colleagues chorused, he would spend his time doing bankruptcies and bills of sale, with an occasional divorce for excitement. They were not entirely wrong.

Joe soon was restive and eagerly accepted Ward's call for help. He flew down to Dallas and threw himself into the case. Going south to help his brother, Joe soon found the crucial help he needed himself. Though he did not know it at the time, Ward was about to resolve all his brother's career uncertainties by providing him the opportunity to enter, in Idaho, a corporate realm far more promising and enthralling than anything going on in New York.

As the litigation proceeded, British qualms about their new project were further allayed by testimony against Inmos from none other than Robert Noyce of Intel. Noyce even buttressed the antitrust charge—the concern that Inmos was monopolizing talent. He dwelled particularly on Pitman, who emerged from the trial as a virtual walking monopoly of talent who had "laid out every high-volume runner that Mostek had."

Nonetheless, halfway through the proceeding, Joe Parkinson managed to get his brother and Pitman dropped from the suit and the injunction lifted against their practice of engineering. This success so impressed Petritz that he hired Parkinson to represent Inmos as well. By the end, three weeks later, Inmos had won on nearly every point and Joe Parkinson was beginning to show severe incipient symptoms of silicon fever.

Inmos's legal victory, however, turned out to be pyrrhic. At least it cost them any claim to a monopoly of memory talent. "One thing you get out of a lawsuit," Ward Parkinson recalls, "is you get to know what's going on." As Inmos's tangled purposes emerged in the testimony, Parkinson, Pitman, and another leading former Mostek memory designer named Dennis Wilson became increasingly disaffected with the company.

In any case, one week after the trial, Ward Parkinson, Dennis Wilson, and Doug Pitman met with Joe Parkinson in the living room of Ward's house in Dallas—three miles from TI headquarters—and took initial steps toward founding Micron Technology as a firm of design consultants. Although Joe did not join in the scheme at the time, the excitement of his brother's entrepreneurial break encouraged him to leave his employer in Boise and strike out on his own shingle. Joe opened offices near the capitol and stood ready to help Ward as needed.

At the time, Micron had no money or work, but its founders

hoped that the publicity from the trial would have served as adequate advertisement of their talents. As they considered their situation, the image of a perfect client began to form in their minds: a firm that produced MOS memories, preferably nearby; a firm with a healthy respect for the talents of Parkinson, Wilson and Pitman; a firm that had heard the tributes from the trial. Three companies came to mind. After rejecting the possibility of Inmos and contemplating the vast mazes of TI, Ward said: "Hey, why not call L.J." He did, and Sevin—for whom the suit had already served its purpose of weakening Inmos—immediately offered a contract for designing memories. The pay seemed too low, so Parkinson demanded free licenses to produce any designs they might develop. As a company without so much as an office, Micron did not strike Sevin as any threat to Mostek as a producer of chips. Sevin readily agreed, and within two weeks after the trial, Micron was on its way.

For a year, Parkinson, Wilson, and Pitman worked in Dallas on various Mostek memory designs, including a 64K dynamic RAM. It was satisfying work but a scarce improvement on working directly for the company. They dreamed of manufacturing memories—"It was a gleam in our eyes," said Parkinson—but they had no source of capital and no realistic plans. Now with four children under school age, Pitman and his wife both had tired of Dallas and longed to return to the mountains. Finally, in November 1978, Parkinson told Pitman to go north and find an office for them.

After stops in Utah and Montana, Pitman arrived in Idaho and was not surprised to discover he liked the environment. He called back to Dallas and told Parkinson that Boise was the place, but that the office market was desperately tight and expensive. Parkinson said, "Give it another day."

Pitman called the next night and said that there was no ordinary space in Boise at a price easily affordable by Micron, but that he had found an unfinished basement in a dentist's office building.

"A what?" asked Parkinson.

"A dentist's basement. We could fix it up," said Pitman. He paused, then added, "I also bought a house."

There was another, longer pause. "Well, I guess we're going to Boise," said Ward. "I hope I can persuade Dennis."

"Don't worry," replied Pitman. "I've got some pictures of the scenery. He'll love it."

Dennis Wilson had been inclined to leave Dallas, but the pictures, which consisted entirely of artful renditions of sagebrush in bloom, prompted him to make a reconnaissance first. Luckily, he, too, decided he wanted to stay in Idaho.

So it was that for the next several months Micron Technology developed semiconductor circuits for a Dallas company in the basement of a dental center in Boise. Then in August 1979, Mostek sold out to United Technologies, which was ignorant of the memory business and hostile to irregular relationships with consultants. Within weeks the deal with Micron was terminated. Micron was cast loose among the mountains and potato fields of Idaho, without even a bit line to Dallas.

As semiconductor firms recently have begun to discover, however, Idaho offers many surprising benisons beyond its ravishing scenery, its ski resorts, and its potatoes galore. For example, its population is tough, hardworking, and open to enterprise. Within that hardy populace, moreover, is the nation's highest concentration of millionaires. A few months before the wind-down with Mostek, Ward Parkinson had done one of them a favor.

The man's name was Allen Noble, one of the state's more phenomenal entrepreneurs. A farmer who had run away from his home in Montana at age fourteen, Noble parlayed the few acres of potatoes with which he started into a vast business in farm development and irrigation projects. Most famous in Idaho is the Snake River hi-lift, which brought water up some 500 feet to transform a desert region called Dry Lake into a booming producer of potatoes and other vegetables. Frustrated with the limitations of existing watering systems, Noble also started a company, Noble Linear Irrigation, which manufactures irrigation equipment.

One day he faced a problem with the electronic controller for a new sprinkler machine he had invented and patented to replace the circular sprinklers prevalent in the business. A huge robot with an arm span half a mile wide, it moved up and down a field spraying more evenly than circular devices, and reaching into corners which other equipment missed. Fabrication of the system had been contracted to a local machine shop run by Ron Yanke, who previously had hired Joe Parkinson. Yanke had built his company from a small firm into a manufacturer of everything in heavy equipment from logging mills to missile containers and mining gear. Yanke had asked Joe Parkinson whether Ward might help out in solving the sprinkler problem.

Ward met with Noble and Yanke and, after warning them that microprocessor applications were not in his area, spent a month working part-time with the two men on the project. They developed a high mutual respect for one another. In due course the design problem was solved and Parkinson returned to his Mostek assignments, which seemed likely to continue indefinitely. The abrupt cancellation of the contract—so Parkinson now believes—was the best thing that ever happened to him. "If I had stayed with Mostek," he says, "it would have been too easy to get fat and happy."

Feeling lean and resolute, if a mite manic, the Parkinsons, Wilson, and Pitman decided in that autumn of 1979 to go into the business of manufacturing 64K dynamic RAMs. They had nothing in hand but a set of unfinished design ideas, which were freely available to them under the Mostek contract, but which had been rejected by Mostek as unsatisfactory. Mostek favored a more ambitious part, "full of bells and whistles." Micron's competitors on three continents—and enlisting four governments in the effort—collectively had spent nearly $2 billion gearing up to produce 64K DRAMs, and several were already distributing sample prototypes. TI had announced impending production of its device. Fujitsu already was in production, albeit with a cumbersome part requiring three different voltage inputs. All the established firms seemed several years ahead of Micron.

Even without the obvious and apparently prohibitive problems of time and finance, the technical challenge was awesome. Several of the leading technical firms in the world struggled mightily, spent lavishly, and failed to do so much as produce a workable part for three years. It was a major technological threshold for the industry.

Yet Micron went ahead. While developing the plans for construction and negotiating with Benitez, Ward Parkinson set out in search of finance. After many dead ends in the circles of sophisticated venture capital, and many articulate explanations of the futility of fighting the Japanese, he was shocked to discover that American semiconductor experts in general had given up on DRAMs, by far the largest market in the industry. In desperation Parkinson turned to his new friends, Yanke and Noble. To his surprise they were enthusiastic about the idea of starting a chip firm. It helped that they had a working relationship with both Parkinsons, a personal knowledge of impossible dreams, and no expertise whatsoever about semiconductors.

But Ward Parkinson was in a dilemma. Although the two magnates seemed eager to proceed, he hesitated to let them put up funds without exposure to a cogent exposition of the formidable facts of the industry. Yet, he thought, the facts likely would end their interest. Nonetheless, Parkinson called L. J. Sevin and shortly afterward the three entrepreneurs—two successful and one foolhardy—left for the Boise airport to fly to Dallas.

They met Sevin in his office at Mostek on August 7, 1979, the day before Mostek's stock doubled in false anticipation of a buy-out by Gould Corporation, a billion-dollar Chicago conglomerate. The slim brown-haired former chip designer greeted them cordially and then gave the appalling news on DRAMs. As Noble remembers, he said it would cost maybe $100 million, and "you'll still be way too late. The Japanese have spent billions and are still expanding their commitment. Heck, you're even so far behind us at Mostek that you don't have a prayer. The industry already lost nearly $300 million on 16K RAMs in 1981 alone. The pricing out there has fallen so far off the learning curve it's on the kamikaze curve, and the Japs will make it crazier in 64Ks. Some of the Japanese firms are ready to offer samples of 256Ks." So it went.

Then Sevin turned to Parkinson. He said he could not give any more work to Micron without "causing a mutiny" among his own designers, but he would surely like to have Ward return to Mostek. Ward shook his head sadly. Sevin looked glum. Finally Noble asked why, if it was so bad, was Mostek in the race? "What hope do you have?"

"Well, you've got to be nimble," said L. J. Sevin with the kind of lame smile that so many semiconductor executives offered when explaining their commitment to this frenzied rivalry of men and nations. "But sometimes I wonder."

Parkinson thought that it was all over. "What do you think?" he asked Noble and Yanke as they settled into the seat of their rented car and headed for the Dallas airport. What they thought was that it was all very exciting. What somehow happened during their morning in Dallas with that charming silicon adventurer, L. J. Sevin, was that they ignored the message and marched off to the music. Feeling the onset of silicon fever, they decided to go ahead despite all the hulking obstacles, or—if the truth be known—perhaps in part because of them. Both men signed up for Micron's board of directors and set out to arrange for "a little finance."

From that point on, Micron was embroiled in a fierce race against time. During the next several months it had to come up with some $6 million in loans and investments. It had to get a workable design for a 64K, a detail still far from finished in early 1980. It had to find land, erect a building, assemble the equipment, attract, hire, and train personnel. And it had to coordinate all these efforts into a crescendo of technical virtuosity and productivity unequaled in the history of industry. Anything short of this climactic triumph would leave Micron as just another listing in the endless annals of entrepreneurial overreach, just another forgotten name in the record-breaking catalogs of bankruptcy in the worldwide recession of the early 1980s.

Noble and Yanke began by putting up enough money to keep the company going and to start construction. They brought in a friend, Thomas Nicholson, a handsome farmer with steel-gray hair, who had developed his spread into one of the largest sheep ranches in the country. He put up some land in a desert area to the east of Boise. Yanke witched for water and hit a prophetic gusher. They arranged for a $1 million loan from a local bank. They summoned Benitez.

But all their heroic labors, if the truth be known, could not have launched Micron as a maker of 64K DRAMs if they had not also contacted, in March 1980, through Yanke and Noble, one of the few men in Idaho who by himself was capable of finance on a global scale. That man was the crusty self-made entrepreneur of pigs and potatoes named J. R. Simplot. By then a salty man in his early seventies, with a sandy-haired crewcut, freckles, an infectious smile, and bountiful optimism and confidence, he was ready for a new adventure in enterprise. His son Scott had told him about Micron. "The farm boys," as he referred to Noble, Yanke, and Nicholson, "had put up everything they got," J.R. recalls. "We decided to give it a run."

"What'll it take to get her rolling?" he asked.

"Four million," he was told.

"All right. We'll go for it," he replied, and so they did.

Thus by May 1980 the Micron board of directors, though free of experts in silicon or sophisticated venture capital, did boast some of the world's greatest authorities on sheep and potatoes. Beyond J.R. himself, Nicholson, Yanke, and Noble was A. Dale Dunn, president of Simplot (and conveniently a director of the First Security Bank of Idaho), and Scott Simplot, executive vice-president of Simplot and a computer buff. In a bold move, Scott had just shifted the company from IBM mainframes to Digital Equipment Corporation (DEC) minicomputers and was increasingly intrigued by chips.

However, $4 million quickly dissolved as the building emerged from the hard desert ground and Micron's engineers struggled with their refractory designs. The investors, with Simplot's weighty signature in tow, soon found themselves arranging a $7.5 million bank loan to finish construction of the building and purchase of equipment. Simplot and the others also invested directly in the development of designs for the 64K. Over the next two years total outlays would mount to over $20 million, a handsome sum for a start-up firm, but less than one-fifth of what was estimated for every other company manufacturing 64K DRAMs. As the investments multiplied, however, Joe Parkinson arranged the financing terms, in a series of R&D partnerships and other devices which always kept 50 percent of the equity in Micron for what Simplot called the knowledge side. "Capital is worthless," he said, "if you don't have the brains to go with it."

As it happened, brain and brawn, building and design, came together just in time. Parkinson, Pitman, Wilson, and their growing staff managed to create and debug a satisfactory 64K DRAM design just one month before Benitez and Yanke finished constructing, equipping, and debugging the fabrication area. Micron was on the verge of becoming a manufacturing company at last.

All these feats of entrepreneurship, however, would have failed to make Micron a viable company without a Micron revolution in the industry's usual chain of command. From the beginning, Ward Parkinson had installed Douglas Pitman, the high school graduate draftsman, as a director and vice-president of the company and had given him a central role in the design of the chip.

Pitman was a mere layout man, and layout men occupy a place in the semiconductor pecking order well below the designers of chip architecture, logic, and cell structure. The designers are the "inventors" of the product; they are physicists and mathematicians and electrical engineers with advanced degrees who author the large binders full of schematics—hundreds of pages for a major new memory—which hold the specifications of the chip. For one major memory product this work can take many hundreds of man-years, defining in detail every transistor and connection on the device, labyrinthine displays that entail the kind of endless, painstaking symbolic writing that pinches the fingers and gives new meaning to the words "digital electronics."

But all this work provides relatively little guidance about how the transistors, in their many layers, actually will fit on the chip. For all the awesome detail of the schematics, these diagrams leave wide creative latitude to the layout man, who must figure out how and where to place and interconnect the elements in the physical topography of the ten-layered device.

In most companies, though, layout is considered routine. Indeed, for devices that will be sold in relatively small numbers, much of this work can be relegated to computer-aided design (CAD) machines which translate electronic symbols into conventional layouts derived from previous designs. In microprocessor chips, for example, it is the logic that chiefly matters. The layout, though important, may not be the decisive factor in the success or failure of the product.

In commodity memories, which may be sold in the billions, however, all that matters is how many functioning cells can be crammed into how little space. The size of the chip will determine the number that can be produced on a single wafer, and thus what each one will cost to manufacture. Depending on the ingenuity of the layout, for example, a particular memory design might turn out to take up anywhere from 20,000 to 50,000 square mils. It easily might fit in a conventional plastic package, costing a few pennies; or like Motorola's and Intel's early 64Ks it might squeeze into plastic only with costly adjustments or risk of damage; or it might demand custom ceramic containers from Kyocera that would price it out of the market. The layout map can determine what share of a memory die consists of actual memory cell arrays and what proportion is used up in peripheral random logic (unrepeated logic specific to a particular task on the chip). Many memory products end up only 40 percent memory cells; others approach 60 percent. This difference is clearly visible in micropictographs of the chips. Best and most beautiful are usually the devices dominated by dark rectangular fields of memory cells.

Like a compact automobile, a memory should be roomy inside and tiny outside; it should have as capacious as possible memory cells, as easy as possible to read, in as small as possible a chip area. These relationships largely reflect the layout design. By having Pitman deeply involved in all phases of the design of the chip, Micron produced a scheme optimized for the practical demands of layout rather than the elegant visions of engineers. It would be a compact, not a Cadillac.

With the design complete, Pitman went to work on the layout itself. Leaning over his board like a keen-eyed bird of prey, his small sharp features accentuated by his black hair and neat black mustache, he has the rare ability of the supreme artist to join a conceptual vision of general patterns to a remorseless particular concern for detail. He immerses himself in the baffling three-dimensional intricacies of each transistor on a multilayered chip without ever for an instant losing intuitive track of the overall balance and design. It is an aesthetic sense, and the product in the end, as is easily ascertained by looking at it through a microscope, is a work of art.

Before him is his canvas, a series of gridded Mylar sheets, one for each layer of the design. On it he inscribes precise polygons, in an array of colors at a scale of two thousand to one, depicting every element on the chip. The work must be exact, for these Mylar sheets will be read by a cursor and transcribed onto magnetic tapes that will drive an electron beam photomask writing machine at Ultratech in California, where Micron contracted out the mask-making job. This machine will reduce each design by a factor of 2,000 and transcribe or "step" it hundreds of times into a photolithographic mask, which patterns each layer of the actual silicon wafer in manufacturing.

In the end, like the Micron building, the chip was cheaper to produce than any comparable Silicon Valley architecture. Because of Pitman's spare layouts and a relatively sizable memory charge, Parkinson and Wilson felt they could adopt an architecture of daringly minimalist inspiration. Like the World Trade Center, Micron's uniquely capacious device would hold its crucial contents in just two tall and uninterrupted arrays. All the other companies except TI had gone to a four-array system. Four arrays meant four sets of peripherals servicing the memory cells, rather than the two sets in Micron's simpler system. Because Micron's individual cells were larger than most other 64K cells, Micron's memory thus could dispense with half their surrounding peripherals. An excellent tradeoff that allowed Micron and TI to achieve the smallest chips, it was missed by many designers who were preoccupied above all with reducing each cell as much as possible on this unprecedentedly dense memory device.

Where Micron pulled ahead of TI was in processing and functioning tolerances. Because Micron initially used some of the industry's least advanced equipment, the Micron design had to offer the industry's largest latitude for error and misalignment among the ten layers; its 1.5 micron alignment leeway was triple that of TI. Its functioning tolerances, moreover, made Micron's chip more suitable for the rough-and-tumble world of personal computers, which Parkinson had targeted as the most promising market. Micron put nearly the most capacious and thus most readable cells in the industry on the smallest and thus most cheaply producible chip. The purchasers of 64K DRAMs, Parkinson reasoned, wanted not an ambitious display of special effects, but a reliable commodity product at the lowest possible cost. Through brilliance in design and layout, Micron aimed to use plant and equipment costing onefifth its rivals' capital outlays and get production yields more than twice as high. This was Ward Parkinson's impossible, world-beating dream, as the Micron staff struggled out of the dental-center basement in the spring and summer of 1981 and moved into the anonymous new building in the desert.

Through the fall of that year, however, all dreams of glory on the experience curve—all inspiring projections of unit costs dropping in a majestic swoop—gave way to a consuming and costly drive to produce just one functioning unit. A fabrication chief, with an electronic engineering doctorate and a long record for a leading rival, came to Boise to work out the problems. But he moved so slowly and communicated so little that a team of fabrication engineers came to Joe Parkinson—the man who did all of Micron's firing—and requested the man's removal. The man left, issuing fiery predictions that Micron never would produce a workable chip. Parkinson learned a key lesson in personnel management: "You don't bring in outsiders to run your plant. You promote the people who your workers want to follow." Parkinson promoted Juan Benitez to head of manufacturing and put him on the board. Benitez brought in Randal Chance, a burly young Texan from TI and Mostek, to focus on wafer fabrication.

But it seemed almost too late. Day by day, as summer turned to autumn, the money drained away at a rate of $27,000 every twenty-four hours, $800,000 a month. It was becoming clear that they would need to raise more money before they had so much as produced a single chip.

Meanwhile, back at the ranches of the leading investors and in the tall white tower of Simplot, Incorporated, in downtown Boise, doubt and dissatisfaction mounted. The Simplots never had quite understood the need to begin building a facility before the chip design was finished. They were worried further by the resignation of Dennis Wilson, a key figure and founder, who tumbled into a lengthy distracting divorce after he completed his work on the schematics. Now the financial division at Simplot, always dubious of their boss's wild venture into new territory, argued forcefully against investing another dime before Micron was producing workable devices. Scott Simplot made calls to E. F. Hutton, Sutter Hill, and Hambrecht and Quist, leading sources of venture capital, but they all blanched at investing in commodity memories in the face of the formidable Japanese. Simplot's president, Dale Dunn, was shaken by a chance meeting in an airplane with the head of the huge Boise facility of Hewlett-Packard and the city's chief authority on electronic technologies. "Can't be done," he said of Micron's plans. "It will be a white elephant. To start a real RAM facility would cost $50 million. You'll never get a working chip out of that plant." Tom Nicholson was counseled by his Idahoan friend William Agee of Bendix to stay away from the commodity memory business: "Be a consumer of chips, not a producer of them."

Scott Simplot got similar lectures from all the leading venturers of Silicon Valley. The man from Hambrecht and Quist asked him, "Have you done anything like this before? What formula did you use in placing a price on this company? Aren't you disappointed by the progress to date? What's your financial model?" Scandalizing the ghosts of his Wharton teachers, Scott replied that he had "an internal Micron model." But like Parkinson before him, he was driven to conclude that in the model of the American venture capital industry, this potential $4 billion market had been given up to the Japanese. Then in October 1981 the yen fell again, and the price of 64K DRAMs, predicted by Ben Rosen at $10, fell below $4, shaking even Scott Simplot's doughty model. The Simplot commitment to the project was weakening seriously.

Finally, late that same month, there was good news from Micron. The first working chips came off the production line. They were slow and accompanied by hordes of stillborn neighbors, but they demonstrably functioned as 64K dynamic RAM memories. The investors were called from their doleful contemplation of the price of the yen and summoned to the plant to celebrate the great event. All five came—J. R. and Scott Simplot, Allen Noble, Tom Nicholson, Ron Yanke—and were shown the nondescript gray slivers of silicon. Then they looked at the chip through a microscope. Allen Noble went first. He remembers not knowing what to expect. A furrowed field of gray sand? A metallic pattern of dark cells surrounded by swirls of circuitry and hooked with tiny wires of gold?

One's first microscopic view of a chip is always a revelation. Noble peered through the lenses and initially imagined there was something wrong, some chromatic test pattern interposed between his eyes and the tiny gray rectangle below.

Then he realized that what he saw from this optic pinnacle was the chip itself. A tiny patch of sand, it blossomed before his magnified gaze in a phantasmagorical grid of gay colors, a field of flowers—oranges, pinks, greens and silvers—like an irrigator's dream of iridescent springtime on a high desert plateau. But that glimpse, it turned out, caught just one corner of the array. From a longer microscopic view the chip unfolded as two great rectangular fields in bloom—the homogeneous cells of memory—surrounded by long opalescent beds of artfully patterned blossoms, interwoven with verdant hedges and silvery paths. Retreating farther in focus, the colors resolved into two dark parterres of purple bordered with a weave of blue and azure figures repeated symmetrically along the sides and down the center. The view most resembled a handsome rug of Persian design, with rows of white boxes at each end for the wires of gold.

Allen was startled by the beauty of the world he suddenly had entered. The men stood silent as they looked at it one by one. "It was a great day," said J.R. Then they had a party. The men were committed. Micron had surmounted its first key hurdle. But there would be many more before anyone could dream of profit.

Scott Simplot sums up the next few months as a time when the chip suffered "speed problems, production problems, yield problems, and recall problems." These were months when Simplot had exhausted its ready venture funds and reached deep into its pockets for what J.R. called "our real gambling money," and the financial department was becoming ever more insistent that Simplot "pull the plug" on the Parkinsons. "We were sure pawing the air for a while," remembers J.R. "It was touch and go."

Simplot was particularly distressed by the low speed of the memory. That would mean low prices and possibly no profits. To Tom Trent back in the plant, though, everything seemed to be proceeding extraordinarily well. A recent arrival at Micron after long service as a chip designer at Motorola—some of it under Ward Parkinson—Trent is a lucid and articulate man who views the world shrewdly over a large sandy beard. He saw the vicissitudes of the Micron device as typical, if somewhat accelerated, passages in the life of a new chip. He acknowledged the business problem of low-speed devices at a time of plummeting prices for ordinary parts and a premium for faster ones. But he knew that the production of functioning chips, however slow, was the first priority. Until the chips worked, improvement was impossible. Once the chips began to function, then he could focus on their speed.

With slow chips in hand—and a speed "crisis" declared—Trent proceeded to solve it. He knew that the problems probably could be overcome by manufacturing changes that used up some of the processing tolerances. But he thought that this production leeway would be precious later in the life of the chip. He turned to changes in the design. There were many possibilities, and he focused on the simplest: "tweaking" or adjusting the some sixty clock circuits or delay elements that time the some thirty clocked events in each "read" cycle of the memory. The change would have to avoid disrupting any of Pitman's laborious symmetries. It would have to accord with all the other timing functions on the device. It should entail revisions, if possible, on only the two top layers. The problem completely absorbed the young designer. A week of days and nights, poring over the clock schematics and layouts, slipped by before Trent at last left the plant to deliver two new drawings to Ultratech in Santa Clara. There they would be digitized on the CAD machine and transcribed on new photomasks.

As chips are produced, they are tested for speed and according to the results assigned to a fast or slower category. After delivery of the new masks the proportion of slow to fast chips shifted overnight from 70–30 to 30–70. Production yields already had begun rising sharply. The fourfold production crisis was essentially over. The first 1,000 chips were dispatched to a distributor during the first week of January 1982, and by the second quarter production yields had risen to more than 100,000 per month.

If J. R. Simplot ever had wavered in support of "the boys," Trent's feat dispelled his doubts. "I always said they just had to give us a run for our money. They sure were giving us a run." Scott added, "It was an emotional thing. How in the world could you ask for more effort from those guys?"

Effort alone might not have sufficed, however, without Ward Parkinson's apparently endless repertory of technical surprises. One day late in 1981, he called the Simplots down to the plant to see a new device he had invented using 64K DRAMs. Parkinson had figured out a way to sell "bad" or slightly defective chips at about ten times the price of good ones. Building on his experience at Reticon, Parkinson created an "optic RAM," based on the discovery that the rate of leakage from the memory cell capacitors is directly proportional to their exposure to light. The optic RAMs—slightly defective ordinary DRAMs encased in packages with clear quartz windows—therefore can be made to function as cheap and efficient light sensors. They can be used in robots and other industrial equipment or in a Micron attachment to a personal computer. Called a Micron eye camera, it attaches to either an Apple ("teaches your Apple to read") or an IBM personal computer and enables it to transcribe words or other images directly to the screen or over a telephone modem to other machines. It turns the computer into a crude but effective facsimile machine. Since each camera uses at least three RAMs, Micron hopes that this item will swell significantly the demand for DRAMs, lead to the replacement of charge-coupled devices for many imaging uses, from TVs to toys, and demonstrate the technological benefits of participation in the mass memory business.

The commercial benefits came more quickly. As J. R. Simplot said: "We went down and saw them send pictures through telephone lines. We bought exclusive rights for $2 million." Simplot purchased personal equity in this technology outside his role in Micron's corporate structure. With DRAM prices plummeting and charge-coupled devices nearly one hundred times more expensive for imaging, this investment by Simplot may well be cheap at the price. That February Noble and J.R. went down together to the International Solid State Circuits Conference in San Francisco to see the Micron eye exhibited at the Commodore booth. Although still unknown outside the narrow circles of chip design, Micron was beginning to attract notice in the profession. One of the world's leading computer firms gave it a $1 million contract to design a pioneering new device combining several types of memory on one chip. The assignment went to Pitman and to Jim O'Toole, the new design chief, who had followed Parkinson from Motorola to Mostek, but avoided all the machinations of the Inmos breakaway ("I just closed my door and got some good design work done, debugging Parkinson's static RAM"). A tall gangly engineer with horn-rimmed glasses and a warm smile, O'Toole had replaced Dennis Wilson. O'Toole and Pitman completed the new assignment successfully by the end of that year—bringing in crucial new money to keep the company going. Pitman managed to do the layout work in spite of his preoccupation with the illness of his wife, who needed open heart surgery for the insertion of a new carbon-steel valve.

While these alarums and diversions—of finances, technologies, and personalities—were erupting, production yields at the plant rose relentlessly, month by month, in line with Parkinson's projections. Still, Micron was losing money on every chip it sold. By the fall of 1982, it was time to solve this problem or go out of business. Parkinson resolved to solve it by a drastic shrink. He would reduce the size of the chip—and thus increase the number on each wafer that was processed. This drop in unit costs could transform Micron's 64K from a remarkable technical feat into a lucrative product. If the effort succeeded, it could change Micron from a struggling company, with margins always under pressure from rivals with larger economies of scale, into a fully profitable firm capable of competing with anyone in subsequent generations of commodity memories.

A successful shrink is more a reward for previous virtue than a virtuoso feat in itself. If the design is consistent and symmetrical, and the process margins are sufficient, a shrink just requires a new size order at the photomask stepper. If the design is tricky and complex and process tolerances tight, however, a shrink may well entail complete redesign of the chip. On memory chips that are full of brilliant anomalies—that are essentially defined by Ph.D.s of engineering and then pushed over the transom for a group of layout peons to execute—a shrinkage will create an instant chaos of voltages and connections that will take many man-months to unravel. But at Micron the layout peon was a vice-president and director who had helped optimize the design for a balanced and symmetrical layout. On the Micron layout, Parkinson and Pitman believed, a shrinkage would have an equal and calculable impact on all parts of the chip.

The benefits of the layout were enhanced by Parkinson's conservative decisions on design and processing. The simple two-array architecture and expanded electrical tolerances—giving room for error and misalignment, granting leeway for erratic power flows, protecting the data under stress, enlarging cell capacitances and readability—all converged in a revolutionary result. Micron's chip, already one of the industry's smallest, turned out also to be the industry's most suitable for shrinkage.

The large firms had achieved small chips by pushing their fabrication teams and new production equipment to the utmost, but they had no additional room to maneuver. TI struggled at 35,000 square mils and Motorola had to blow up its 33,000-square-mil die to 50,000 when yields were too low at the small size. But Micron, despite less advanced equipment in its fabs, was able to reduce its 30,000-square-mil die by more than a quarter, to 22,000 square mils. The shrink merely required Trent and Pitman to use up some of the manufacturing leeway or tolerances no longer needed by Randal Chance's increasingly proficient fabrication team. Pitman and Trent "tweaked" a few peripheral features, and Trent flew down to Ultratech to create the new masks.

The first miniaturized chips emerged in December, and through early 1983 Chance shifted more of his production line daily to the new device. The first set of wafers averaged nearly 100 good chips out of some 500 possibles and included one with 140, a phenomenal yield at this stage. Then in a bold move, Micron decided to move the small chip directly from 4-inch wafers to the 5-inch wafers being tentatively adopted in the industry. Since it costs little more to produce a larger wafer than a smaller one once the production gear is developed and in place, the move to larger wafers can greatly increase the yield (the number of good chips per wafer) and thus further reduce the cost per chip. Still, the change was perilous because it would disrupt every part of the fabrication process. But Micron again succeeded, increasing the number of possibles on each wafer to more than 800, by far the highest in the industry.

The Idaho firm had completed its revolution in semiconductors. By May 1983, as the semiconductor industry entered a long siege of orders that month after month broke all records, Micron had become profitable and a private financing by Montgomery Securities in November valued the company's shares at more than $300 million. In early 1984, the company completed its unique 256K design and was producing more than 2 million 64K DRAMs a month, earning a *monthly* profit of $4 million, and was generating revenues at an annual rate of $108 million.

Since Micron's original device probably had led the industry in its combination of desirable characteristics, the one-third-smaller chip available in 1983 demanded that the rest of the industry try some quantum-leaping of their own. Large established companies, though, are rarely agile enough for acrobatics.

In turning the semiconductor world upside down, Micron also capsized most of the conventional wisdom about the requirements of success in this most advanced of modern technologies. For example, Micron's lower-end strategy—accepting snubs from the mainframe companies that are believed to rule the memory business and pursuing the personal computer trade—has proved a dramatic success. Apple Computer was Micron's first major purchaser, ordering a million chips for its new Lisa and Macintosh models. The color photographs of the Macintosh "mother board" that Apple proudly distributed in early 1984 bore sixteen 64K DRAMs from Micron. Commodore proved a tougher customer at first. But after a friendly meeting between Jack Tramiel and Joe Parkinson, Tramiel intervened with his sales department to assure Micron an order of millions at an adequate price. Later Commodore bought the rights to produce the chip at its own facilities. Terry Bowman, Micron's marketing manager and the man who brought the Parkinsons to Columbia, believes that the personal computer market will grow so rapidly that Micron could become a dominant force in the industry without selling a chip for a mainframe. Nonetheless, Digital Equipment eventually became a large purchaser of Micron's chips.

Micron also has flouted the belief that chips can be assembled into packages more cheaply in offshore plants than at home. This notion has sent many U.S. semiconductor executives to join the worldwide circuit of surfers, hopping beaches through the islands of Asia in an endless quest for the perfect wage. Although many industry leaders acknowledge that automation eventually will bring this job back to the United States, the usual estimates foresee no major change for at least seven years.

Micron, however, shocked buyers such as Apple by quoting a lower price for delivery at home than in Asia. Although assembling both in Boise and at Dynetics in the Philippines, Micron does all its final testing in the United States and has discovered to its surprise that assembly is just as cheap and efficient with Idaho labor. While other companies are following their assembly operations abroad with increasing flows of designers, Micron is bringing it all back home and focusing its sales on American manufacturers of home and personal computers.

Whatever happens to Micron in coming years, however, this unlikely team—a pair of twins from Blackfoot, Idaho, a displaced Cuban, and a college dropout—have demonstrated anew the extraordinary creativity and efficiency possible in a small company. The intimate interplay among four or five men, in design, layout, and fabrication, engineered a part superior to the product of the vaunted labs of IBM or Bell, a part better than the product of Japan's research and development cartels, a part beyond the expectations of any expert in the industry.

Micron gave the lie to all the authoritative researches of five governments, of scores of university scholars, of hundreds of politicians who once again—in longing or lamentation—proclaimed the necessary bureaucratization of creativity. Micron even defied the expertise of the dominant centers of venture capital. Just as it took a copper company to appreciate the oil and gas insights of John Masters of Canadian Hunter—one of the world's leading finders of natural gas—so it took a bunch of potato growers and sheep farmers to take the measure of Micron.

Platoons of scholars from MIT, the Sorbonne, Stanford, and Tokyo U., lavishly financed by the richest corporations and governments of the world, succumbed to a motley team from Utah State, Idaho State, and Missouri Rolla.

Late in 1982, wise men and scoundrels from around the world began coming to see for themselves—to pay implicit tribute to the newborn king of semiconductor memories. The DRAM design group from one of the world's most prestigious electronics firms—including its director of DRAM development—quietly checked into the Red Lion Riverside Motel in Boise. Two earnest Swedes from a leading robotics firm flew in from Stockholm. A brilliant British semiconductor engineer from a world-leading multinational went out to the Micron plant and negotiated an agreement with Joe Parkinson to license the chip. With a strong position in the European market for 16K DRAMs, his multinational had labored for years to mass-produce a 64K and had failed. The Briton's German boss read the contract with incredulity and flew in to investigate the unknown firm and extort a more favorable agreement. Expertly shuffling papers, he told Joe Parkinson to sign on the dotted line, all was in order. After Joe spotted key changes and rejected them, the tall suave German was seen stalking the corridors of the Red Lion in a dark suit, muttering to himself.

One of Micron's fears early in 1983 was that some large company would steal the design. As Jim O'Toole observed, "It is disgustingly simple to copy a chip. There were eight copies made by other companies of Pitman's 16K layout at Mostek." The plagiarist merely strips off each layer with acids and photographs the one below. Without much ado, the photographs can be enlarged, digitized, and plugged into a photomask etching machine. Although this process does not specify all the processing techniques, it can lead to an acceptable copy in six months. This fear is not unfounded. Seeing the chip for the first time, a group of memory designers at a U.S. mainframe company resolved to break and steal it. They were fired by their boss after intervention by Joe Parkinson.

The only answer to the threat and sincere flattery of plagiarism is wide licensing and rapid movement to still-better technologies. Micron has licensed its chip to several companies and hopes that its final answer will be an industry-standard 256K DRAM.

Meanwhile, though, Joe Parkinson's role in the company is becoming ever more crucial. As the company moves into the realm of international rivalry and intrigue, its sales contracts and legal briefs bulk larger even than its binders of schematics. Joe moved back into his old Park Avenue role, at a still-higher level, handling complex negotiations with the legal departments of companies from around the world. More and more they came to him in Boise with petitions as often as with demands. Joe's role in defending his brother's interests and keeping him out of trouble had thrust him, as an entrepreneurial lawyer, onto the world stage of international commerce and industry.

The story of Micron proves once again—as if proof were still necessary—that progress and achievement are the unpredictable result of individual will and faith, diligence and ingenuity, against which all the powers and principalities ultimately must stand impotent and in awe.

In business as in art, the individual vision prevails over the corporate leviathan; the small company—or the creative group in a large firm—confounds the industrial policy; the entrepreneur dominates the hierarch. The hubristic determinisms of the academy and the state—the secular monoliths of science and planning, the imperial sovereigns of force and finance—give way to one man working in the corner of a lab or a library.

This is the real message that Joe Parkinson delivered to an indifferent press on January 3, 1983, when he announced the release of the MT4264A Dynamic Random Access Memory, 65,536 cells in a chip of 22,000 square mils, one-fifth of a square inch in size. He was declaring the indomitable openness of the world. If it is possible for four true believers from Micron to surpass all the looming establishments bestriding the globe, it is possible for you—ladies and gentlemen, entrepreneurs—to achieve what you will, if it is right. That is the message of Micron, and it is a central lesson of human life and history.

THE DYNAMICS OF
ENTREPRENEURSHIP

In the recent history of entrepreneurship in America, perhaps the exemplary moment came on a morning in 1966 when a man in Houston named Thomas J. Fatjo found himself immersed up to his armpits in garbage. Driving a door-to-door route in the city, he had jumped into the bin to stomp down the contents after the compactor broke down with seventy more houses to go. His immersion in muck climaxed the initiation into business for the young accountant, who had seen high opportunities in the field of solid waste disposal and had bought a garbage truck to enter the trade. Several times he skirted mental breakdowns and financial bankruptcy. But in the end he emerged as probably the nation's only CPA with an intimate knowledge of refuse, or the nation's only garbage man with a mastery of accounting.

Within ten years, Fatjo parlayed this rare combination of skills in money and garbage into creation of the world's largest solid waste disposal firm. Called Browning-Ferris Industries, it brought in $500 million in revenues by 1980, was listed on the New York Stock Exchange, and commanded units in most of the nation's cities. As Fatjo explains in his book, *With No Fear of Failure*, however, the key to its growth was the detailed mastery of the garbage business he gained on his route, from door to door in the late 1960s. Day by day, drowsy in the front seat of a secondhand garbage truck as the sun rose over the misty streets, he developed the concept of a national company. Also at the wheel he acquired the sure sense of costs and values that made it possible for him to forge Browning-Ferris from local firms across the land.

Similarly, J. R. Simplot came upon the most crucial insight of his career while sorting potatoes tediously by hand in a local warehouse. This task gave him an instant and all but overwhelming sense of the value of the invention of the electric potato sorter, the device that thrust him into the food-processing trade that he later came to master. Douglas Pitman, the key contributor to Micron's 64K dynamic random access memory, rose to leadership in the semiconductor industry on the basis of experience in its most menial work: the tedious drawing of intricate physical layout patterns. In most companies, layout men, as draftsmen with only high school diplomas, have scant influence on the development of chips. Giving the layout man a major input in chip design was a key move in Micron's own revolution in the industry.

In the same way, Henry Ford and Soichiro Honda of the auto industry, Gordon Moore and Mark Shepherd in semiconductors, and Kenneth Olson and Steve Wozniak in computers all began in the "skunkworks" of their trade, with their hands on the intricate machinery that would determine the fate of their companies. Familiarity with the very material substance, the grit and grease and garbage of their businesses, liberated all of these men from the grip of established expertise and gave them the insight and confidence to turn their industries in new directions. All of them had to stoop to conquer the American economy.

Still, one of the key principles of entrepreneurship—the business of breaking the settled mold—is the absence of clear and fast rules. Some successful entrepreneurs, following in the footsteps of Andrew Carnegie, a man famously ignorant in the technology of steel, have launched companies in fields that they little understood. Carnegie explained his achievement in a suggested epitaph: "Here lies the man who knew how to gather around him men who were more clever than himself."

Carnegie's real enterprise was not steel but industrial combination, and even he was humble enough to listen to the voices from the skunkworks and in the marketplace. Entrepreneurs can be pompous and vain where it doesn't count; but in their own enterprise, the first law is to listen. They must be men meek enough— and shrewd enough—to endure the humbling eclipse of self that comes in the process of profound learning from others.

In all the history of enterprise, most of the protagonists of major new products and companies began their education—and discovered the secrets of their later breakthroughs—not in the classroom, where the old ways are taught, but in the factories and labs, where new ways are wrought. Among all the legions of lawyers, financiers, bureaucrats, and masters of business administration strutting into the American economy from the nation's leading schools, nothing has been so rare in recent years as an Ivy League graduate who has made a significant innovation in American enterprise. (Tom Gates, though, dropped out of Harvard to start Microsoft.) The reason seems simple. It is nearly impossible to capture an industry from the top, where the leading graduates like to start. Proof of value and profitability—major assets of the firms that attract the stars—virtually define an absence of opportunity. With no such proofs, a whole industry may be yours for the asking. Starting from the bottom, you do not have to capture the top; you—like Ford, Morita, Noyce, and Jobs—become it.

The entrepreneurial start-up is the most creative domain in American enterprise largely because it affords the best learning process. A man who builds a company from scratch acquires a depth of understanding of what makes it work that an imported chief executive, however effective his management information systems, however many cases he has explored in depth at the Harvard Business School, cannot easily command. The entrepreneur gains a dynamic and integrated view of his company and a realistic view of enterprise.

Because he started in rebellion against established firms, he bears a natural skepticism toward settled expertise. Because he had to make scores of decisions before all the information was in, he recognizes that enterprise always consists of action in uncertainty. The entrepreneur prevails not by understanding an existing situation in all its complex particulars, but by creating a new situation which others must try to comprehend. The enterprise is an aggressive action, not a reaction. When it is successfully launched, all the rest of society—government, labor, other businesses—will have to react. In a sense, entrepreneurship is the creation of surprises. It entails breaking the looking glass of established ideas—even the gleaming mirrors of executive suites—and stepping into the often greasy and fetid bins of creation.

In the entrepreneur's contrarian domains, he needs most of all a willingness to accept failure, learn from it, and act boldly in the shadows of doubt. He inhabits a realm where the last become first, where supply creates demand, where belief precedes knowledge. It is a world where expertise may be a form of ignorance and the best possibilities spring from a consensus of impossibility. It is a world where service of others—solving their problems and taking on new ones for yourself—is the prime source of leadership and wealth. It is a world where bankruptcies can serve as an index of growth, large setbacks as a portent of large gains, and stability as a precur-

of failure—where other people's garbage is your wealth and l is often a richer resource than gold. It is a world where unit s can indeed be made up by volume, where low profit margins lead to the largest profits, and where giving is the rule of highest returns. A world rarely penetrated by any economist, it is yet the very center of all economic life.

David L. Birch and his associates at MIT gained a glimpse of this topsy-turvy domain during the late 1970s when they themselves entered the statistical skunkworks of the economy by conducting the most comprehensive and detailed analysis ever performed on the facts of American small business. Using records from a Dun & Bradstreet sample of 5.6 million firms, the Birch team reached the highly publicized conclusion that companies with fewer than a hundred employees created 80 percent of the net new jobs in the U.S. economy during the 1970s. Data from the early 1980s confirmed these findings. In launching jobs, the last were manifestly first in U.S. capitalism.

Nonetheless, the significance of such statistics should not be exaggerated. A similar study in Massachusetts concluded that high technology was unimportant for the revival of the state because high-tech firms created only 3 percent of the new jobs. Yet these firms, large and small, generated the wealth and developed the skills and forged the markets without which many of the job-creating smaller firms would have failed. Large firms usually got that way by being productive, and their productivity is obviously vital to creation of employment.

As larger firms move down the curve of growth, increasing their own productivity, they may even destroy jobs in their own companies or move them overseas. But only by the enhanced productivity generated by new ideas and technologies can new jobs be durably created. As the prices of routine products drop through automation or offshore manufacture, wealth is released to purchase new products and sustain the new small firms where the jobs are. Even when the statistics seem to say otherwise, it is always the innovative firms, of all sizes, that are creating the jobs.

More important than the findings on employment, therefore, were the Birch discoveries on the dynamics of growth. The team began with the usual anthropomorphic notion of business evolution: "We had thought that a company grows and develops much like a human being: It starts small, grows smoothly and rapidly during a 'growth phase,' matures and stabilizes for some period and eventually becomes outdated and falls off." This is the familiar Kuznets curve of a business life cycle. Although many companies do run through a Kuznets curve, the MIT scholars discovered that the fastest-growing firms more often show a pattern of growth quite different from the intuitively plausible.

The entrepreneur may follow a diving-board model. There is often a certain amount of preening on the plank before he discovers that he will have to finance the company himself. This chastening fact ends many a quest for independence. But many are spurred by a vision so compelling—and a frustration so sore—that they mortgage their house and borrow from their uncle. Then comes the entrepreneurial splash . . . or splat. There often follows a terrible period of submergence—its silence broken only by appeals for money, as losses pile up.

During this stretch, which can easily last for years, and during which the entrepreneur is rarely seen even by his family, established firms confidently declare his demise. That sound you heard, they all maintain, was a splat; the idea did not hold water. Venture capitalists rejected it, as they usually do; experts, as always, laughed; banks nervously eyed the entrepreneur's dwelling. But the entrepreneur himself, desperate for funds, has learned how to cut costs and bring a product to market.

It is a splendid product, perhaps. It will change the world. But alas, the unit cost is far above the price the world will pay to be changed. The firm loses money on each item sold and the number is all too few. Losses mount and inventories grow. Finally the firm cuts prices dramatically to clear the shop. Demand "surprisingly" surges. Sales soar, personnel are hired, new equipment is purchased, losses accelerate, until the magic moment of reversal on the learning curve, when costs sink below the price and profits come in.

For a few years the company undergoes runaway expansion. Then it suffers its crisis of growth. Although it is selling all it can produce, it cannot finance itself out of its own earnings. Inventory costs rise rapidly; borrowing soars; capital outlays increase; competition rears its head; and the world sours on change. Unless the entrepreneur can take decisive action at this point (Thomas Fatjo, for example, replaced himself as CEO), the firm will struggle and possibly fail. The winners will enter a new trajectory of growth.

The pattern will vary drastically, of course, from company to company, industry to industry. But almost nowhere can one discover a smooth and predictable evolution of growth. The smooth ascent of aggregates conceals a violent flux of particular firms. The gyrations are clear in the Birch study. Focusing on 1.4 million companies most reliably documented over the seven-year period of the analysis, the Birch team compared their performance from 1969 through 1972 with their later results from 1974 through 1976. They found that established companies, which had growth of more than 50 percent during the first three years, were by far the most likely to suffer losses at a similar pace during the last three years. They found that stable companies, which changed little in the initial period, were most prone to bankruptcy. Nearly 25 percent went out of business during the subsequent span; stable companies were about twice as likely to fail as companies that suffered losses of more than 50 percent in the early period. Some 22 percent of these firms with large losses, however, subsequently experienced rapid growth. The Birch study indicated, in fact, that a three-year period of large losses was the single best indicator of three subsequent years of total growth of more than 50 percent.

Needless to say, losses are not a sufficient predictor of success. Rapid losses were equally likely to lead to still more rapid losses or bankruptcy. But rapid losses correlated twice as well as rapid gains with a later period of 50 percent growth. Large gains in the first three-year period, moreover, portended rapid losses in 16.5 percent of the sample. Here we find the familiar crisis of growth when the entrepreneur discovers he can't do it all himself but refuses to relinquish control. It might be followed by submergence or new success. Instability is the predictable condition of the business of entrepreneurial surprise.

The reversals and gyrations of the diving-board model—the need to go under before you can rise up—may explain the baffled and traumatized look of many owners of small business and the refusal of most banks to invest in them without full collateral. But instability and surprise is the entrepreneurial law. The extraordinary pace of growth—more than 50 percent over a three-year period—won by over 40 percent of the sample companies explains both the job-creating skills of small firms and the persistence of entrepreneurs in starting and sustaining them.

The far more spectacular statistics of growth and survival among high-tech firms in Silicon Valley—90 percent financed by personal savings—shows that opportunity still beckons. That nearly all the semiconductor companies begun in the late 1960s are still in business in one form or another after the tumultuous decade of the 1970s indicates, in fact, that innovation against the odds, as appraised by bankers and venture capitalists, is a surer route to riches than riding the surf of commodity markets or joining an executive training course. The tempestuous history of these companies, however, attests that the threat of failure and the experience of losses contributed as much to their triumphs as the promise of success.

The Birch study shows that the need for failure is as characteristic of whole economies as of small companies. Shedding new light on local and regional data on business breakdown, Birch's analysis of a five-year period in the mid-1970s found that the most rapidly growing cities tended to have higher levels of business failure than economically stagnant areas. The prime example was Houston, which led a Birch list of ten representative metropolitan areas in the number of new firms created during the 1970s and was second in the percent of failures.

Far more important than the rate of failures, however, was the rate of new business formations. The bulk of the variation in growth from one city or region to another came from greater fertility in creating new companies, not from movements of existing companies, or from differing rates of bankruptcy. Birch's data suggest that the high rate of business failure in the United States in the early 1980s—accompanied as it was by unprecedented levels of business starts and venture capital—signified not a declining economy but a dynamically changing one. This Birch conclusion will not surprise students of Japan, an economy that underwent rates of business failure twice as high as in the United States for twenty-five years while growing some three times as fast. Like successful people, thriving economies have more failures than failures do.

The alternation of losses and gains reflects the central dynamic of entrepreneurship. Entrepreneurs launch new companies or transform old companies by losing money. The process is often termed investment. It is analogous to giving, because there is no predetermined return. As Birch shows, the losses as often lead to more losses and to bankruptcy as they lead to growth. An investment, though, in those terms, is not simply a purchase of durable equipment. It may be any expenditure that enhances learning and experience. An entrepreneur may invest in a price cut, a marketing ploy, a training program, a consultant, or even, like Intel in 1982, in wages and salaries to keep the staff together during a business downturn.

Whether "investment" or "expense," any outlay that contributes to the accumulation of valuable knowledge and skills in the firm can serve to expand the real capital of the company, while the purchase of an unneeded "capital good" may in fact constitute consumption. Perhaps the single most common "capital" purchase by prosperous businesses in the late 1970s, for example, was the company Mercedes. (Rapidly depreciable on the books yet losing little sales value, it came nearly free of charge after inflation and taxes.) Computer software, by contrast, was all expensed. Countries around the world that indulged the universal planner's fetish for steel—a product rapidly giving way to rival materials—were in fact consuming wealth despite the huge capital plants they created and the steel they sold. Losses incurred to keep a firm in business, avoiding necessary changes in product and personnel, can also represent mere waste, just as "profits" generated by failure to maintain or restore equipment can conceal real losses. The difference between capital and consumption is rarely evident on a company's (or country's) income statement or even much of the time on its balance sheet.

A loss becomes an investment when it is compensated for in the mind of the investor by a plausible promise of future success. The invisible counterparts of the statistics of loss are expectations of gain. Investors allowed Xicor and Zilog, Ford and Digital Equipment to run losses for half a decade or more. Genentech, the biotechnology venture headed by Robert Swanson, ran losses for eight years and then raised more than $100 million in the market by going public. The unmeasured asset that balances the red ink is entrepreneurial imagination and creativity.

Without persuasive new ideas, companies large or small are required to produce profits reliably every quarter on pain of drastic devaluation of their shares. With good reason much of the time, their losses are seen not as investments but as inadvertent consumption. Investors are right to impose this requirement on unimaginative companies. The frequent business failures in ostensibly stable firms studied by Birch reflect the precariousness of apparently secure niches for both large and small businesses.

Bankruptcies play the same role in economic progress that falsification plays in the progress of ideas. The key reason the U.S. economy is more successful than the Soviet economy is that the United States allows more failure. The key reason that U.S. scientists outproduce Soviet scientists, who vastly outnumber them, is that U.S. researchers don't know all the answers; they seek to overthrow rather than affirm established views. Both sciences and economies advance as much by disproof as by affirmation.

The eminent philosopher of science Karl Popper, in fact, identifies a valid scientific hypothesis chiefly by whether it is stated in a form in which it could possibly be disproved. If a theory—such as that people born in August under the sign of Leo tend to be temperamental—is too general or flexible to be proved wrong by logic or contrary evidence, it is incapable of generating new knowledge. It is a scientifically sterile proposition. Similarly, the presence of a testable hypothesis differentiates investment from gambling. A true gamble does not test a refutable principle, but merely tries a random chance. Therefore, it cannot produce valuable knowledge.

Every entrepreneurial venture, however, embodies and tests a hypothesis about products or markets. By launching the Lisa computer in early 1983 at a price of nearly $10,000, after investment approaching $50 million, Apple asserted it could persuade sufficient numbers of people to pay that amount to acquire Lisa's integrated software and other features. This was an eminently testable hypothesis and it was soon proved false. Once Lisa failed in its initial form, Apple introduced other hypotheses, such as the notion that enough more people would buy Lisa at half the price to change it into a successful product, and that the same technology would win for Macintosh at $2,495. At every step Apple would be gaining valuable information and transmitting much of it to the public.

In the month of Lisa's debut, the U.S. government enacted a $4.6 billion "jobs bill." Jobs would be seen as "created" regardless of whether total employment in the economy was increased or diminished by this diversion of $4.6 billion from the private sector. Whatever the implicit hypothesis of the program, it would not be experimentally tested in this application, since it would be impossible to determine either the source of changes in the number of jobs or the behavior of job markets in the absence of the bill. Unlike Apple's $50 million investment in the specific and testable Lisa, the government's investment in "jobs" is epistemologically barren.

Between these two polar projects, there are many intermediate investments with less clear implications for the creation of economic knowledge. A large investment in a totally new product or line of research can produce a huge profit of economically valuable information. It can point the way for valuable investment by hundreds of other entrepreneurs. It can absorb all its own financial profits in promising new projects, refining the original idea. On the other hand, an investment in a well-tested product—a new fast-food franchise in a well-developed shopping center or an oil well in a working field—is unlikely to produce major gains in knowledge or financial power. Because the investor has not exposed himself to major reverses, either financial or epistemological, he is unlikely to win huge gains.

His role is similar to what philosopher of science Thomas Kuhn calls "normal science": He is conducting experiments that further refine and apply the propositions previously launched and tested in only slightly different form by other entrepreneurs. Entrepreneurial pioneers play the role of "revolutionary science," launching wholly new ventures that can transform the economic environment. Because they take large risks, their yield of knowledge may be great, as may be their need for profits to finance further investment. A government project, however—or a subsidized and protected private venture—is like an experiment with skewed results. It yields little knowledge.

Every capitalist investment has the potential for a dual yield: a financial profit and an epistemological profit. One without the other is sterile. Economies progress when the process of investment is informed by the results of previous investments. What makes the capitalist entrepreneur uniquely valuable as a force for growth and progress is that he combines in one person these two yields of enterprise. If his venture succeeds, he also gains the power—through profits—to make further investments, further experiments in the light of his initial venture. Under capitalism, the power flows to precisely the people who are willing to stake their money not on gambles or sure things but on testable hypotheses, thus generating knowledge and wealth for the society.

An understanding of the primacy of entrepreneurship is indispensable to any theory of economic development in stagnant economies, where there is no spur of demand or evidence of an invisible hand. The usual theories, in fact, explain economic growth only by assuming it is already under way, creating markets and demand. But it is the spontaneously acting entrepreneurs, with no assurance of demand or markets, who provide the hands that lift up an economy. Their decision whether to invest, the quantity they commit, and the quality of their ideas determine the pace and substance of growth, evoking markets and demand by launching unanticipated goods.

Entrepreneurs understand the inexorable reality of risk and change. They begin by saving, forgoing consumption, not to create an ersatz security but to gain the wherewithal for a life of productive risks and opportunities. Their chief desire is not money to waste on consumption but the freedom and power to consummate their entrepreneurial ideas.

Whether sorting potatoes or writing software, they are movers and shakers, doers and givers, brimming with visions of creation and opportunity. They are optimists, who see in every patch of sand a potential garden, in every man a potential worker, in every problem a possible profit. Their self-interest succumbs to their deeper interest and engagement in the world beyond themselves, impelled by their curiosity, imagination, and faith.

Entrepreneurs seek money chiefly for positive reasons: to perform their central role in economic growth. Just as a sociologist needs free time and access to libraries and research aides, and a scientist needs a laboratory and assistants, and a doctor needs power to prescribe medicine and perform surgery—just as intellectuals need freedom to write and publish—capitalists need economic freedom and access to capital to perform their role in launching and financing enterprise. Entrepreneurs must be allowed to retain the wealth they create because only they, collectively, can possibly know how to invest it productively among the millions of existing businesses and the innumerable visions of new enterprise in the world economy.

By the very process of acquiring profits, they learned how to use them. By the very process of building businesses, they gained the discipline to avoid waste and the knowledge to see value. By the process of creating and responding to markets, they orient their lives toward the service of others. Entrepreneurs who hoard their wealth or seek governmental protection from rivals or revel in vain consumption or retreat to selfish isolation betray the very essence of their role and responsibility in the world. To that degree, they are no longer entrepreneurs or capitalists but relics of the feudal and static societies of the precapitalist era.

Entrepreneurs provide a continuing challenge both to men who refuse a practical engagement in the world, on the grounds that it is too dangerous or corrupt, and to men who demand power over others in the name of ideology or expertise without first giving or risking their wealth. Capitalism offers nothing but frustrations and rebuffs to those who wish—because of claimed superiority of intelligence, birth, credentials, or ideals—to get without giving, to take without risking, to profit without sacrifice, to be exalted without humbling themselves to understand others and meet their needs.

Entrepreneurs, though many are not churchgoers, emerge from a culture shaped by religious values. The optimism and trust, the commitment and faith, the discipline and altruism that their lives evince and their works require all can flourish only in the midst of a moral order, with religious foundations. Secular culture has yet to produce a satisfactory rationale for a life of work, risk, and commitment oriented toward the needs of others—a life of thrift and trust leading to investments with uncertain returns. Secular culture, in the name of charity, can only summon envy; in the name of service, can only offer coercion; in the name of giving, can achieve only the sterility of income redistribution.

The value of a society's goods ultimately derives from the values of its people. A society of morbid materialism will suppress the spirit of enterprise that sustains the creation of material wealth. A society of secular hedonism will summon a sordid commerce hostile to the spirit of creation and the discipline of work. A culture of cynicism and selfishness will destroy the trust and erode the faith and deny the sacrifice on which all human advances rely. Entrepreneurs bear a heavy responsibility for the quality of the goods they create. But the religious culture ultimately shapes the moral order in which entrepreneurs thrive or fail, defines the order of value that informs the prices and worth of a society's goods.

In *Why I Am Not a Socialist* (1908), G. K. Chesterton wrote: "If I were a poet writing an Utopia, if I were a magician waving a wand, if I were a God making a Planet, I would deliberately make it a world of give and take, rather than a world of sharing. I do not wish Jones and Brown to share the same cigar box; I do not want it as an ideal; I do not want it as a very remote ideal. I do not want it at all. I want Jones by one mystical and godlike act to give a cigar to Brown, and Brown by another mystical and godlike act to give a cigar to Jones. Thus it seems to me instead of one act of fellowship (of which the memory would slowly fade), we should have a continual play and energy of new acts of fellowship keeping up the circulation of society. Now I have read some tons of Socialist eloquence in my time, but it is literally true that I have never seen any serious allusion to or clear consciousness of this creative altruism of personal giving."

In the harsh struggles and remorseless battles of their lives, entrepreneurs are no saints, and far from sinless. They bear scars and have inflicted many. Since their every decision has met an empirical test beyond appeal, they are necessarily the world's true realists, most proven pragmatists. Yet more than any other class of men, they embody and fulfill the sweet and mysterious consolations of the Sermon on the Mount and the most farfetched affirmations of the democratic dream. They come, like Andrew Grove, Armando Codina, Juan Benitez, and a million others—now Koreans, Haitians, and Vietnamese—as outcasts and refugees; they end as the most quintessential and rooted denizens of their new homeland, defining its nature and promise for natives who have lost, amid the cluttered comforts of their lives, the spiritual ties and meanings of national identity.

They begin, like Jack Simplot and Jack Tramiel, with nothing; they scrap and struggle in the wilderness; they learn the grit and texture of the dirt; they inherit the world. Like John Masters and Soichiro Honda, they learn the central truths of their success during their periods of greatest anguish and rejection, in the face of the derision of all established authority. Like Roberto Goizueta, they learn that their only inalienable wealth is mind and spirit. All of them deeply know that to reach the top, you have first to get to the bottom of things. To lead, you have first to listen. To save yourself, you must serve others and solve their problems.

Most of all, the entrepreneurs learn the deepest truths of giving and sacrifice, the miraculous powers of commitment and faith. They give themselves, their time, their wealth, their sleep; they give it year after year, reinvesting every profit, mortgaging every property. They leverage their lives to their private belief in a redemptive idea. And their long outpouring of belief and faith and funds and sacrifices, seemingly wasted and lost in the maws and middens of the world economy, somehow mysteriously coheres and collects. Beyond the horizons of calculation or prophecy, at last the mountain moves; and there unfurls a great returning tide of vindication that overflows all plans and expectations. It is an irrational process, but it is the classic experience of the entrepreneur, the endlessly recurrent miracle of capitalism, by which orphans and outcasts vastly and repeatedly excel the works and wealth of emperors, the reach and rule of armies, the dreams of kings, the calculus of expertise, the visions of state.

"Do unto others as you would have them do unto you" and "Give and you will be given unto" are the central rules of the life of enterprise. They require the institutions of property (you cannot give what you do not own) and personal freedom (a planned economy cannot allow the surprising gifts of entrepreneurs). But it is a life that most deeply springs from religious faith and culture. The act of thrift, suppressing your own desires in order to serve the desires of others—the act of committing your work and wealth, over a period of years, to bring into the world a new good which the world may well reject—the act of putting your own fate into the hands of unknown others, freely deciding your future in a market of free choice—these are the essential acts of a religious person. It is a commitment made in the darkness of time to a process of dangerous creation unfolding in an unknown future; and it partakes of that "mystical and godlike" impulse of personal giving, that "continual play and energy of new acts of fellowship," which makes possible the progress of men and nations.

In the 1980s in the United States, during a time when leading economists on all sides of the political spectrum were predicting worldwide depression, America's entrepreneurs made a defiant statement of their optimism and faith. They started new companies at a rate of nearly 600,000 a year, more than ever before in history and more than six times the number begun annually in the supposedly thriving years of the 1950s. Venture capitalists poured unprecedented billions into thousands of start-ups in a range of radically new technologies, from bioengineering to fiber optics. Scores of new semiconductor and computer firms rose up in the face of massive efforts by giant Japanese corporations in league with a commercially ambitious government. Wildcat oil and gas prospectors fanned out across the country and around the world in the face of sinking prices and a short-term glut of oil. Immigrants from Latin America, Asia, Europe, Russia, and the Middle East continued to press to the shores of the United States, starting companies and creating jobs, in the face of perennial xenophobia and unbelief from the prophets and protectionists of the welfare state.

Entrepreneurs everywhere ignored the suave voices of expertise: the economists who deny their role as the driving force of all economic growth; the psychologists who identify their work and sacrifice as an expression of greed; the sociologists who see their dreams as nostalgia for a lost frontier; the politicians who call their profits unearned, their riches pure luck.

Bullheaded, defiant, tenacious, creative, entrepreneurs continued to solve the problems of the world even faster than the world could create them. The achievements of enterprise remained the highest testimony to the mysterious strength of the human spirit. Confronting the perennial perils of human life, the scientific odds against human triumph, the rationalistic counsels of despair, the entrepreneur finds a higher source of hope than reason, a deeper well of faith than science, a farther reach of charity than welfare. His success is the triumph of the spirit of enterprise—a thrust beyond the powers and principalities of the established world to the transcendent sources of creation and truth.

These men are legion, the true legislators for the silent and silenced majorities of the globe. They come by the millions and throng every mecca of freedom. Today America and the West are the prime beneficiaries of their inestimably precious gifts. But as the West loses the faith of its fathers, there are millions of Asians who are discovering it anew—some on our shores, some beyond. The tide of surprise now increasingly comes from the East. But it reflects most deeply an American faith and Judeo-Christian truth.

The spirit of enterprise wells up from the wisdom of the ages and the history of the West and infuses the most modern of technological adventures. It joins the old and new frontiers. It asserts a firm hierarchy of values and demands a hard discipline. It requires a life of labor and listening, aspiration and courage. But it is the source of all we are and can become, the saving grace of democratic politics and free men, the hope of the poor and the obligation of the fortunate, the redemption of an oppressed and desperate world.

AFTERWORD

"The great cloud wagons move Westward still,
dreaming of a Pacific."—Louis Simpson

J. R. Simplot's patch of Idaho sand, reached by covered wagon, became a silicon sliver that opened a new world market. Today the covered wagons are 747s, serving a thousand frontiers of technology and enterprise. As the constraints of time and space slip away, pioneers move into the limitless domains of mind, and range the world in pursuit of ideas and other men.

They throng the airports and file into the great humped birds of hope. Some are immigrants. Moving to America, they regain not merely the freedom of thought but what is more important, the potency of thought; not merely the soapbox symbol of liberty, but the capitalist realization of it. Some came as Boat People; within a decade they leave—and return—as Boeing people. Many ply the crowded skies between Tokyo and San Francisco. For America's great rival and partner on the new frontier of mind is now Japan.

Take any Japan Air flight to the United States and you will see them, the followers of Soichiro Honda and Sony's Ibuka, intent among the sleeping faces. Enclosed in their small pools of light, they are studying a technical abstract from the International Solid State Circuits Conference or a seminar transcript on High Vacuum technology, or perusing with moving lips a technical brochure from Intel Corporation. Like generations of their forebears since World War II, they still come, clutching phrase books and computer printouts, bearing cameras to film the slides at technical meetings in case they cannot catch the words. They seem deceptively naive, even slow, to Americans amused at their fumbles of English; but many of those Americans cannot read the technical papers in English as well as the Japanese can.

This is still the usual traffic, these Japanese headed for America.

259

Now, however, in the next episode of the spirit of enterprise, there is a new traffic of Americans on the 747s, headed for Tokyo. A young researcher from Bell Labs is there, poring over Japanese papers on gallium arsenide laser diodes (fortunately in English), on his way to Japan for two years of study. So are young executives from a computer company, off to learn Japanese refinements on laser printing. So too are increasing numbers of entrepreneurs from U.S. firms determined to break into the pullulating Japanese markets in capital equipment and office electronics.

With this group is my friend Whitmore (Nick) Kelley, head of Berkshire Corporation, the manufacturer of clean room disposable products, such as wipers and swabs, whom we met in the introduction to this book. Like many U.S. entrepreneurs, he expanded his company vigorously through the 1981 and 1982 recession. Now in 1985, with sluggish semiconductor markets in the United States, he is spending more than half his time in Asia, discovering an immense new capitalist arena open to his products.

It seems like an unusually aggressive move. But Kelley, like scores of other American leaders of small businesses, now comprehends that in enterprise the first rule is to keep moving and that the field of play is global. Fewer American firms will now make the error of U.S. auto companies (and anti-trust prosecutors) who imagined the United States to be an economic island. For suppliers to high technology companies in particular, as Kelley understood, Japan's electronic leviathans have become a mandatory market. If you don't penetrate Japan, your competitors probably will, enlarging their share of world business and moving down the curve of growth.

Your Japanese rivals, moreover, now command a market in high technology capital goods nearly as large as America's. They will soon move into the United States, if only to supply the U.S. facilities of their Japanese customers. In the age of the 747, anyone making your product, or a substitute for it, anywhere, is your rival.

In a deeper sense, though, all these travellers partake of a worldwide solidarity. For all the fierce energies and bitter grievances unleashed by capitalist competition, its final gift is to bring people together in a common venture on a global frontier, with universal laws and mutual gains. The devout nationalists of Micron Technology, in a vicious struggle to prevail among the crashing tides and undertows of the world traffic in computer memory chips, have moments when they hate their competitors in Japan. Yet they may find more sincere and sophisticated admirers at an industry seminar in Tokyo than in the boardrooms of Silicon Valley.

In Japan, as in Boise, they live and die for memory chips. In Tokyo and on Kyushu (Silicon Island), people fully comprehend the heroic improbability of Micron's innovations and achievements. In their efforts to understand and surpass Micron, they come to respect it and share in its struggles more than American companies in other businesses ever do.

Beyond this common ground of a shared technology, there is the common ground of shared markets. Even IBM's line of personal computers, a $7 billion business that sprang up in three years, could not have succeeded without the Japanese chips and other parts that comprised some 60 per cent of the machine. The PC's success generated huge markets for peripherals and other complementary technologies, including memory chips from Micron. In addition, Japanese and other Asian firms comprised some 40 per cent of the market for the U.S. semiconductor capital equipment companies that supply U.S. firms such as Micron. Even Berkshire Corporation, a supplier of Micron's cleanrooms, will be able to enhance quality and lower its prices as a result of the larger markets and learning processes it gains in Japan.

When capitalism is working well, the cheapest products are usually the best products and the best products are the least expensive. Because cheapness is usually an effect of experience—of total unit volumes—the items with the best features, which respond most successfully to the needs of consumers, will achieve both the biggest markets and the lowest prices. American entrepreneurs are relearning the secret of Japanese success—the old American way of Henry Ford. It doesn't matter how cheap you make your product if it doesn't do the job. But if it does do the job better than the competition, you will sell so many that each one will be cheap. It will be cheap because it will be better, and because it is cheap you will sell still more of them; and make the product better yet; and make even more money.

U.S. firms that meet the test of the innovation will prosper more in a world electronics market that is being steadily enriched by products from Asia than they would in a protected America. Commerce is not a zero sum game, a limited pie, in which each gain for one player necessarily means a loss for another. Capitalism is a game of mutual gains. As long as prices drop, products improve, and markets grow, entrepreneurial rivalry is partly collaborative, and enterprise is more a communal adventure than a continuation of war by other means.

The spirit of enterprise embraces these contradictions and resolves them in a way that the spirit of politics cannot. Far more than in the international posturings at the United Nations or the confabulations on arms control at Geneva, the hopes of world unity and survival reside in the solidarity of the silver eagle, plying the horizons of commerce.

This communal spirit—the commercial imagination—is now carrying well beyond commerce to renew America's intellectual life, and through America, to enrich the realm of ideas everywhere. After recent decades of often abusive introspection, the United States has ceased to turn in upon itself, ruminating on death and decadence, with its Easy Riders aiming their motorcycles back toward the eastern seaboard and into the past. America's real intellectuals no longer bow toward the dismal necropolis of European philosophy, pursuing the infantile regress of Marx and Sartre into a tantrum of impotent mind.

Instead, the world now turns in upon America—the mecca of migrants seeking to recover the lost powers of thought—and America explodes upon the world its glittering shards of electrified sand, pregnant with new worlds within, as the 747 masters the world without. Meanwhile the United States' culture of entrepreneurial creativity offers terms of reconciliation beyond the sterile words of conflict.

Struggling out of the shadows of European nihilism and materialism, mobs and masses, iron laws of history and reductive trends of science and society, there emerges a bird of peace, silvery against the blue, and a piece of sand, inscribed with new hope. Together they restore to individual men and women around the globe the heroic stature of new creation: the ability once again to fuse idea and act, and redeem the dignity of the race.

BIBLIOGRAPHIC NOTES

GENERAL SOURCES

John Chamberlain preceded me on this path with two inspiring works: *The Roots of Capitalism* (Indianapolis: Liberty Press, 1976) and *The Enterprising Americans: A Business History of the United States* (New York: Harper & Row, 1974). His influence is evident both in the conception of the project and in several chapters, particularly on the significance of Henry Ford in "The Curve of Growth."

In many articles, books, and essays—most recently in *Forbes* (May 23, 1983)— Peter F. Drucker has called for, and often provided, the kind of entrepreneurial economics I attempt to expound in these pages. Of all the writers on economics of this era, he has demonstrated most luminously that the way to comprehend economies is first to master the ways of business.

Karl H. Vesper of the University of Washington has long been a one-man institution of entrepreneurial studies. Among his many publications, *New Venture Strategies* (Englewood Cliffs, N.J.: Prentice-Hall, 1980) and his annual proceedings of the conferences on entrepreneurship at Babson College in Wellesley, Massachusetts, were especially valuable. Edited by Vesper, the proceedings are published yearly by Babson under the title *Frontiers of Entrepreneurship Research*. Also useful was the *Encyclopedia of Entrepreneurship*, edited by Vesper, Calvin A. Kent, and Donald L. Sexton (Englewood Cliffs, N.J.: Prentice-Hall, 1982).

On a less academic level, Joseph R. Mancuso has also been a leader in the entrepreneurial movement through his excellent book *How to Start, Finance, and Manage Your Own Small Business* (Englewood Cliffs, N.J.: Prentice Hall, 1978) and through his Center for Entrepreneurial Management (83 Spring Street, New York, N.Y. 10012), which publishes the *Entrepreneurial Managers Newsletter* and offers a useful forum for discussion.

Anyone who writes on businesses and the real American economy—the economy of entrepreneurs—must rely heavily on journalistic sources. I have long depended on the *Wall Street Journal*, particularly Bob Bartley's splendid editorial pages, for daily intellectual sustenance and inspiration. The *San Jose Mercury-News*, particularly David Sylvester on semiconductors, provides excellent coverage of the entrepreneurial scene in Silicon Valley. Various chapters of the book were enriched by *Forbes, Fortune, Business Week, Barron's*, the *Harvard Business Review*, the *Economist, Electronics, Electronics News, Infoworld*, the *National Review*, the *American Spectator*, and a host of other publications that overflow my office into other rooms of my house. Warren Brookes's column in the *Boston Herald-American* and his book *The Economy in Mind* were especially useful, as was David Warsh's unfailingly intelligent coverage of the world of economists in the *Boston Globe*. Warsh also introduced me to the world of the Boston consultancies. And for daily coverage, I found that Maxwell Newton of the *New York Post* provides the most succinct and pithy business analysis in America.

SOURCES BY CHAPTER

Prologue: The Entrepreneur The theme of this chapter springs from an aperçu of Irving Kristol, whose views are epitomized in *Reflections of a Neoconservative* (New York: Basic Books, 1983). Kristol observed that analysis of economic life divides into two disciplines: the study of business, conducted largely by journalists and business schools, and the study of economics by economists. According to Kristol, economists assume the existence of an "economy" that can be governed by economic policy shaped by economists, and that transcends the behavior of businesses, run by mere businessmen. I was surprised to discover that Adam Smith in *The Wealth of Nations* and *The Theory of Moral Sentiments* displayed a disdain for mere businessmen typical of contemporary economists on the left and the right.

The one group of economists most cognizant of entrepreneurs is the Austrian school, comprising such early figures as Eugen Von Boehm-Bawerk and reaching a pinnacle with the contributions of Ludwig Von Mises (*Human Action*, Chicago: Henry Regnery Company, 1963), Friedrich Von Hayek, and Joseph Schumpeter, particularly in *The Theory of Economic Development* (London: Oxford University Press, paperback edition, 1961) and *The History of Economic Analysis* (London: George Allen & Unwin, 1954). In his *Capitalism, Socialism and Democracy*, Schumpeter introduced the invaluable concept of entrepreneurial "creative destruction" and then amazingly predicted that it might end, without at the same time ending economic development. I was surprised to find that even Schumpeter presented the entrepreneur as somehow responding to opportunities created by the market. Schumpeter predicted that the entrepreneurial role would decline as technology advanced and large organizations took a larger place in modern economies and as the satisfaction of material wants undermined the disciplines of capitalism. Schumpeter is certainly the greatest economist of the twentieth century and the most telling prophet of the trials and contradictions of democratic capitalism under what he called the "tax state." Let us hope he will be proved wrong in his dire predictions for a bureaucratized America plundered by a new class of redistributionist intellectuals.

Israel Kirzner and Ludwig Lachman are leading current "Austrians," and Kirzner in particular has done much important work on entrepreneurs; see especially *Competition and Entrepreneurship* (Chicago: University of Chicago Press, 1973) and *Perception, Opportunity, and Profit: Studies in the Theory of Entrepreneurship* (Chicago: University of Chicago Press, 1979). But again, he seems to see the entrepreneur as an "opportunity scout," alertly reacting to disequilibria, rather than creating them by aggressive and original initiative. Nearly all economists try to avoid the epistemological murk that lies beyond the recognition that entrepreneurs, like artists and intellectuals, act spontaneously and unpredictably and that the quality of their creations matters far more than the quantity of "capital" they form.

José Ortega y Gasset, *The Revolt of the Masses* (New York: Norton, 1932), is perhaps the single most brilliant and prophetic work of this century and inspired a key theme of this book: the general unawareness on the part of the public and its political and intellectual leaders of the sources of the wealth they take for granted.

The studies of the psychology of entrepreneurs cited occasionally in the book mostly come from A. David Silver, *The Entrepreneurial Life* (New York: John Wiley & Sons, 1983), an excellent compendium of observations and insights on entrepreneurs and their activities.

PART ONE: THE ECONOMY OF HEROES

Chapter 1: A Patch of Sand This chapter was chiefly based on interviews with the principals in Boise and elsewhere. Especially helpful were Scott Simplot and Allen Noble. The opening lines were suggested by an epigram recited to me by John Baden of the Center for Political Economy and Natural Resources, at Montana State University.

Chapter 2: The Real Economy Throughout this book, the economic data come chiefly from the regular analyses of Evans Economics (Michael Evans) and from the Economic Reports of the American Institute for Economic Research in Great Barrington, Massachusetts (Larry Pratt and Ernest Welker). The data on high-technology capital formation come largely from the pathbreaking work of Stephen Roach of Morgan Stanley. The conceptual guidance as usual comes from Laffer Associates (Arthur Laffer and Charles Kadlec) and Polyconomics (Alan Reynolds and Jude Wanniski). Reynolds has been relentlessly incisive in sorting out the causes and effects of deficits and in attacking the new mercantilism in America.

Much of the data on the service economy derive from Thomas M. Stanback, Jr., *Understanding the Service Economy* (Baltimore: Johns Hopkins University Press, 1979), and essays by Theodore Levitt, including in particular "The Emerging Fecundity of Service," in *The Future of Productivity* (Washington, D.C.: National Center for Productivity and Quality of Working Life, 1978).

Chapter 3: The Explorer This narrative was chiefly based on interviews with the principals, on journalistic coverage in Canadian and industry publications, and on *The Hunters* by John Masters (Canadian Hunter, 1981). I also found inspiration in *The Ultimate Resource* by Julian L. Simon (Princeton, N.J.: Princeton University Press, 1982), one of the key books in the recent history of economics for its demolition of neo-Malthusian fears of population growth and resource exhaustion. Many of the data on natural gas reserves and prospects came from E. N. Tiratsoo, *Natural Gas: Fuel for the Future? A World Survey* (Houston: Gulf Publishing Company, 3rd ed., 1979).

Chapter 4: The Man Who Wanted to Clean the Water Based on interviews with the principals and *Berkshire Eagle* coverage by Judy Katz and an interview with Katz. The concept of the tragedy of the commons was introduced to me by John Baden, Richard Stroup, and their colleagues at the Center for Political Economy and Natural Resources in Bozeman, Montana, and in *Managing the Commons*, Baden and Garrett Hardin, eds. (San Francisco: W. H. Freeman, 1977). The center's unique approach to environmental issues is summed up in an extended essay by Richard Stroup and John Baden, "Property Rights and Natural Resource Management," in *Literature of Liberty* (Menlo Park, Calif.: Cato Institute); in Stroup and Baden, *Natural Resources: Bureaucratic Myths and Environmental Management* (Cambridge, Mass.: Ballinger, 1983); and in Baden, ed., *Earth Day Reconsidered* (Washington, D.C.: Heritage Foundation).

Chapter 5: The Cuban Miracle   This chapter was based on interviews with the principals and on coverage in the *Miami Herald;* also, for Ogden and the city projectors, see Daniel Boorstin, *The Americans: The National Experience* (New York: Random House, 1965); for the immigrant experience, see Thomas Sowell, *Ethnic America* (New York: Basic Books, 1981) and *The Economics and Politics of Race: An International Perspective* (New York: Morrow, 1983); also, for a detailed and original study, see Ivan H. Light, *Ethnic Enterprise in America: Business and Welfare Among Chinese, Japanese, and Blacks* (Berkeley: University of California Press, 1972).

PART TWO: THE EUTHANASIA OF THE ENTREPRENEUR

Chapter 6: A Sad Heart in a Personal Jet   This chapter was based on interviews with the principals. Material on the effects of a flatter tax come from Michael Evans, *The Truth About Supply Side Economics* (New York: Basic Books, 1983), an excellent book unfortunately much ignored; from Laffer Associates; and from Alvin Rabushka and Robert E. Hall, "The Flat Rate Tax: A Proposal for Tax Simplification," in *New Directions in Federal Tax Policy for the 1980s,* Charles E. Walker and Mark A. Bloomfield, eds. (Cambridge, Mass.: Ballinger, 1983), the proceedings of a conference of the American Council on Capital Formation, which also presents much valuable data on the capital gains tax and other issues. Further evidence on the underground economy is collected in Vito Tanzi, ed., *The Underground Economy in the United States and Abroad* (Lexington, Mass.: D. C. Heath, 1982).

The tax shelter material comes from personal interviews and observations, various journalistic sources, and Robert G. Allen's two books on real estate investing, *Nothing Down* (New York: Simon and Schuster, 1981) and *Creating Wealth* (Simon and Schuster, 1983). *Creating Wealth,* which is a broader view of its topic, begins with two valuable chapters on the rules of wealth creation which might be summed up "Be an entrepreneur." For a massively comprehensive catalog of the variety of shelters, I consulted William C. Drollinger, *Tax Shelters and Tax-Free Income for Everyone,* 4th ed., Vols. 1 and 2 (Orchard Lake, Mich.: Epic Publications, 1979, 1981). Also of use was *Tax Shelter Digest,* and for the offshore scene, Adam Starchild, *Tax Havens* (New Rochelle, N.Y.: Arlington House, 1979). For a more combative and entertaining treatment of the subject, there is Bill Greene, *Win Your Personal Tax Revolt* (San Francisco: Harbor Publishing Company, 1981) and *101 New Loopholes: The 1982 Reagan Tax Package* (Harbor, 1981).

Chapter 7: Capitalism Without Capitalists   Material on the effects of the U.S. tax system appeared in Martin Feldstein, ed., *The American Economy in Transition* (Chicago: University of Chicago Press, 1980), Henry J. Aaron and Joseph A. Pechman, eds., *How Taxes Affect Economic Behavior* (Washington, D.C.: Brookings Institution,

1981), and Bruce Bartlett, *Reaganomics: Supply Side Economics in Action* (New Rochelle, N.Y.: Arlington House, 1981).

The featured chapter in the Brookings volume, by Jerry A. Hausman of MIT, concluded that "the combination of federal and state income taxes and the payroll tax leads husbands to reduce the amount they work significantly—about 8 percent for men who earned between $8,000 and $12,000 in 1975—and imposes significant inefficiencies as measured by 'deadweight loss' [the distortion of behavior caused by efforts to avoid the progressive effects of taxation]. For a worker earning $10 an hour (in 1975) the deadweight loss is 54 percent of revenue collected." These findings, together with other studies by Hausman, Michael Evans, Laffer Associates, and other economists, lead inexorably to the conclusion that the high progressivity of income taxes in the United States and Britain is a principal cause of sluggish growth. But even some of these economists shy away from the larger implications of their studies.

The surge in relative tax payments by the rich in 1982 and 1983 after the cut in the top rate was first noticed by Lawrence Pratt of the American Institute for Economic Research, Great Barrington, Massachusetts. As a proxy for top-bracket revenues, he uses the "other" or "non-withheld" category of treasury revenue reports, which captures payments by the rich every quarter as well as the census or Treasury analyses published years after the event.

The British tax data were assembled and computed by Ronald Burgess of the Economic Study Association in London and York, who is one of the very few British supply-siders (and even he underestimates the significance of the high marginal tax rates in Britain).

The Ishibashi material came from Chalmers Johnson, *MITI and the Japanese Miracle* (Stanford, Calif.: Stanford University Press, 1982), a superb work of scholarship that nonetheless exaggerates the significance of the governmental measures it describes and underestimates the creative contributions of entrepreneurs. Most of the data on Japanese tax policy during the Ishibashi era came from Kozo Yamamura, *Economic Policy in Postwar Japan* (Berkeley: University of California Press, 1967), and Ryutaro Komiya, ed., *Postwar Economic Growth in Japan*, Robert S. Osaki, trans. (Berkeley: University of California Press, 1966). The international comparisons of tax policy came from *Individual Taxes in 80 Countries* (New York: Price Waterhouse, 1981) and, especially, Keith Marsden, "Taxes and Growth," in *Finance and Development* (Washington, D.C.: International Monetary Fund and the World Bank, September 1983). The results of the study were presented in *Capital Formation* (Washington, D.C.: American Council for Capital Formation, September 1983). Other important material appeared in Vito Tanzi, *Inflation and the Personal Income Tax: An International Perspective* (Cambridge, G.B.: Cambridge University Press, 1980).

PART THREE: THE GREAT TRANSITION

Chapter 8: The Curve of Growth   The theme of this chapter originated in a series of interviews at Bain and Company, with Bill Bain, Coleman Andrews, Patrick Graham, David Parsons, Vernon Altman, Ralph Willard, and others. Among works on business strategy I found particularly useful were Michael E. Porter, *Competitive Strategy* (New York: Free Press, 1980), which is skeptical about the experience curve; Ira C. Magaziner and Robert B. Reich, *Minding America's Business* (New York: Harcourt Brace Jovanovich, 1982), which applies it incisively to both domestic and international competition and also offers a trenchant critique of existing productivity data; Derek F. Abell and John S. Hammond, *Strategic Market Planning* (Englewood Cliffs, N.J.: Prentice-Hall, 1979), particularly for its detailed presentation of PIMs data and conclusions; Abell, *Defining the Business: The Starting Point of Strategic Planning* (Prentice-Hall, 1980); Kenichi Ohmae, *The Mind of the Strategist* (New York: McGraw-Hill, 1982), an interesting appraisal of the limits of the experience curve as seen by the competition at McKenzie Japan; Hunter Lewis and Donald Allison, *The Real World War* (New York: Coward, McCann & Geoghegan, 1982), an alarmist case that sees the United States lagging on the curve everywhere. Among magazines, the debate over the experience curve has been treated most thoroughly in the *Harvard Business Review*. Walter Kiechel of *Fortune* has also offered intelligently skeptical coverage.

The material on the computer industry came from a large variety of sources, including (for an IBM-oriented history) Katharine Davis Fishman, *The Computer Establishment* (New York: Harper & Row, 1981), and Jack B. Rochester and John Gantz, *The Naked Computer* (New York: Morrow, 1983). The concept of software share emerged in part from an interview with Adam Osborne. Fred Bucy, Mark Shepherd, and William Sick of Texas Instruments provided crucial material on that company's experiences on the curve, as did Mariann Jelinek, *Institutionalizing Innovation: A Study of Organizational Learning Systems* (New York: Praeger, 1979). Burton Klein, *Dynamic Economics* (Cambridge, Mass.: Harvard University Press, 1977), is a crucial work in entrepreneurial economics and also presents valuable material on early history of the automobile industry as well as insights on semiconductors. Also useful on the auto industry history was Ed Cray, *Chrome Colossus: General Motors and Its Times* (New York: McGraw-Hill, 1980). Esther Dyson, *RELease 1.0* (formerly *Rosen Electronics Letter*), is the most literate and intelligent of the current analysts of the personal computer industry (EDventure Holdings, 375 Park Avenue, New York, N.Y. 10152). *Infoworld, Popular Computing, Byte,* and *Personal Computing* are among the many computer magazines I read regularly; *High Technology* is a superbly edited magazine on its subject. *Electronics Business, Electronics Magazine,* and *Electronics News* are necessary to cover the field. For many interesting observations about the investment implications of the rise of high technology on the experience curve, see Robert Metz, *Future Stocks* (New York: Harper & Row, 1983).

Chapter 9: Japan's Entrepreneurs Much excellent Honda material came from Sol Sanders, *Honda: The Man and His Machines* (Rutland, Vt.: Charles E. Tuttle Company, 1977; also Little, Brown, 1975), and from Tetsuo Sakika, *Honda Motor: The Men, The Management, The Machines* (Tokyo, New York, and San Francisco: Kodansha International, 1982). Most of the Sony material came from Nick Lyons, *The Sony Vision* (New York: Crown, 1976). The material on Japanese robots came to a great extent from Kuni Sadamoto, ed., *Robots in the Japanese Economy* (Tokyo: Survey Japan, 1981). For the MITI role in these events I relied heavily on Chalmers Johnson, *MITI (op. cit.)*. For small business data on Japan, I relied on Robert C. Wood of Modern Economics Co., Scituate, Massachusetts.

Chapter 10: America as Number One I got the title from Ezra F. Vogel, *Japan as Number One* (Cambridge, Mass.: Harvard University Press, 1979). Benjamin J. Rosen in the *Rosen Electronics Letter* set a standard for coverage of the semiconductor industry that will not be soon equaled; I relied heavily on his observations. In the course of preparation of a forthcoming book on the electronics industry and of covering the industry for *RELease 1.0*, I conducted scores of interviews with semi-conductor executives. Complementing and guiding the interviews in reconstructing the history of the industry were Ernest Braun and Stuart MacDonald, *Revolution in Miniature* (Cambridge, G.B.: Cambridge University Press, 1978), and the chapter on semiconductors in John Zysman and Laura Tyson, eds., *American Industry in International Competition* (Ithaca, N.Y.: Cornell University Press). Joel Popkin was quoted in *Business Week* (Oct. 17, 1983, p. 169) on the colossal error in estimating the price of computing. Many of the statistics on the industry derive from the useful publications of the Semiconductor Industry Association (SIA) under the guidance of Thomas Hinkelman. The high-technology investment data come from Stephen Roach of Morgan Stanley. The comparisons between U.S. and Japanese software capabilities and personnel come from Kenichi Ohmae, ed., *Japan Business: Obstacles and Opportunities*, prepared by McKinsey & Company for the U.S.-Japan Trade Study Group (New York: John Wiley & Sons, 1983), updated from industry sources.

Chapter 11: The Rise of Micron   This chapter is mostly based on extensive interviews with all the principals.

Chapter 12: The Dynamics of Entrepreneurship   The Fatjo story is told in Thomas J. Fatjo and Keith Miller, *With No Fear of Failure* (Waco, Texas: Word Books, 1981). The data on business starts, failures, and job creation are presented in David L. Birch, "Who Creates Jobs?" in *The Public Interest*, No. 65 (Fall 1981).

INDEX

MORE ABOUT PENGUINS, PELICANS, PEREGRINES AND PUFFINS

For further information about books available from Penguins please write to Dept EP, Penguin Books Ltd, Harmondsworth, Middlesex UB7 0DA.

In the U.S.A.: For a complete list of books available from Penguins in the United States write to Dept DG, Penguin Books, 299 Murray Hill Parkway, East Rutherford, New Jersey 07073.

In Canada: For a complete list of books available from Penguins in Canada write to Penguin Books Canada Ltd, 2801 John Street, Markham, Ontario L3R 1B4.

In Australia: For a complete list of books available from Penguins in Australia write to the Marketing Department, Penguin Books Australia Ltd, P.O. Box 257, Ringwood, Victoria 3134.

In New Zealand: For a complete list of books available from Penguins in New Zealand write to the Marketing Department, Penguin Books (N.Z.) Ltd, Private Bag, Takapuna, Auckland 9.

In India: For a complete list of books available from Penguins in India write to Penguin Overseas Ltd, 706 Eros Apartments, 56 Nehru Place, New Delhi 110019.